The High Cost of Dying

RUTH MULVEY HARMER

THE HIGH

COST OF DYING

COLLIER BOOKS, New York, N.Y.

Collier–Macmillan Ltd., London

A hardcover edition of *The High Cost of Dying* was published by
The Crowell-Collier Press

Collier Books is a division of The Crowell-Collier Publishing
Company.

First Collier Books Edition 1963

To the Cooperators

Edward M Searle
11/15/63
95¢ (T.W.B.T.D.!!!) ?!?

Library of Congress Catalog Card Number: 63-13042
Copyright © 1963 by The Crowell-Collier Publishing Company
Published simultaneously by Collier-Macmillan Limited, London
All Rights Reserved
Hecho en los E.E.U.U.
Printed in the United States of America

Contents

To the Cooperators

The High Cost of Dying

Chapter 1

Turnstiles to Eternity

DURING RECENT YEARS protest has been vigorous and vehement against the high cost of living. Yet little has been said —publicly, at any rate—about the even higher cost of dying. Although that has more than tripled during the last quarter of a century, the general attitude has been that to draw a relationship between funerals and finances is neither relevant nor proper: *the right sort of person simply doesn't consider money at a time like this.*

As a consequence, the cost of death and burial has become one of the most crushing expenses facing American families. In 1935, the average cost of an adult funeral was about $350; by 1960 it had risen to $1100. Nationally, the bill rose from about half a billion dollars a year to two billion, and since then the toll charges at the gates to paradise have continued to mount. By mid-1962 the cost was estimated to be almost $1400 —indicating a rise of more than 40 per cent in a decade. In some places it was even higher. Early in 1963, G. J. Klupar, executive director of the Catholic Cemeteries of Chicago, told an Illinois commission studying the subject that the cost of dying—"counting the trimmings"—came to $1545.

Statistics give only a poor indication of what this has meant to millions of families, for the expenditure is required not on at a time of great emotional shock, but frequently at a time of great financial dislocation. Most persons, however frugally they may have lived, are dying beyond their means.

A revealing incident occurred on Thanksgiving Day in 1961, when thousands of persons filed into the Los Angeles Coliseum to pay tribute to the victims, the living and the dead, of the worst accident that had ever involved an American athletic group. Thirteen months earlier a dense fog had enveloped the Toledo Airport, and the chartered plane carrying home members of the defeated California State Polytechnic College football team crashed and burned. Sixteen players and the team's student manager were killed. Five had been married; among their survivors were eleven small children. Not one survivor —and the survivors included several widowed mothers—received any air crash insurance, nor did those students who had been injured, some of them so seriously that they were still incapacitated a year later. Shortly after the crash, the airline company was placed on emergency suspension by the government, and the underwriters refused to pay claims on the grounds that the airline had violated a warranty by operating a non-airworthy plane.

To alleviate the genuine distress—California Polytechnic is about as far from being a rich man's school as a state college can be—sympathetic school officials and staff members organized a memorial fund. The "Mercy Bowl" football game was a bright hope. Previous donations by students and staff and other charitable persons were almost exhausted and the need was still great to provide fifty dollars a month for each fatherless child, to cope with medical bills, and to contribute toward the food and rent and other outstanding expenses of many who had suffered.

The game, to which even the players and members of the press paid full admission in order to swell the gate receipts, netted the California Polytechnic Memorial Fund $151,081. However, more than one-fifth of that sum had already been spoken for by undertakers in Ohio and California who had willingly accepted the task of seeing that the "proper" thing done for the victims—at whatever cost to the living.

All the mortuaries in Toledo, the fund treasurer said, had

received a share of the business: the president of the airline had gone to the scene of the crash on the following day and had signed a contract to cover mortuary costs amounting to $27,000. Curiously enough, the charge for preparing the bodies and providing caskets was almost uniform. Only three bills sent to the fund committee showed variations from the standard $1225 total: one was for $1240, another for $1262.50, a third for $1257.22.

That was just a beginning. The bodies were flown back to California, while other morticians took over for sums ranging from $157 to $884.16. Precise amounts this time widely varied: $649.05, $551.30, $288.40, $653.76, $366.80, $773.98, $650.32 (for an out-of-state funeral), $873.66, $223.52, $314.88, $157, $884.16, $525.74, $538.50, $309.30, $751.96. The amount of one bill is unknown since the family refused to turn it over to the committee for payment.

On the basis of the known figures, it is thus apparent that the average undertaking costs amounted to about $1763. A few of the California morticians included cemetery plots in their totals, and one bill covered the cost of a small headstone. However, most of the usually sizable cemetery bills were paid by the families. In the case of the California Polytechnic College players, there was no major transportation charge—as is often the case in our highly mobile society—since the government released a plane to the airline long enough for the bodies of the students to be flown back to California without charge.

That event took place in a year when thousands of persons in California working through cooperative funeral societies were able to obtain complete funerals for as little as $150, including the casket, embalming, use of the mortuary chapel, and other services. It also occurred shortly before William C. Cowan, president of the Los Angeles County Funeral Directors Association, told a radio and television audience that the "break-even" price for a mortuary was $461 for funeral services and denied that the price was determined by the cost of the casket. The similarity of the charges imposed by Toledo morticians in the instance of the football players provides a rather curious commentary on that.

It may be protested that the incident involving the student

football players was atypical, just as the Centralia mine disaster in 1947—when families of the 111 dead miners had to pay an average of $732.78 for funerals—was held to be atypical.

More representative was the experience of the late John Crawford's family—indeed, so representative that it was featured in the *Ladies' Home Journal* in December, 1961, under the heading "How America Spends Its Money."

On a spring day in 1956 the car in which the young mining equipment worker was being driven by a friend missed a turn on a mountainous Idaho road. John Crawford was killed instantly, leaving a wife and five children, the youngest of whom was three and a half months old. When the widow came out of her first daze of grief, she took stock of their finances. For income, she had $200 a month from Social Security; on the other side of the ledger were a number of debts, including a $225 balance on the bill for the delivery of the youngest child. Her husband, it was reported, had left nothing in the way of tangible assets but a $1200 life insurance policy. "Worst of all," the article pointed out, "Bonnie realized that in the midst of emotional shock she had sanctioned funeral arrangements beyond her means." The funeral expenses amounted to $1567. Although $405 of that amount had been paid by Social Security and Veterans Administration programs (John Crawford had served in the Army Air Force in World War II), the insurance had been virtually wiped out.

Mrs. Crawford later reported fairly: "I don't think I got talked into it. It's just that at a time like that you keep thinking you have to have the best for the person you loved. I wish someone had reasoned with me, or tried to warn me."

Although many unscrupulous morticians have exerted strong pressure to persuade bereaved persons to order elaborate funerals, they have not always needed to exert any pressure at all. For the unusually high sums charged for a funeral are in large measure a reflection of the industry's remarkably successful public relations program—a program that has redefined the ancient concept of respect for the dead to emphasize extravagant display. "It is the task of those in the funeral profession," says the *Psychology of Funeral Service,* an important handbook for morticians, "to educate the public in the right paths."

That "education" has been so effective that the modern American funeral—with its vulgarity, sacrifice of spiritual values to materialistic trappings, immature indulgence in primitive spectacles, unethical business practices, and overwhelming abnegation of rational attitudes—has become for many students of the national scene a symbol of cultural sickness. Commenting on the problem of making *credible* much of the American reality, the novelist Philip Roth wrote: "It stupefies, it sickens, it infuriates, and finally it is even a kind of embarrassment to one's own meager imagination." And the funeral industry, beyond all other forms of actuality, is "continually outdoing our talents."

The public relations campaign has managed to make us not only accept extravagant display, but to demand it under the delusion that lavish send-offs are the precise measure of our religion, family love, true-blue Americanism—all of which concepts they violate in a most basic way. What father, for example, would accept the sacrifice of a child's educational opportunity in the interests of his having a "fine" funeral? Yet, frequently that has been the consequence. What husband would willingly allow his wife to give up the home they both had worked for so that his body could repose in an elaborate casket? That, too, has often happened.

For example, a few years ago, when the father of a young man I know died, he believed that his wife would be reasonably comfortable for the rest of her life. They had clear title to their house; his investment in Social Security would pay for his funeral and provide her with a modest monthly income.

Unfortunately, he had forgotten one thing—how expensive death can be. The undertaker, who had promised the man's distraught widow that he would "take care of everything," did just that. His bill for providing an elaborate show, a casket lined with beige satin and velvet, transportation to the cemetery, flowers, a soloist, and a $400 metal sheath to protect the "everlasting" casket cost the woman her principal inheritance. To pay the bill she had to sell the house which had been their home for thirty years.

Even more modest funerals can create havoc. One of the most satisfied new members of a California credit union is a hotel maid in one of the large cities; her membership ended a kind of bondage that had begun with the death of her husband. Unable to obtain a loan of $300 to pay for his funeral from more conventional sources, she had entered into an arrangement with a loan company, she told Charles Sheline, volunteer credit union organizer. After two years of making monthly interest payments of $15, the principal was still outstanding: "I could never manage to get together the fifty dollars the company said was the least it would accept toward paying off the debt."

In some cases, of course, persons have willingly gone into debt for an elaborate funeral that has provided them with a means of atonement for their failures in family relationships. Several years ago, a Milwaukee clergyman told a reporter for a national magazine that he had encouraged—over the protest of an undertaker—the daughter of a deceased parishioner to go ahead with her plan for a lavish funeral. "My reason was this: I knew the daughter felt she had neglected her mother. The expensive funeral did a lot to relieve her sense of guilt."

This neglect-now, pay-later attitude toward human relationships strikes hard at moral and ethical concepts since it provides easy absolution for all cruelty and coldness, hardness and abuse. In Los Angeles recently, a major "human interest" feature was the story of "Old Pete," an eighty-one-year-old recluse of Buena Park who had died ten days after he was forced out of his borrowed shack because the land had been bought for commercial purposes. Home-owners and shop-keepers in the neighborhood gave themselves a warm and wonderful feeling by donating $98 for his burial. A local mortuary contributed an additional $50 held "necessary" to provide his departure with what one sob sister account called "a sort of splendor." He made his final appearance in a new suit of clothes to replace the old overcoat and the burlap shoes he had worn for twenty-three years. His body was spared what the writer implied would have been a fate worse than death—being sent to the county crematory.

Undoubtedly the contributors were well-intentioned; but one wonders whether the kind of charity that is designed to benefit the giver rather than the receiver can be considered part of the greatest of all virtues. Perhaps H. L. Mencken, that archiconoclast, came closer to the heart of the matter than he knew when he asked his friends—if they wished to remember him at all—to forgive some sinner and wink an eye at a homely girl.

At any rate, from the standpoint of our Jewish and Christian heritage, modern funerals border on the blasphemous in their radical departure from the rites accorded Moses and Jesus, which were to set the pattern for the funerals of succeeding men. Many clergymen have protested present practices as "downright pagan," owing most of their extravagance and elaborateness to the Greeks, Romans, Babylonians, and other Western groups. Certainly the costly, body-centered rituals in America today parallel in a startling fashion the funerary activities in ancient Egypt where—and it is said only partly in jest—the grave robbers saved the nation from bankruptcy by stripping the dead Pharaohs of their treasure and putting it back into circulation.

At first practices were encouraged by clergymen who were alarmed about the excessive drinking and roistering that marked early American funerals as well as the riotous wakes staged by the Scotch, Irish, and other later immigrant groups. However, during the last three decades the funeral rituals in fashion have created growing unrest among church groups. Scattered protests in sermons and in the form of church-sponsored funeral societies were given weight in 1959 by a survey made by Dr. Robert L. Fulton, Los Angeles State College sociologist, at the request of the National Funeral Directors Association. That study revealed that 51 per cent of the Protestant clergymen in America and 41 per cent of the Catholic clergymen are opposed to what has been called in trade circles "the American way of death."

Although the undertakers insist that the country's honor is involved, precisely what relationship exists between patriotism and ostentatious obsequies is not at all clear to most students of American history. Nor was it clear to other social historians—as the comments of Dickens and Dostoyevsky indicate. In the rogue's gallery of Victorian England portrayed in *Oliver Twist*, no figure is more deeply etched in acid than Mr. Sowerberry, the undertaker, to whom little Oliver was apprenticed. The hypocritical, sanctimonious, gaunt man with his air of "professional jocosity" and his determination to make his fortune on the "fair profit" he received from burying the parish dead in undersized coffins is one of the most contemptible of the exploiters Dickens so savagely delineated. And the pitiful reaction of the pretentious poor in Russia is compassionately laid bare in *Crime and Punishment* in the episode of the funeral feast given by the deranged and consumptive widow of Marmeladov. Motivated partly by her desire to honor the memory of the dead alcoholic "suitably," the unfortunate woman compounds the disaster by "wasting" ten of the twenty rubles Raskolnikov has given her. Dostoyevsky commented bitterly: "Perhaps the chief element was that peculiar 'poor man's pride,' which compels many poor people to spend their last savings on some traditional social ceremony, simply in order to do 'like other people,' and not to 'be looked down upon.' " Nevertheless, that equation has been established by the American funeral industry, which has operated in such a bizarre fashion that it has successfully vanquished the economics of the capitalistic, free enterprise system.

Like many other industries, the funeral and burial industry in America received its principal impetus during and after the Civil War, which witnessed the rise of the bier barons. Unlike most other industries, however, it was confronted from the beginning with a rigidly limited market. No amount of salesmanship, no amount of packaging, no amount of product development could serve to expand sales, since they were based on the national death rate, a shrinking rather than an expanding market. Exceptions to fixed volume do occur during periods of disaster. In the two world wars, for example, the undertakers led strong and successful drives to have the bodies of "our boys" brought back home—for a proper funeral. So persuasive were they that even the Navajo Indians violated an ancient taboo and agreed to public burial of their war dead in the interests of prestige. Plans to cope with a nuclear holocaust have already been made; that would represent a real bonanza.

In times of normal economic functioning, the number of operators would be only the number the industry could efficiently support, with marginal operators falling by the wayside. Not so in the funeral industry. During the last half century of dramatically declining death rate, the supply of undertakers has increased with glorious disregard for their need. Between 1900 and 1935, the number of deaths in the country increased by only 3 per cent while the number of undertakers rose by 60 per cent. In 1927, leaders of the industry estimated that 10,000 morticians could do the job efficiently; at that time there were 23,000 funeral homes. In 1950, a spokesman said that 2000 funeral directors could take care of all the business in the country; at that time there were about 24,000 funeral homes.

So many undertakers are now operating that the average number of funerals that could possibly be allotted to each is about fifty-eight a year. Since some establishments count their corpses by the thousand, the less flourishing must make enough on the twenty or thirty they receive to pay off sizable capital investments and to pay themselves and their employees decent salaries.

This "through the looking glass" economy has been brought about largely by trade associations. Sponsored enthusiastically by the manufacturers of caskets and other funerary goods and services, trade associations have worked to keep the number of operators large by urging price "floors" high enough to permit small undertaking establishments to continue in business and to provide larger ones with astronomical profits. To some extent monopoly conditions have been effected in an industry characterized by an oversupply of small businessmen—a genuinely remarkable economic achievement.

In order that this condition be perpetuated, funeral directors offering lower prices than the "suggested" minimum have been read out of trade associations and have had their supply of caskets and other goods curtailed. When a lively price war between one large undertaker in Los Angeles and the rest of the trade broke out several years ago, it was settled in a discreet manner out of court, although not before charges and countercharges in the local press had stirred many persons to inquire about pricing practices. In an epilogue to the affair, a trade journal warned subscribers: "And there is another point. You do not have competitors. You and the others in your profession are 'we.' You know that you have competitors. I know that you have competitors. But the public would hate to think there was rivalry over the dead."

The paradoxical assertions seem less contradictory when considered from the industry's point of view. There is to be no competition that will affect prices; competition may affect only packaging. Within the latter framework, however, competition is fierce; sometimes, ludicrously so. For example, a few years ago a North Carolina undertaker announced that he was giving trading stamps to purchasers of caskets and cerements: "It seems like people just want something more for their money."

That competition has not provided consumer benefits in the form of lower prices or essentially better products and services is due not merely to business practices within the trade, but to emotional attitudes without. Few persons would not be revolted by the notion of bargaining over the body of a friend or relative; few persons would, when a death occurs in the family, set out on a shopping expedition to determine which undertaker was offering the best buy that season.

Needless to say, that attitude has been enhanced by undertaking and cemetery establishments, all the way from pet cemeteries offering "complete funerals," to Forest Lawn, three hundred preposterous acres of trees, ponds, statues, paintings, and bodies—a tourist attraction in southern California outranked only by Disneyland.

As a result of clever public relations, undertakers, after centuries of dwelling on the outer fringes, have gained social status and have been endowed by many with a semiclerical respectability. As they have splendidly climbed the rungs from *undertaker* to *funeral director* to *mortician* and as their once modest "parlors" have been transformed into sanctified country clubs, they have assumed the prerogatives of professional men and clerics.

Much of this has been accomplished through a remarkable, Orwellian type of "newspeak" to match their managed economy—a set of euphemisms so remote from the language of ordinary men that it is possible to spend an evening with a cemetery salesman and never hear a word that suggests death and burial. Persons no longer die, they "pass on" or "go to the final reward" or they "leave" or simply "step out of the picture." The body is no longer a corpse; it is the "departed," the "loved one," or even—with greater liveliness—"Mr. ————." And Mr. ———— is no longer "laid out" for viewing; if he is not actually stretched out on a bed in a "reposing room," he is in the "slumber room" waiting to greet visitors, with his nails carefully manicured, the proper makeup applied, and perhaps holding a pipe or a book in a remarkably "natural" way.

What was once called a funeral service is now a "living memorial," with birds twittering while the organ plays something soothing—not hymns: they are "too depressing." Coffins have become caskets to hold a precious treasure, not the vile dust of outmoded religious notion. More recently, they have become "couches" to banish further all thoughts of death. Cemeteries are no longer for the dead; they are memorial parks for the living. Plots and grave spaces are held to be "one's property." And of what interest is cost compared to the view "one's property" offers and the desirability of the neighbors?

The price of a casket, although industry spokesmen deny it, is still practically the sole determinant of the price of the funeral under the peculiar system of "accounting" favored by most undertakers and recommended by the coffin manufacturing circle. In spite of that, funeral directors blandly reject any suggestion that they are tradesmen selling goods and services. By insisting on their professional status, they have minimized such mundane considerations as dollars and cents. Instead, they concentrate on appealing to snobbery, to affection, and—cruelly—to feelings of guilt. Which among us would not have done more for the departed? Well, here, ladies and gentlemen, is a last chance.

Few are as forthright about their trade connections as the founder of the W. W. Chambers funeral homes was in 1947 when he testified before a Senate investigating committee about the sizable profits still possible. Explaining why he had left his job in a livery stable to become an undertaker earlier in the century, Mr. Chambers said: "What appealed to me mostly was when I saw one of them (undertakers) buy a casket for $17 and sell it to a poor broken widow for $265. I said, 'This is awful sweet. I can't let this go.'"

In spite of their claim to more-than-businessman status, some undertakers have proven themselves very shrewd entrepreneurs, indeed. A principal cry among undertakers is that "this is no way to get rich." And often they show figures to "prove" that. For example, according to a study made for the National Funeral Directors Association, the average profit margin on each funeral for the undertaker in 1960 was held to be $54.50.

It requires no profound knowledge of finances to realize that some relatively fancy accounting is involved. If the average profit is multiplied by sixty funerals a year—an excessive figure for about half the undertakers—the total annual profits for an establishment would amount to $3270. Yet the investment that must be made is sizable; in that same year $67,724 was the average investment in a small funeral home (conducting an average of 57 funerals a year), $366,579 the average investment in a fairly large one. That persons should struggle so fiercely to enter a business or continue in one bringing a return so modest is singular, indeed. & HOW!!

What makes the situation more curious is that frequently the smaller operators charge less than the larger ones. One of the lowest bills submitted for undertaking expenses for the California State Polytechnic College players was from a "small" mortuary in the community whose owner insisted that the bill be discounted 50 per cent because he realized that payment of the total—still among the lowest—would be a hardship.

In spite of their protests that the mortician's lot is not a happy one financially, the bankruptcy rate among them is lower than for almost any other business in the country. Their ability to collect their bills is correspondingly high; less than 2 per cent of their bills are considered noncollectable—an enviable record in the country. Moreover, the condition of industry leaders is so obviously prosperous as to make comment unnecessary. For example, Forest Lawn's promise that one telephone call "does everything" helped to enable that company to realize a net profit for 1960 of about $2,500,000, according to trade circle reports. Ten per cent of the persons listed in the May, 1962, issue of *Ebony* as the richest Negroes in the United States amassed varying shares of their fortunes from mortuaries, cemeteries and allied businesses. That figure is undoubtedly too low, since the source of wealth was in many cases described merely by such vague phrases as "real estate" or "investments."

Not only our attitudes, but most of our laws governing disposal of the dead have also been shaped by undertakers and members of related businesses. Aided by public determination to avoid "unpleasant" talk about death and by the successful lobbying in state capitals, persons in the mortuary and cemetery business are generally free of controls—except for whatever compassion they may possess and whatever degree of integrity with which they pledge to abide by the codes of ethics drawn up by the various trade associations. Most of the leading national and local groups have declared out of bounds such disreputable practices as "bait advertising," "switch selling," and "promoting funerals all out of proportion to the family's way of life." But even the best intentioned reason—correctly—that they are not in business for their health, and such unethical practices are fairly common.

Bait advertising was attacked by the attorney general of New York State in December, 1954, after an investigation showed that in a number of cases "he (the undertaker) sets up a low and extremely attractive price for a complete funeral, which is merely the lure for the unwary public at a time of deep grief. When the bereaved person visits the undertaker's establishment, the undertaker disparages the advertised offering and plays upon the emotions of the family in order to palm off more expensive goods and services."

When the undertaker has possession of the body, he is in an even more advantageous position; it is not likely that the family will resist whatever price is set. If it insists on the advertised price, the suave manners are often replaced by the "hard sell."

The experience of a Los Angeles newspaper reporter several years ago indicates how hard that can be. Deciding to investigate one of the funeral homes advertising a very low "special" after he had heard several unpleasant reports of the place, he went to the establishment, representing himself as a man who had just lost his wife. He was welcomed cordially and led into a "selection" room where he was invited to take his pick of the caskets on display—the price of all of which far exceeded what had been advertised as the total price. When he insisted that he wanted information about the advertised funeral, he was turned over to another salesman. Then he was led down a flight of stairs to a basement room, where a pine box stood partly in a puddle of water beneath the glare of an unshaded light. Beside it on the floor was a small assortment of fruit peelings, seemingly arranged for the most distasteful effect.

"There it is, bud." The salesman kicked the casket. "That's the deal."

When he brought the story into the city room his reception was equally discouraging. The city editor read it, raised an eyebrow, and handed it back. "You're kidding," he said. "You know we can't use this. Look at the ads those people run."

Several years ago, when a committee from the Los Angeles Funeral Society called on funeral directors in the city to arrange a contract for providing final services for members, some of the experiences corroborated the reporter's. One mortician said: "We can show you something cheaper; it's for the sort of person who doesn't mind burying his mother in an orange crate." Another owner of a large establishment—he boasted of almost seven hundred "cases" a year—was equally scornful as he turned away business: "We don't want no soldiers' funerals."

As the California State Polytechnic College incident and the story of Mrs. Crawford indicate, selling funerals all out of proportion to a family's way of life is still a frequent abuse. In 1950, the United Auto Workers made a study of Ford Motor Company pensioners who died during the year; they found that while average life insurance benefits were only $1300, average funeral expenses were more than $800. In

1954, the New York attorney general charged that some low-income families were forced to pay the last cent of a dead person's insurance policy for a funeral service that normally cost half as much. Some undertakers were charged with "padding" funeral bills after they had learned what was in the savings account.

In many cases courts have ruled against excessive sums being spent; by order of the California Court of Appeals some years ago an undertaker's bill for $3101 was reduced to $750 on the grounds that such expenditures were unwarranted by the manner of living of the dead man—a sheepherder.

Perhaps not the least important reason that protest against inflation in funerals has been minimal is that the chief victims, persons with relatively low incomes, are a notably inarticulate group. Of course, other income groups are also affected, as may be inferred from advertisements on Los Angeles buses announcing "complete services—$95 to $4800." Nevertheless, a person who can pay $9700 or even $19,000 for a casket with an "Ever-seal air, watertight construction, and an Ever-Rite adjustable bed, all in zestful champagne finish, with a semi-tailored interior of gold tone, savoy crepe" is less liable to postburial suffering than the widow of a working man who is forced to hand over the insurance benefits.

In an article in the AFL-CIO's *I.U.D. Digest* in 1960, Dr. LeRoy Bowman, Brooklyn College sociologist and author of an outstanding book on funeral practices, described the exploitation of a family of foreign extraction and of less than modest means. The family was charged $3500 for the funeral and burial of their chief wage-earner. A study of 296 funeral bills made in 1961 by the International Ladies Garment Workers Union showed that the average cost was $899, exclusive of the cemetery plot, special transportation, and items of that sort. The survey also showed that Negroes and Spanish-speaking families were "frequent victims" of questionable practices.

Depressing as the situation is, it is certainly not incapable of solution. The idea that the funeral industry is a public utility and as such should be operated by the state or under state regulation has been acknowledged in Europe for years.

Prices and sales are regulated in England; in France, any of six classes of funerals at specified prices may be purchased through private undertakers working in contractual arrangement with the government. In Switzerland, every citizen is entitled to a free state funeral, carried out by municipal employees, with free grave, free casket, free hearse, and a car to follow it. Additional services or more costly merchandise may be purchased at government-fixed prices. The Scandinavian countries exercise strict control over burials.

In the United States, indigents and other public charges are buried at public cost by public agencies; however, great stigma is attached to the idea of a "charity" burial. The same stigma, interestingly enough, does not apply to a person's receiving death benefits, now totaling about $500, provided through Social Security and Veterans Administration programs. The undertakers consider that kind of subsidized funeral eminently acceptable, although the exercise of government control over prices and practices would, in their eyes, be socialism.

Since shortly after the Civil War, the trade associations have worked successfully in this country to prevent government "interference" with their activities at all levels—unless it suited their purposes. Although the return of dead servicemen to their communities had long been an optional matter, during the Korean conflict all were sent back. Veterans Administration allowances have continually increased to accommodate the inflationary tendencies in the undertaking and burial trade, and most local governments have obligingly scaled up the allowances for final rites for persons dying intestate. Actually, a major portion of small estates are diverted to pay mortuary expenses.

Recently, the government has been scrutinizing with a more careful eye the charges of undertakers who submit bills for government payment of funerals, and penalties have become more severe for those convicted of overcharging. However, in view of the general attitudes that have resulted from the educational activities of the trade, there is little likelihood that the government could or would act to curb excesses. A fairly recent incident demonstrates how sensitive reaction of government officials is in such matters. In February, 1957, the Army decided that in the interests of economy it would retire the funeral horses that follow the caisson of a general officer or cavalryman to an Arlington National Cemetery burial in favor of motorized hearses. A considerable saving was involved since the cost of an average caisson funeral was held to be $175 as opposed to $2.15 (two dollars fifteen cents) for a motorized burial. Outcries against the "lack of respect" for the country's dead were so violent that the then Secretary of the Army Wilber M. Brucker reversed his decision because "the economies were outweighed by intangible values." The horses stayed.

With public action unlikely, a private solution has been advanced by church groups, labor unions, consumer cooperatives, and interested individuals bent on reform. Memorial societies and funeral cooperatives working to obtain for members simple, dignified funerals at modest cost have grown extraordinarily rapidly during the last ten years in the United States and Canada. Although they differ widely in structure and scope, all emphasize the importance of pre-need arrangements. All stress education and group action.

The latter points are important because many undertaking establishments and cemetery owners have found pre-need plans exceedingly profitable ventures. Being able to accomplish a glorious exit on the installment plan has had great appeal, particularly to older persons who are determined to compensate for unsatisfactory lives by obtaining the best of everything in death. What a burden that can be was revealed by some elderly neighbors of mine recently. The couple, living on his Social Security allowance and her earnings as a practical nurse working part-time, pay $50 a month under a five-year contract to a Los Angeles establishment that advertises complete undertaking for less than $150.

"Of course, that includes everything," the woman explained cheerfully, "even the clergyman."

The idea of a businessman selling the services of a clergyman along with caskets, flowers, cemetery plots, and assorted items is so extraordinary that recently many—Catholic, Protestant, and Jewish, alike—have uttered sharp protests. The trade has countered with equal sharpness. An editorial in the March, 1962, issue of *Casket and Sunnyside*, the oldest and perhaps most influential trade journal in the mortuary business, exhorted funeral directors to protect themselves: "Shall control of funeral service be left to the dictatorial orders of the uninformed or self-seeking members of the clergy? Or shall the American people have the right to bury their dead with dignity and after their own conscience in keeping with their financial needs?" Meantime, the morticians continue their effort to acquire semiclerical status by constructing elaborate chapels and even churches—as necessary business facilities.

By making arrangements in advance it is possible to insure that decisions are rational, as they frequently are not during periods of grief when there is a strong desire to escape reality and to ignore practical matters. Even when grief is not overwhelming, however, persons respond to sales pressures applied by members of the trade with greater readiness than in other circumstances. For example, last year a Los Angeles teacher showed me the bill for the funeral of his father-in-law, who had died in California after an illness. Although Mr. and Mrs. George Lyon are not extravagant people, "something happened" when they made the arrangements. What happened precisely was that they were persuaded to pay $744.50 for the casket and professional services, $10 for permits, $5 for five certified copies of the death certificate, and $10 for an organist—although the service was extremely simple since the dead man's home had been in Boston and he had made relatively few friends during his California visit. Publications cost another $12.50, and the charge for a travel case for shipping the body to Boston was $75. Transportation amounted to $482.72, $234 of which was the price of a round-trip ticket for the daughter to accompany the body. (To send a body unaccompanied usually costs even more.) When they reached Boston, another mortician took over and charged several hundred dollars to rearrange the hair and apply more rouge and to provide other modest services.

The only bargain item on the Los Angeles bill had been the clergyman's fee, originally set at $5. Mr. and Mrs. Lyon insisted on increasing that substantially, although the undertaker said that it was not necessary. "We felt that it would have been an affront to our pastor to do otherwise after all the time he spent and the kindness he showed us."

If the teacher and his wife had belonged to the Los Angeles Funeral Society, a consumer group organized in 1957, they would have been able to obtain a funeral for less than $150, including the casket, embalming, viewing, use of the mortuary chapel, and delivery of the body to the airport. Instead, they paid almost $1000 for these services, exclusive of the Boston costs.

Financial benefits offered by the cooperative and church groups are undoubtedly great. One member of the Bay Area group in Berkeley, California, reported that eight months before he joined the association he had arranged for the burial of his mother through a mortuary. A few months after joining, he had to arrange for the burial of his father. Services for the former, he said, were inferior to the services he received through the association, and the cost had been $800 in contrast to the $150 cost for his father's funeral.

Because a return to simplicity shifts the focus from the body to the spiritual significance of death and of life, many clergymen have enthusiastically supported the societies. For example, six clergymen volunteered to serve on the advisory council of the Bay Area association: Dr. Josiah Bartlett, Jr., dean of the Starr King School of the Ministry, pastors of two Unitarian churches, a Lutheran minister, and a Methodist minister.

The industry, of course, has strenuously opposed the efforts of churches, unions, and consumer cooperatives to organize such groups. Most of them have had very real difficulty finding an undertaker willing to work with them. For more than fifteen years burial cooperatives in the Middle West were hampered by having supplies withheld. In Chicago and several other cities it has been impossible for groups to obtain contracts from undertakers, who have been frank about fear of reprisals. Their association with the Bay Area cooperative was a principal reason for two California undertakers having been written out of their trade association in 1961. The Los Angeles group spent months going from one mortuary to another before they finally encountered an undertaker willing to risk the wrath of the trade. "I heard you people were coming," more than one mortician said. "I can't have anything to do with you."

The Palo Alto group, now one of the largest in the country, met similar discouragement. Mrs. Londa S. Fletcher, who had been appointed by the Friends Meeting to work out a simple arrangement after she had been revolted by the "mock mourning" of the undertakers at her grandmother's funeral, was rebuffed by a number of the local undertakers before finding an "excellent" man. "We have no minimum price," was their standard answer to her inquiry. That was sometimes supplemented with: "We know your group are generally able to have a *good* funeral, and we think you should," or "We don't like the funerals of your people; what we like are the Portuguese and Spanish."

Mrs. Fletcher's reports of progress quickly acquired allies, and within a few weeks thirteen residents of the college community, including six leading clergymen, helped her to work out a plan that resulted in the formation of the Peninsula Memorial Society on a nonprofit, nondenominational basis. Within less than ten years the group had acquired 1200 member families, who were able to obtain what they considered proper funerals for as little as $150.

The word "proper" with respect to funerals is an important word. Many—perhaps most of the members of the funeral societies—have enough money to spend on an elaborate funeral if they desire one. Some do; some do not. All feel, however, that they are entitled to the freedom of rational choice.

A number of undertakers agree. Those who have entered into contracts with the memorial societies and funeral cooperatives have generally reported themselves satisfied with the arrangement. The Seattle mortician who has worked with the People's Memorial Association there since 1939, over the protests of his colleagues, feels that the association has been "of extraordinary value." Although he has been able to realize only a "modest profit" on the minimum arrangement —$100 for immediate cremation—members have brought other business.

In Los Angeles, where about four hundred are plying the

trade, the tables were recently turned when several under-takers sought out the funeral society to try to work out a contract. But many continue to be frightened and to react in a hostile way to what they consider a threat to their existence. The means some have employed have violated rules of fair play—circulating scurrilous and sometimes libelous comments about members of the associations, employing private in-vestigators to get "inside" reports on the open meetings and complete records of officers and members. More frequently, however, they have protested against the associations, claim-ing them to be irreligious and unpatriotic.

The industry's position is neatly summarized in a letter sent by the president of one of the largest mortuary firms in the United States to a Los Angeles television commentator who had devoted a program to a discussion of the memorial so-cieties in California, where there are now ten.

"I have no desire," the letter began, "to become a part directly or indirectly of the controversy being stirred up on the subject of memorial societies who advocate quick un-ceremonious disposal of the body much as we dispose of refuse and trash. However, I do think you should be re-minded, simply for your own thinking, that the funeral cere-mony is a religious service and that the idea of quick disposal of the body will go a long way toward eliminating any observ-ance of faith in God, in the hereafter, and in the immortality of the soul." He concluded with an assertion that 30 per cent of the families served by the company spend less than $400 for the complete funeral, and with an expression of confidence in the fairness of the commentator.

That letter, a masterly exercise in rhetoric, was written by the president of the company which had sent the bill for $1419.74 for the Los Angeles services rendered the teacher's father-in-law and which had to be instructed to increase the clergyman's fee to a "fitting" amount. The sentiments might also have been more convincing if the company had not been indicted by a federal grand jury some years ago and five executives fined $9000 by a United States district judge on charges of conspiracy to defraud the government in the han-dling of veterans' funerals.

In spite of the scope and intensity of the funeral industry's protest, the reform program is growing to such extent that there is genuine hope that the costly and barbaric shows for the dead may be abolished in the interests of the living. It will, as one California clergyman said, require a "long, slow process of education." For it must be remembered that in the present system, the industry has on its side not only the laws it has helped to write, but our attitudes that it has remolded to conform to its own interests: respect for the dead, the need for ritualistic expression of grief, the desire to conform to socially approved standards, the yearning for tangible evidence of immortality. It has also exploited the worst of our motivations and desires: snobbery, vanity, the chance to rid ourselves of feelings of guilt through a payoff.

We are and we have been, in all fairness, our own chief victimizers.

SO LETS WAKE UP; B4 WE DROPDEAD!!

Chapter 2

Epic Beginnings of Epic Endings

WHO ARE WE? Why are we? What are we?

Because they attempt to provide us with answers to those overwhelming questions, art, history, and archaeology offer exciting and absorbing discovery routes. To an even greater extent so does literature, which emphasizes not differences nor distances, but the sameness of evolving men—the human verities that are eternal.

So it is that the epic, the oldest and most spacious of all literary forms, continues to surprise and delight us by holding up a mirror of man not as he *was* but as he *is*. Gilgamesh, Ulysses, Achilles, Aeneas, Beowulf, Roland—those epic heroes speak to us across a thousand, two thousand, even four thousand years in the comprehensible idiom of the psyche, of the heart. Our ability to understand them indicates our ability to understand ourselves and our contemporaries; for more than any other single force, I think, they have molded our desires, have shaped our ideals of conduct, virtue, courage, love, dignity, ambition, friendship. They have provided us with our concept of the great life—and the even greater death.

It is something of a surprise to realize how preoccupied are the epic celebrations of the heroic life with celebrations of the heroic death. Much of the *Odyssey*, the entire conclusion of

31

Beowulf, thousands of the clay tablets on which the *Gilgamesh Epic* was inscribed, many of the most moving *laisses* of the *Song of Roland*, much of the *Aeneid*, and the last third of the *Iliad* are concerned exclusively with the funerals and burials of the heroes.

The reason is that the heroes of all of them—Babylonian-Sumerian, Greek, Roman, Alexandrian, and medieval European—are linked to each other and to us by their central quest: the search for immortality. All are defeated in their effort to find it here on earth—by fate, by the gods, by the nature of things. But all make their departure richly assured of everlastingness in a permanent afterward that is, in most instances, a literal translation of impermanent now. The guarantee is the elaborately conducted burial ritual that gives to the shadow all the rights and privileges possessed by the substance—a guarantee, incidentally, that is as much in demand today as it was in the glorious Greece of Homer more than 2500 years ago or in archaic Sumer more than four thousand years ago when Gilgamesh, "in the dark month, the month of shadows," set off for the kingdom of dust with his offerings of bread and ale.

Although most men lead lives bearing more resemblance to that of James Joyce's Leopold Bloom than to that of Homer's Ulysses of the hyacinth beard, in death they insist upon their heroic due. Far from regarding that natural phenomenon—death—as the great leveler, they have come to visualize it as the great elevator—the one opportunity to participate in the epic tradition. They have never trod the plains before Troy nor seen Calypso's isle; they have never, even briefly, possessed the flower of eternal youth, nor manned the Pass of Roncevaux. But they can know what it is like to cross the Styx in style; and—by Jupiter—most insist they will.

That is why, in spite of a few thousand years of secular and religious education and in spite of our avowed adherence to the Judaic-Christian tradition, the themes and rituals that characterize modern funerals are rooted firmly in pagan and primitive ceremonies and rites so lovingly detailed in the ancient epics as models and guides for the living: the elaborate preparation of the corpse, its ceremonial disposal, and the commemorative activities.

Although they may have varied in other respects, all of the ancient societies that are recreated in the Western epics were agreed that the most terrible misfortune that could befall a man is that which climaxes the curse for disobedience in the Bible: "The Lord saith. And thy carcass shall be meat unto all fowls of the air, and unto the beasts of the field, and no man shall *fray* them away."

Proper burial, on the contrary, was regarded as a blessing —a triumph over death—since it was the only way to achieve status and security in the underworld, where the shades appeared precisely as they did at the moment of departure. That notion, of course, accounts for the ambivalent attitude that has always prevailed. Although the Sumerians and Babylonians, as much as the Greeks and Romans, resisted the idea of mortality, all felt that it was better to enter the spirit world while life was at its peak in order to perpetuate that condition eternally. Since the obligation to construct a bridge between the hereafter and the here-and-now was with the living, every effort was made to provide a king or hero with the lavish send-off that was considered his due and would serve as his passport. The more demonstrably he was a hero, the more lavish the send-off. Commoners, of course, could not hope to improve their position, and their burials were, consequently, stark affairs. Children, ancients, and women (except in the Norse systems) fared little better since they were destined to sit below the salt in the underworld as they had in the upper. A notable exception was Dido, but then she was an exotic queen, who could and did treat herself to a splendid farewell appearance.

Without the approved ceremony, the shade could not even gain admittance to the kingdom of the dead, to say nothing of continuing an honored no-existence as a lively shade. Moreover, omission of the rites could affect the living as much as the dead—just in case further prodding was needed. Elpenor, one of Ulysses' men who fell off Circe's roof in a drunken bout, warned his leader when they met in the kingdom of the dead: "Do not leave me unmourned and unburied; do not desert me, or I may draw God's vengeance upon you!" Failure to provide a hero with a proper burial, according to "divine decree," was regarded as a cosmic offense. Even long-patient Zeus was forced to intervene in the Trojan War by sending Thetis to the wrathful Achilles with an ultimatum that he surrender Hector's body to his father.

Gaining possession of the body from the hands of the enemy who might outrage it was the first step in the complex series of incidents leading to final disposal. This need is described most vividly in the *Iliad*, in which Books Seventeen through Twenty-four—one-third of the entire work—are devoted to the struggle between Greeks and Trojans over the bodies of their respective heroes, Patroclos and Hector. Those two episodes brought the ten-year war to a climax, with Achilles abandoning his nine-year sulk after being warned by emissaries of Zeus and Hera against allowing the Trojan dogs to tumble and tear his friend. When Achilles finally confronted Hector, he cried to him vengefully: "I have brought you low. Now you shall be mauled by vultures and dogs, and he (Patroclos) shall be buried by a mourning nation." When Achilles dragged the body of her son in the dust to dishonor it, the mother of Hector threatened to eat his liver in revenge—a genuinely shocking threat among the Greeks.

The Romans, whose respect for the dead was so great that leaving the Christians' burial grounds unmolested was the only surcease from persecution accorded them, were deeply concerned with fine, friendly burials. In the *Aeneid* a whole series of incidents reveals that. The leader and his men gave Polydorus, who had been slain and improperly buried by the King of Thrace, a new burial before they left that country, and promised to make amends to the helmsman who drowned on the voyage so that his spirit would not be forced to wander for a century—the fate of the unburied dead. Aeneas, who undoubtedly holds the undertaking record among ancient heroes, having buried father, nurse, comrades, friends, and allies with fitting honors, reached the height of vindictiveness after the death of his friend, Pallas. In a rage he kicked the decapitated body of Tarquitus, the slayer: "Lie where you are, you who expected us to fear you. Your mother shall never lay you fondly in the earth, or consign your remains to any stately family tomb." In epic tradition, he later recovered his magnanimity and declared a time out of war so that all the dead might be buried properly.

The importance of being buried by friends and family was as great to Gilgamesh, the legendary king who ruled Uruk in the third millenium B.C., as it was to Charlemagne's vassals who battled against the Saracens in 778 A.D. According to that most ancient epic, the spirit of him whose body lies unburied will find no rest in the underworld and it will be forced to eat garbage thrown into the streets. Oliver permitted his friend to blow the horn to summon Charlemagne only after Archbishop Turpin reminded him that after exacting vengeance their emperor would bury them properly in the close of the church.

Once the body was in friendly hands, preparations for the final ceremonies began. The extent of preparations and the time devoted to predisposal mourning and ritual varied considerably. For the commoners, it was enough to wrap them in a covering and burn or bury them immediately. For heroes and kings, a long time was of the essence. Any indication of haste was regarded as unseemly. Although embalming was not practiced by the Greeks, they believed that the gods indicated their favor toward a person like Patroclos by preserving him to meet the need for time. Although the Trojan War was still being fought, Priam told Achilles, who had volunteered to hold off his Greek host long enough to permit Hector a proper burial, that it would take at least eleven days: "We would mourn him nine days in the house, on the tenth day we would bury him and feast the people, on the eleventh we would build a barrow, and on the twelfth we will fight, if we must."

Achilles, himself, as Agamemnon reminded him enviously when they met on the meadow of asphodel in the *Odyssey*, had had a glorious exit: "Seventeen days and seventeen nights we mourned you, mortal men and immortal gods together; on the eighteenth day we gave you to the fire, and slew around you fatted cattle and sheep."

The record for the longest pre-interment period is held by *El Cid*, in the *Chronica*, which Southey incorporated into his translation of the Spanish epic. According to that version, the body of Cid Ruydiez, after traveling half the breadth of Spain propped up in his saddle, sat for ten years on an ivory chair in the monastery of San Pedro de Cardeña. But by the end of the thirteenth century when that was written, North African customs and influences had transformed the simple ceremony favored by Jewish and Christian rites into a necrophile's delight.

Western attitudes toward death have not been notable for their consistency. On the one hand, it has been visualized as more of the lively hours; on the other, it has been conceived of as a kind of rest and sleep. An indication of the latter is that in the Western epics the bodies were almost always stretched out on some kind of bier (bed of fate), washed ritualistically with warm water, and anointed with oil; eyes and mouth were closed. Although the significance of that is a matter of speculation, its importance is not. Agamemnon's rage against his murdering wife rose to a crescendo when he described his wretched end to Achilles: as he lay dying with a sword through his body, "the bitch turned her back, she would not take the trouble to draw down my eyelids or to close my mouth in death."

Sartorial elegance was stressed—even when cremation was to follow. Gilgamesh laid a veil, "as one veils a bride," over his friend. Achilles was burned in "raiment of the gods," and he, himself, to demonstrate what a generous enemy he could be, provided a fine tunic for Hector's body. Aeneas did honor to the body of Pallas by wrapping it in one of the gold-embroidered purple garments Dido had given him and by covering his hair with the other. Although Christian tradition favored only a simple shroud, Charlemagne had Roland, Oliver, and Bishop Turpin washed with spices and wine and wrapped about in roebuck's hide, with rich Oriental materials covering them. The body of *El Cid*, at the king's command, was clad in a succession of splendid robes.

While death was considered on the one hand similar to rest and sleep, it was also regarded—as John Donne noted—as a short sleep after which "we wake eternally." And it was that duality that accounted for the heroes' being sent off with all the equipment and impedimenta they would need on a journey to any strange land.

At Ur, the royal dead were carried off to their tombs on the bed of fate astonishingly well provided with food, drink, clothing, and other personal effects. Distressingly, they also took their retinue along with them on the theory that servants and wives and aides would be just as useful in death as in life. The dead king or noble was under obligation to provide for them in the hereafter, and thus he alone was required to take the necessary store of bread and wine to feed his followers. Faulkner's short story "Red Leaves" indicates how common and how widespread that custom was.

Fifteen hundred years later, the Homeric Greeks were just as concerned about proper provisions for the dead. For Patroclos' "journey," Achilles had the Myrmidons kill flocks of sheep and herds of cattle, which were cut up and heaped about the body beside jars of oil and honey. In addition, he provided the body of his dead friend with four horses, two of his nine dogs, and twelve noble young Trojans to serve as bodyguards and attendants.

The Alexandrians were not remiss in such matters. When Idmon, the soothsayer, was killed by a boar in the course of the *Voyage of Argo,* the Argonauts slaughtered many sheep at his grave, "as is a dead man's due."

Similar provision was made in the Rome of Augustus. To honor Pallas, Aeneas had his bier heaped high with the prizes he had won and with some horses and weapons that were gifts of the Trojans. Aeneas also thoughtfully provided a contingent of captives to be sent as death offerings to the shade, "the blood of whose slaying was to sprinkle the flames." In *Beowulf,* essentially outside the Christian tradition, the custom persists. His people hung around the funeral pyre the helmets, battle shields, and other war trophies he had requested. And in the subsequently built monument they laid gold and gems and the treasure he had wrested from the serpent in his last great battle. The *Song of Roland* alone is characterized by the traditional simplicity of Christian burial, so notably demonstrated by the unmarked niches in the cata-combs.

Two symbols that recur constantly through the accounts of death in Western society are hair, significant perhaps because it continues to grow beyond death, and blood, the essence of life. Offering hair to the dead is perhaps the oldest and most pervasive of all gestures. Gilgamesh lamented the death of Enkidu by tearing out his hair; the Myrmidons covered the body of Patroclos with their hair, "like a shroud"; Achilles added to the heap the golden tress he had kept uncut to sacrifice to the god of the river that had given him near-immortality. The curious Roman belief in the strong bond between earthly life and hair was illustrated when Iris flew down to Dido, who had fallen on her sword; the goddess cut a lock of the queen's golden hair "to assign her life to Stygian Orcus."

Blood was as important to the shades as it was to their substantial antecedents. It was much more important than food since it gave them the *vitality* they needed to enjoy the delights of the afterworld in a worldly manner. In Greek and Roman epics much emphasis is laid upon sprinkling the pyre with the blood of enemies and animals. Ulysses took great pains to follow Circe's instructions on his visit to the kingdom of the dead, refusing to allow any—even the bloodthirsty spirit of his mother—to come near the blood of the black ram and the black ewe he had sacrificed until the soothsayer had drunk his fill and told Ulysses what he wanted to know about his homeward journey.

The burial ceremony proper was, of course, the high point in the rites. Of the six methods universally prevalent for disposing of the dead—inhumation, cremation, preservation, exposure, water burial, artificial decomposition—only the first two were employed in the Western cultures described in the epics, both of which ceremonies provided the ancients with plenty of opportunity for conspicuous consumption.

For the Sumerians, to whom death meant the journey to the house "whose people sit in darkness," burial meant the elaborate ritual of carrying to the underground tomb the bed of fate, with all provisions and as many as eighty attendants. The attendants were not stretched out in the tomb, but were buried in a crouched position so that they would be ready to spring to service at the nod of the master shade.

Although the Greeks and Romans practiced earth burial on occasion—indeed, as the *Antigone* emphasizes, a mere ceremonial sprinkling of earth on the corpse was sufficient to guarantee passage—the proper end of the heroic life was cremation. The bigger the hero, the bigger the pyre. Like many other primitive people, they may have preferred this partly because the dead were to be feared; mostly, however, they believed that the fire would help to speed the spirit on its way more quickly. As Ulysses' mother explained to him when they met in the kingdom of the dead: "As soon as the spirit leaves the white bones, the sinews no longer hold the flesh and bones together—the blazing fire consumes them all; but the soul flits away fluttering like a dream."

Cremations were extremely elaborate, as accounts in the *Odyssey, Iliad,* and *Aeneid* testify. Contrasting the glorious farewell of Achilles with his own miserable exit, the shade of Agamemnon told the shade of Achilles: "You were burnt in raiment of the gods, with honey and oil in abundance; troops of armed warriors marched around the pyre, both horse and footmen, with a loud resounding noise." The morning after the flames had consumed him, the Greeks gathered the bones and laid them with pure wine and oil in a golden urn, mingled with the body of his dead friend, Patroclos. Patroclos' pyre had been one hundred feet each way, so large that Iris had had to persuade the winds to go.

Hector was cremated in a glowing manner. On the tenth day, his body was laid on a pyre, and on the eleventh the flame was quenched with wine. Then the bones were placed in a golden casket and wrapped in soft purple cloth; the casket was laid in a hollow space so that a memorial could be erected over it. Aeneas carried on the Trojan tradition in a fittingly Roman spirit. Observing the traditional rites of the Greeks, the Romans draped the pyres with dark green leaves and fronted them with funeral cypresses. They carefully averted their faces when they fired the great piles of tree trunks, and after washing the ashes in wine and enclosing them in urns they had to submit themselves to purification: clean water was carried around them three times and then sprinkled on the participants with the bough of a fertile olive tree.

The *Aeneid* scornfully contrasts the Trojan-Roman customs with those of the "unhappy" Latins during the twelve-day truce declared to enable both sides to dispose of their dead warriors. The Latins built numberless pyres, although they buried some of the bodies in the earth and removed others to nearby ground so that they could be sent home to their own cities. The rest "they cremated without ritual or count, a huge, chaotic heap of carnage." On the third day, they heaped the bones together and piled over them a mound of earth. The Trojans, on the other hand, scrupulously observed the proper formalities in their incineration, "all following the fashion of their forbears." Black-smoking brands were applied to the base of the pyres. Then troops, wearing shining arms, rode on horseback three times around the fire, crying the lament. Men shouted and trumpets brayed while they cast on the fire the trophies of war taken from slain Latins—helmets, swords, bridles, wheels, shields, and other offerings. Then they killed many bulls as a sacrifice to Death, and cut the throats of bristle-haired boars and flocks which they had seized from every field "to spout their blood into the flame" and gratify the spirits' unspiritual thirst.

Although *Beowulf*, the Anglo-Saxon epic about a man's search for immortalizing honor, is usually considered to be a mixture of pagan fairy tale and historical tradition "passed through the refining fire of Christianity," consideration of his death and burial indicates that the Christian element is a thin veneer. After his struggle to wrest the treasure from the serpent that has mortally wounded him, the seventh-century hero gave detailed instructions to his loyal kinsman, Wiglaf, about his departure. Consequently, the Geats prepared for their leader "a noble pyre," hung—as he had desired—with helmets and battle shields, and with lamentations the soldiers set alight "the greatest funeral fire." Those lavish pyres, designed to guarantee complete incineration, undoubtedly did much to produce a scarcity of wood. That shortage was so serious that many early peoples considered wood as precious as fine metals or gems. Indeed, one French scholar—with more truth than humor—has estimated that if the custom had been continued the Mediterranean peoples might have died out because of lack of fuel. *Hm-m-m-m-m..*

The Jewish people, with greater respect for resources, held cremation taboo, as did the Christians. Curiously enough, the Alexandrians exhibited a distaste for the practice. Although they drew heavily upon both Greece and Egypt, where the death cult reached its most elaborate form, their burials seem remarkably restrained compared to those of other Western groups. Although the Alexandrians continued the practice of slaying animals to provide the spirits with blood, they favored inhumation and they placed chief emphasis on personal grief. In the land of the Mariandyni, where they lost Tiphys as well as Idmon, their attitude is described in a moving passage in the *Voyage of Argo* after the former's death: "Their grief at this catastrophe was profound, and when they had buried him also, close to the other, they cast themselves down by the sea in despair and lay there wrapped up like figures cut in stone, without a word and with no thought of food or drink."

A relatively simple earth burial was accorded the heroes in the *Song of Roland*. Charlemagne's terrible grief at the death of Roland and his valiant troops was assuaged by his determination to provide all the men and lords who fell in battle with a proper burial. When they had been found, all were laid "in one great trench." The bishops, canons, monks, and priests who had accompanied the army absolved the dead and made the sign of the cross over them. Then they kindled myrrh and incense in thick clouds, and censed the bodies "with a lavish hand," perhaps in the belief that the spirit would be wafted aloft with the smoke.

"So there they leave them; what else were in their power?" This curious question in the epic, apologetically appended to the account, is some revelation that by the end of the eleventh century, when the poem is said to have taken final shape, social distinctions that were unknown to the early Christians had come to dominate death and burial ceremonies.

Although an on-the-spot burial had to suffice even the great Peers of France, Charlemagne had Roland, Oliver, and Bishop Turpin prepared for a special interment after the defeat of the Emir. He had their bodies opened before his eyes and their hearts removed and wrapped in fine silk before they were placed in white marble urns. That curious custom, reminiscent of early Egyptian embalming practices, had become so extensive in Christendom by the thirteenth century that in 1294 Pope Boniface VIII issued a papal decree forbidding separate burial of the heart—a decree rescinded by one of his successors in answer to public demand. The epic further emphasizes that the bodies of the three "greats" were carried back to France for a splendid burial in white tombs at St. Romayne's.

Perhaps the only traditional aspect of the burial of *El Cid* was that it occurred in "sanctified ground." In proper pagan fashion, he went to his reward with elaborate trappings; even the body of his horse was buried nearby.

The building of a barrow over the bones or body by no means meant the end of the affair. After the weeping and lamentations and the ceremonial marches three times around the burial spot, funeral feasts were held and elaborate funeral games were staged to honor the dead. Earliest accounts of funeral repasts emphasize that the food and liquor—in large quantities—were entombed with the dead. However, in a more practical spirit the Greeks instituted the custom of having the living partake of the good things to eat and drink—a custom that soon became characterized by lavish and extravagant display.

After Achilles had led the cavalcade around the bier of Patroclos, but before the burial, he invited the thousands of Myrmidons to sit down beside his ship and share the funeral feast of bulls, sheep, goats, and boars. Spirit food was also thoughtfully set out: "Around the dead body the blood of the victims poured out in cupfuls was running all over the ground." Priam, too, was mindful that custom required him to be a gracious host to both the living and the dead; after Hector's bones were buried, all returned to the city, "and the whole assemblage had a famous feast in the palace of Priam their King. That was the funeral of Hector."

Funeral feasts were supplemented with elaborate games to honor the dead and to provide something of value for the lucky mourners. In the anniversary ceremony Aeneas staged with filial piety for his father, he and his men celebrated the "joyful duty" with prayer and feasting for eight days. On the ninth, Aeneas summoned the shade of his father—whose spirit had been released from Acheron for the rite—and ordered the funeral games to begin. He thus provided the shade with one of its favorite diversions in life and offered good evidence that he was the proper son of a priest.

The funeral games in which friends and allies of the dead man competed for costly prizes climaxed the elaborate pagan death ceremonies. Both Virgil and Homer stress the importance of the magnanimous gesture: Aeneas and Achilles demonstrated themselves thoroughly aware of the responsibility placed upon them by exhibiting the generosity of a potlatch host in awarding prizes for the boat races, boxing matches, foot races, wrestling matches, discus hurling, archery, and fencing competitions. Achilles gave not only first and second prizes for the chariot races, but third, fourth, and fifth.

In other cultures, however, games were less favored than commemorative gestures of a more permanent nature. Poets from Horace to Shakespeare vaunted their ability to provide monuments "more lasting than bronze," but according to many, few spirits seem to have been satisfied with anything less.

The Egyptians, of course, built their own mausoleums; but in most societies a build-it-yourself monument has been considered bad form. The ultimate test of friendship has been the amount of money and imagination expended on a remembrance. Gilgamesh ended his seven-day lament for his friend in a manner that earned him an enviable reputation: he summoned goldsmiths and stoneworkers from all parts of the land to make a statue of Enkidu. Achilles sympathized with Agamemnon that he had not been killed at Troy instead of returning home to be murdered: "Then the whole Achaian nation would have built you a tomb to keep a glorious memory of you and your son both."

Agamemnon graciously retorted that the gods had given Achilles proof of their love through the funeral games and the "great and notable" tomb built for him on a headland above the Hellespont. The drowned helmsman in the *Aeneid* was consoled for having to wander a century because he had not received burial with the Cumean Sybil's promise that "people will make atonement" by erecting a tomb. The emperor provided a tomb for Roland and his two friends, and the king of Spain did similar honor to *El Cid*. Perhaps the noblest of the epic tombs was Beowulf's barrow of Hronesness—to guide the seafarers who sail "across the darkness of the flood."

In considering present funeral practices in relation to the epics, the "persistence of memory" has all the acute surrealism of a Dali painting. Any current account of a celebrity reveals the strength of those ancient influences—the $800,000 tomb of Irving Thalberg in Forest Lawn; the tomb of Lenin in the Kremlin, from which the body of Stalin was recently unceremoniously dumped; the vast mausoleum and church in Los Angeles patterned after St. Sophia's, built by a famous movie-maker to honor God and himself; Generalissimo Franco's multimillion-dollar monument in the Guadarrama Mountains—Spain's only public work of any consequence since the dictator seized power. All of those and millions of other lesser efforts to achieve immortality indicate the profound influence the epic conception of death has had on Western culture.

In what sharp contrast to those lavish farewells is the simple account of Socrates' departure—or, for that matter, of those of the Old Testament prophets and of Christ. But those persons were quickly recognized as dangerous men, concerned with the good life rather than with material ambitions or the kind of "immortal longings" that masquerade in robe and crown. Socrates' admonition to his sorrowing friends to "be of good cheer and say that you are burying my body only" carries little weight with most men compared to the promises held out by epic poets of the chance to lead, on the other side of the Styx, the heroic life that they have never known.

Chapter 3

The World, the Flesh, and the Funeral

THEORETICALLY, the attitude toward death and burial of the Greeks and Romans and of such predecessors as the Sumerians and the Egyptians seem absurd—naïve and irrelevant—to us in the light of our Judaic-Christian tradition. Practically, however, those attitudes have become our attitudes to an extraordinary degree.

There are, to be sure, some parallels between Old and New Testament eschatological beliefs and those of the important pagan groups that helped to mold Western culture. All share the conception that death is inevitable, that the spirit continues to exist after having shuffled off the mortal coil, that judgment of some kind will be rendered on the conduct of life. Among the early Hebrews, burial places were regarded as sacred, and offerings of material treasures—spices, incense, food—were made to the dead. The anxiety of the ancient Hebrew to have a son originated in part, as Robert W. Habenstein and William M. Lamers have pointed out in *The History of American Funeral Directing,* from the fear that there would be no one after his death to provide him with the gifts he needed so that his soul could enjoy rest. The Hebrews also considered that a grave was essential; to have a body left unburied is one of the most dreadful fates mentioned in the Old Testament.

BOO!!

45

On the other hand, both the Old and the New Testament reject the notion that different gods control the worlds of the living and the dead or that the departed can harm or help the living. More dramatically different is the Biblical conception of a resurrection of the flesh. Although the Egyptians believed that the various elements that left the body at death could be reconstituted, as had occurred with Osiris, many consider that the effect of this belief—which gave rise to the practice of embalming—had been to "mortalize" the soul. All of the arts of religion and science were employed by the Egyptians to make the body so attractive and so well preserved that it would lure the Soul, the Name, the Shadow, and the Heart to "cohabit with it."

Moreover, the Judaic-Christian conceptions of life and death also evolved with a growing emphasis on spiritual egalitarianism. The upper-caste pagan ancients might not have agreed that this was the best of all possible worlds, but it was the world in which one was alive, enjoying certain privileges. Consequently, it was so much more desirable than the terrifying afterworld of death that they used every item that came to hand and mind—food, animals, slaves, wine, blood, clothing, hair, women, jewels, weapons—as links to bind the two existences inseparably and in such a way as to keep their social status intact.

Morally more sophisticated, the Jewish and later the Christian leaders looked upon the world and found it wanting. Where, under the sun, was justice? Unable to free themselves from the knowledge that hunger, sickness, poverty, and misery were inescapable facts of the world to which a Creator had exposed them, a world in which vice was often more handsomely rewarded than virtue, they fashioned an afterward that contradicted the *status quo:* a world of perfect justice where the will of a just and perfect God would be done. Life was, therefore, a kind of extended birth struggle; the grave was not the end, but the beginning of the real life.

The Judaic-Christian conception of the hereafter was not merely a *spirit* world, but a genuinely *spiritual* one. Intellectually and imaginatively more subtle in spite of their relatively late arival on the historical scene (Egypt had its pyramids by

3000 B.C. and Sumer was also at that time a great empire), the Jews were able to distinguish between *kinds* of existences; their predecessors, simpler-minded, had not been able to. Such distinctions have been beyond many of the Jews' successors, too—bringing to mind the child of one of my neighbors whose natural religious perplexities have been compounded in this space age by "getting the angels all mixed up with the Martians."

To the more rigorous Jewish leaders, all the values and triumphs of the material world were perfectly irrelevant in the spiritual world; therefore, admittance could not be gained by materialistic bribes, nor could status be determined by material possessions. Consequently, lavish funerary display was not merely beside the point, but blasphemous.

Observances were modified by theological doctrine and by contact with neighboring cultures; for example, after the Babylonian captivity (597-547 B.C.) coffins came into general use, shrouds became fashionable, and after the manner of Greeks and Romans some Jewish officials during later centuries were buried with ornaments and gold and silver, according to their historian Flavius Josephus.

In spite of the modifications and deviations, however, their religious beliefs dictated the generally stark and simple nature of the traditional funeral and burial rites. Other important influences were sanitary and hygienic concerns, and the belief that the dead were dead so far as this world was concerned: "They no longer have a share forever in anything that is done under the sun" (Ecclesiastes 9:6). While there was no need for appeasement because of fear—a profoundly important motivation for most lavish funerals—there was a need for respectful mourning: "With what is death comparable?" asks the *Jewish Code of Laws.* "With the burning of a Scroll of the Torah, as there is none so worthless in Israel who neither possessed some degree of knowledge, nor had fulfilled some of its commandments."

These varying influences resulted in a certain amount of ambivalence in the Jewish attitude toward death—an ambivalence that has characterized every major religion and every major culture. The attitude gave rise to religious laws and rituals that have been observed for thousands of years by the orthodox and that very largely determined Christian practices for centuries, since Christ—whose death as whose life became a model for followers—received essentially a Jewish burial. ✓

In reaching a conclusion about what constituted the proper observances when death occurred, Jewish and Christian leaders had to resolve seemingly irresolvable antitheses. Since men had been promised everlasting life, death was an unnatural interruption that gave deep cause for mourning and weeping. On the other hand, since death was the beginning of everlasting life, that birth-death had to be celebrated in a fitting manner. The soul alone was held to be of concern to God; the flesh was "unclean." If the soul departed at the moment of death, nothing remained but earthly vileness. On the other hand, since death and decay would be vanquished through the miracle of resurrection on the great day, the body had to be treated in such a way that it would be worthy of reunion with the soul.

Biblical resolution of those paradoxes was the orientation of funeral and burial ceremonies away from the body and toward the spirit—a dramatic reversal of most pagan answers. The delicacy of the point of balance gave rise to a rigid code among the Jews which is still binding on the faithful after long centuries of their wide dispersal. All of the rites and ceremonies prescribed in the *Code of Laws* are governed by the belief in resurrection and in the supremacy of the spiritual aspect of man. COMING OF THE MESSIAH —

The flesh itself is so loathsome and so corrupt that priests may not participate in funeral and burial rites; indeed, no Jew may handle a body on the Sabbath or on religious holidays. It is forbidden to pronounce any benediction in the presence of the dead, to partake of any food where the dead lies. Custom has even decreed that any vessel containing water that has been in the vicinity of the dead must be emptied.

The rejection of food in the presence of death was continued and even extended in many Christian communities. For example, in Scotland even up to the eighteenth century when a death occurred all milk, butter, and onions in the house had to be thrown away in the belief that the dead spirit had corrupted them. In Brittany, even more unusual attitudes were common into the twentieth century. Milk could remain in the room with the dead, but water had to be removed so that the spirit in its wanderings would not drown. In his interesting book on *Funeral Customs,* Bertram Puckle reports that butter was deliberately placed in the room with the body of a person who had died of cancer; after waiting a suitable amount of time for the disease to enter the butter, the butter was then taken out and buried.

The Jewish ritualistic pattern begins, whenever possible, before the moment of death; ten male adults are required to gather around the deathbed in prayer and supplication because "the soul is astounded when departing from the body." As in Biblical times, orthodox believers today follow the procedure of cleansing the body, which is placed in a standing position, with nine measures of warm water, washing the head with beaten egg and wine, and finally dressing the body in a shroud of fine, white linen, made with unknotted thread to indicate the belief in the resurrection of the dead. But even that sole item of funerary display may not be too costly, "for that is forbidden." Males are permitted to be buried in the kind of *tallith* (shawl) each was accustomed to wear at prayer, although its fringes must be made unfit for religious use. Cleansing practices are forbidden if blood has been spilled in the dying; the bloody garments are worn to the grave, and the earth that has been stained "with the blood of the soul" has to be gathered up and interred.

According to ancient law, the dead may not remain unburied overnight except for such imperative reasons as the necessity to procure a coffin, await the arrival of a close relative, obtain a shroud, or wait for a holiday to end. Embalming was clearly out; about the only Old Testament figure subjected to that was Joseph, but that was after his sojourn in Egypt, where it was the general custom. Moreover, since embalming preserves the body to varying degrees after burial as it does before burial, the practice has been severely frowned upon. The period of decay is a period of penance, and is not to be deliberately prolonged. Curiously enough, Jewish persons in the United States today have become so conditioned by the "American way," in spite of their religious doctrines, that, according to Jewish welfare authorities, all except a few of the very old and very orthodox are embalmed.

Cremation, of course, has always been taboo because of the belief in a literal resurrection. The *Torah* specifies that interment must be in the earth itself, although many of the earlier Jewish leaders were buried in caves. Coffins, which became fairly standard after the Babylonian captivity, must be made of wood and must contain some kind of opening to facilitate the return of dust to dust.

The grave which contains the flesh was also held to be unclean. A few Biblical personages (Samuel, Joab, and others) were interred in their houses, but in such a manner that defilement could be avoided. Even today, mourners returning from the cemetery are required to purify themselves by plucking some grass—the symbol of resurrection—and washing their hands in water, the ashes of a cow, and hyssop. Instead of honoring the flesh, the principal practices of Jewish believers have been designed to help the spirit through the painful twelve months (*jahrzeit*) after death, during which judgment is rendered on its earthly life.

The *Torah* holds that mourning for any virtuous man is proper: "He who beholds a funeral and does not accompany it is guilty of sneering at the poor and deserves to be excommunicated." However, intense mourning is obligatory for seven types of close relatives: father, mother, son, daughter, brother, sister, wife or husband. All other relatives keep partial mourning during the first week after a death, but the person who is required to observe full mourning has rigid obligations. For the seven days of intensive mourning following the death and burial, those in rigid mourning are not permitted to work, bathe, change their clothing, mend the garments they have rent, or comb their hair. The person keeping full mourning is required to say special prayers publicly in order to help save the soul of his parent from judgment. Since judgment is believed to be particularly rigorous in the evening, the mourner is given special privileges in the synagogue for seven days: whether minor or adult, member or stranger, he is entitled to say all the *kadishim* (mourners' prayers).

The prayers are required to be said three times a day for

eleven months thereafter—twelve months if the mourner has knowledge that his parent was an evildoer. And each year on the anniversary of the death, he is required to pray in the synagogue and to light the *jahrzeit* candles at home. The emphasis on humility and piety during the twelve months when the soul is experiencing "anxiety" is further reflected in the urging to avoid putting up any kind of tombstone until after that period.

Relatively few Jewish persons in the United States adhere so carefully to the defined observances and rituals. Embalming is a standard practice; shrouds have been discarded in favor of more fashionable burial garb; bodies are shipped from one city to another, which was formerly not permissible unless the destination was Jerusalem. All in all, there has been general reorientation toward the body, over the strong protests of traditionalists. Not long ago, a young Jewish friend told me with distress and disgust of having attended the funeral of a coreligionist who had been one of his college instructors: "I found myself in a long line in the room in the funeral home where a service was being held. After a while, I was directed to join a long line that was moving past the casket. The casket was open and I could see her propped up, with make-up on and her hair all waved. She was wearing some kind of evening gown. It was terrible, terrible," he repeated sadly. "She was a very good woman. Very religious. She would have been horrified."

As the Jews have, ironically, adopted many of the customs and practices of the hated Egyptians, so the Christians have incorporated many of the attitudes and observances of their pagan Roman persecutors. Total meaning, for the Christians, was revealed on that Easter Sunday morning after the crucifixion when Mary and the other women went to the sepulcher with their spices and found inside the tomb two in shining garments who asked: "Why seek ye the living among the dead?" At that moment the stature of Jesus, the significance of life and death were made manifest to Christians. With the grave absolutely vanquished, with death's sting utterly removed, why should obeisance be made? Why should tribute be paid? For centuries it was not.

Christ's simple burial in the linen shroud, which the Christians also regarded as a symbol of resurrection, became the pattern for succeeding men. While their Roman oppressors continued to bury their dead with varying degrees of splendor along the Appian Way and other highways—their tombstones still providing comfortable vantage points for Lollobrigida fans on her triumphal returns—the Christians went beyond their Jewish predecessors in their disregard for the things of this world. Rigidly ascetic in life, they saw no reason to indulge the body in death what it had carefully avoided in life. Austerity was all.

Like the Jews, the early Christians held that death—not burial—was the significant moment in man's spiritual as well as in his earthly life. One of the seven sacraments still acknowledged by the Roman Catholic Church is *extreme unction,* which prepares the soul for its departure. The early Christians also believed that the flesh was linked with the world and the devil; that once the tenant soul had departed, the "temple" that had sheltered it was of little consequence. Like the Jews, they believed that the body would be reunited with the soul—a doctrine that led them to reject cremation and to insist upon some kind of protection for the body.

Influenced partly by the conditions of their persecution and partly by the democratic spiritual concept that all are equal in the sight of God, the Christians found in the catacombs a perfect way of expressing their ideas about death and burial. Although some early believers were buried in graves provided for them by fellow religionists in family plots, most were buried anonymously and indistinguishably in the winding labyrinths under Rome that offered a reasonably safe place of worship. Only occasionally was one grave set apart from another, by the rude scratching of a name or a design pressed into the wet mortar. Many were not "buried" at all, but simply heaped up on shelves to remind the faithful worshiping nearby that all was vanity. Their presence indicated a major departure from Judaic tradition, since the notion of having a body in the synagogue was utterly repugnant, and, in many minds, still is.

The early toleration of the dead by the Christians became

something more as the persecutors invaded the catacombs and martyred many of the secret worshipers. They began to celebrate the ritual of the Mass on the tombs of those martyrs, whose remains became such a significant part of the altar that even when they left their underground "churches" their places of worship invariably accommodated one or more altars containing relics of the honored dead. For a period, too, the Christians developed in their burial service a formal rite called "the kiss of peace."

Although the Christians continued the practice of washing the corpse and anointing it with spices, and also associated white with death rather than the preferred pagan colors, black and purple, another departure from Judaic tradition with respect to the dead was the idea of an extended deathwatch or wake. At first burial took place immediately; the body of Christ, in accordance with Jewish custom had been placed in the sepulcher at once. Also in accordance with Jewish custom, the survivors and mourners made frequent visits to the unsealed sepulcher for three days to determine that live burial had not occurred. The interval between death and burial was soon extended to eight hours, and gradually the Roman custom of allowing three days to elapse before burial became standard. As with the Greeks and other non-Christians, the faithful made exceptions to that customary period to permit full honors to be accorded the "important" persons who died.

The tone of the Christian funeral was quiet, instead of the wild lamenting that had characterized others, hymns were sung by the family and friends to acknowledge that the body had passed into a new state of glory. Torches, originally used by the Romans to light the way of the nocturnal processions to dusty death, became symbols of the brighter world into which the dead had been translated. The funeral involved neither hired mourners nor morticians, since all of the members of the little Christian communities shared this responsibility, including the ranking officials. Tradition and ritual required simply that the body be laid out decently; that lights be placed nearby; that a cross be placed upon the breast, or the hands be arranged to form a cross; that holy water be sprinkled on the body; and that it be interred.

Those duties were later carried out by the companies of functionaries established during the days of Constantine, since by the fourth century funeral practices had become more elaborate, involving rites in the house, services in the church, and ceremonies at the cemetery. Every member of the church was guaranteed a coffin and a funeral procession that included three minor clerics. Another measure during the regime of Constantine had important consequences: the Edict of Toleration in 313 A.D. sanctioned burial within the walls of a city. This was a radical step. Constantine himself was buried in the Church of the Holy Apostles he had built.

The growing concern of the church with funeral and burial ceremonies indicated a growing concern for "proper funerals" among the members. The latter, of course, in relatively brief time had come to regard themselves less as dedicated members of a community than as individual supplicants for divine favor; the early conception of absolute spiritual democracy was modified by the desire of many persons to preserve the *status quo* beyond earthly limits. That happened so quickly that by the end of the fourth century laws had been made to protect persons from overcharges and to prohibit funeral banquets and the growing custom of dressing the corpse in rich garments as "sacrilegious."

It had been one thing to declare theologically that all men were equal in the sight of God. But kings and persons of high degree proved their ultimate inability to accept that notion by leaving for the grave decked in imperial finery. Warriors decided to forego the customary white shroud in favor of more impressive garb, and clerics clung to their vestments: what could be more influential in the life ahead? The final rites for the Empress Theodolinda, friend of Pope Gregory the Great, in 595 A.D., contrast remarkably with those of Christ and his early followers. The rites lasted for more than a week, centering around her richly dressed body which lay in state in the Cathedral of Monza. The cathedral had been hung in the Roman manner with black drapes.

Generally, Italian funerals have been more elaborate than those of any other Western European country; it was there that Roman influence made itself most acutely felt. How Romanesque, for example, the observances in January, 1962, to honor in death Charles ("Lucky") Luciano, the Italian emigrant who had reigned as vice lord of New York before he was deported to his homeland. His elaborate mahogany casket, the focal point in the requiem service, was surrounded by huge funeral pieces from such traditionalist friends as Joe ("Cock-Eyed John") Raimondi, Nick di Marzio, and Joe Adonis, who was described in the obituary notice as "the New Jersey gambling czar." After the Mass, the corpse was carried to the English cemetery in Rome in an ornately carved silver-and-black funeral carriage with huge silver lanterns mounted near the doors. The carriage was pulled by eight black horses.

An interesting protest against pagan black was registered by the late Dutch Queen Wilhelmina. The funeral of her husband, Prince Hendrik, in 1934 and her own funeral in December, 1962 were all in white in accordance with a pledge the royal couple had made to each other. Both white-draped coffins were carried to the mausoleum of the ancient Royal House of Orange on carriages painted white by horses covered with white cloths and white hoods. Coachmen, in blue ceremonial uniforms, pulled white reins with their white-gloved hands. A communiqué issued by the government ordered women mourners to forego black in favor of white or light-colored clothing, and men were instructed to leave off mourning bands. In her memoirs, *Lonely but not Alone,* published in 1959, Wilhelmina had explained that she and her German prince had long before decided that they believed that death is the beginning of life "and therefore had promised each other that we would have white funerals." She added that Hendrik's white funeral, his last gesture to the Dutch people, had "made a profound impression and set many people thinking."

Burial *à la Romana,* however, has gained a tremendous following among even the most devout in many Western countries. It does stagger the imagination to compare the death and burial of early Christian saints and martyrs with that of members of many religious communities today. The pomp, the pageantry, and the preoccupation with the body are remarkably out of keeping with basic principles, as this rather astonishing "prize-winning" suggestion submitted to one of the trade magazines by a mortuary college student indicates:

I have a suggestion for anyone having the experience of attempting to put makeup on a nun of the Catholic Church. If you have ever had the experience, you will wonder when to put the cosmetics on—whether before or after the habit has been placed. It is much easier to let the other nuns put it on. Then after they complete their work, take three pieces of wax paper and insert them on the top and sides with a spatula or orange stick and fold them back. This will allow you to get your cosmetics right up to the edge of the habit, and you won't smear it around or get any on the habit. It also prevents you from getting any light spots on the edge.

It is not necessary, of course, to return to the past to find contrasts. There are some orders of nuns and monks, the Trappists, for example, who have perpetuated early austere customs for almost two thousand years, some living with their simple coffin always in sight and even turning daily a spadeful of the earth from the place that will eventually serve as the grave.

From the fall of Rome in the fifth century to the fall of Constantinople in 1453, funeral and burial rituals all over Europe continued to grow in size and scope, with the "poor souls" being more widely separated from the rich by increasing luxury before interment and by post-burial memorials that would have inspired envy in any pagan breast. The Roman way moved up gradually from Italy to the Scandinavian countries and westward to France and England. In Spain it collided with the Egyptian practices and observances that had been introduced by the Moors.

Curiously enough, the French attitude toward death has always been more restrained than the Romanesque, as evidenced in early prohibitions against sumptuous displays and in the current nationalized condition of the funeral industry. There have been pressures there, too, to have things done more fashionably.

In 1958, for example, the Bishop of Angiers issued a ruling of funerary equality for persons in his diocese. In the rest of the country persons might continue to select from six classes of funerals, ranging from $30 for Class 6 to $3000 for Class 1; in Angiers, the bishop decreed, there would be only one type of funeral. That, corresponding to Class 4 in the undertaking category, provided for two priests, one cantor, two choirboys, six candles on the altar and six on the catafalque. No deacon or archdeacon, no draperies, no crepe.

Immediate protest from the trade, which works privately under government regulation and supervision, about carrying *égalité* too far was answered sharply by *Le Monde:* "It may seem too cruel to force those *in extremis* who have never traveled third class or used the public transport services or had to go steerage to go to their last destination in circumstances which nothing in their lifetime had prepared them for, and to inflict on them a dying so completely contrary to their living. It would be charity to accustom them to equality at a slightly earlier date in their lives."

By 1962, distinctions had become even more pronounced in some churches in France, which were offering ten classes of funerals ranging from an austere, if dignified, ten-dollar minimum favored by the nation's workingmen to a lavish $1500-and-up ceremony for wealthier parishioners—a funeral with tolling bells, a chorus of thirty voices, and black silk draperies embossed with the initials of the deceased. Maurice Cardinal Feltin, Archbishop of Paris, decreed that as of January 1, 1963, Paris churches will offer only one class of funeral: "We shall invite the faithful to forget the useless pomp and ceremony of the past and to accept evangelical simplicity. Indeed, death does remind us of our fundamental equality before God."

The church officials' austerity program called to mind Charlemagne's effort at the beginning of the ninth century to roll back the tide. They decreed that burial within churches be absolutely forbidden, and they even ordered the destruction of tombs, forbidding them to be built rising above the ground. Their efforts were doomed to failure. By the end of the ninth century, even the Pope bowed to the almost universal desire for church burial. And in the *Song of Roland,* which took final shape toward the end of the eleventh century, Charlemagne is presented as ordering the body of Aude entombed near a church altar and transporting the bodies of the three heroes from the pass at Roncevaux to a church at Blaye, where they were laid to rest in white sarcophagi.

That poem also indicates to what extent Egyptian customs had influenced Western Europe, since it has Charlemagne ordering the bodies of Roland, Oliver, and Bishop Turpin opened and their hearts removed. That unusual custom, which not even papal decree had been able to stamp out, became exceedingly popular in England, where it extended through the nineteenth and into the twentieth century, as the burials of Shelley and Thomas Hardy testify. It had particular appeal for those in high places, of course, since it multiplied the opportunities for extravagant display. For example, King Edward I of England (1239–1307) had parts of Queen Eleanore's body deposited in three different tombs he erected in her honor.

Although we consider Spain somewhat in the shallows of the main stream of Western culture, it, too, made major contributions to western European and subsequently American funeral and burial practices. By the time the Moors were driven from their last stronghold in 1492, the ideal burial in that Catholic country bore less resemblance to that of Christ than to that of Ramses II. *El Cid*, according to the thirteenth-century chronicle, was embalmed with such skill that his body sat for ten years on an ivory chair in the monastery of San Pedro de Cardeña, after having traveled half the breadth of Spain tied to his horse. Then, still seated on the ivory chair and clad in richest garments, it was placed in a huge vault dug before the monastery's high altar.

The Spaniards succeeded in imposing their ideal upon the Indians of Latin America, where burial customs were generally stark, although in a few cultures the important priests and nobles were sent off in style. An insight in the belief that the grave is a path of glory was given to me in Mexico in 1960 at the funeral of a child in an Indian village. The emaciated little body—it is the custom in the region to starve children for forty days after they have contracted the measles —lay stretched out on the household altar in the single-room house. Clad in a sleazy silk dress, it was wearing shoes made of metal foil, a matching crown, and a pair of gauze wings.

More important from the standpoint of the American funeral, however, was the extension of the custom of embalming to Spain's enemy, England. The rapid decay of the body had always been a restraint that could not be ignored. Other methods of preservation had been tried and rejected as impossibly costly or incredibly savage. For example, the body of Alexander the Great had been returned to Macedonia preserved in honey. During the Middle Ages, when wars were frequent and political leaders took to the battlefield, there was strong desire to find a method of shipping the illustrious back home for burial. That gave rise to a custom that was cheaper than shipping the body in honey or wine, but one which was denounced by many church leaders: boiling the body so that the bones could be extracted and sent home in a chest. The fluids and other portions were interred on the spot.

King Henry V, the victor of Agincourt and Shakespeare's ideal monarch, was among the boiled. Special pains were taken in his case to obtain an intact skeleton for transportation from France to England, and he was given a glorious burial in Westminster Abbey, where his tomb was crowned with a silver effigy. A number of other medieval monarchs had been embalmed, however, including Charlemagne, King Edward I of England, and King Canute. However, many centuries were to pass before embalming became the order of the final day for ordinary persons and the basis of the extravagant modern American funeral.

In addition to the Egyptian, Jewish, Greek, Roman, and Sumerian influences that helped to mold the "Christian" funeral, Norse beliefs and observances introduced new notes into English and subsequently American practices. Perhaps the most extraordinary contribution of Norse paganism to burial extravaganzas was the ship burial, a custom that was widespread from Iceland to England during the seventh and eighth centuries and continued until the Icelandic Conversion in 1000 A.D.

Some years ago, archaeological excavations at Sutton Hoo,

near Woodbridge in Suffolk, England, revealed the lengths to which the Norse belief in an afterworld patterned on this world carried them. In one mound was a clinker-built boat for thirty-eight rowers—a boat eighty-five feet long that had been dragged up from the river about half a mile away and lowered into the ground.

In Norway at Oseberg, excavations revealed that a ship burial had even been accorded a woman during the Viking age. No one knows whose grave the ship was, since ghouls had ruthlessly scattered the bones of two women found in the burial chamber. In addition to the bones, the burial chamber contained jewels, chests, a bed, equipment for weaving, and buckets of wild apples. Also aboard the ship were the remains of an ox, four dogs, and a heap of horse skeletons. The after-part of the ship had been fitted up like a kitchen, and in the forepart were other provisions and an elaborate little wagon that had been employed in the funeral procession.

Since the Norse religion promised that every man should enter Valhalla with as much wealth as he had on his pyre and should also enjoy everything he had buried in the earth, it was up to his survivors to see that he went well prepared. This belief conflicted with the admonition that "you can't take it with you," and triumphed over it since grave goods became very important in early English burials. Even today many persons are buried with their favorite possessions and valuable jewelry.

As each culture provided another overlay, the Christian funeral grew in luxury and ostentation during the Middle Ages. This progress was occasionally retarded by a strong desire on the part of some lay persons as well as some clerics to maintain the forms as well as the basic teachings of Christianity.

In *Medieval People,* a charming account of six ordinary lives during the Middle Ages, the two attitudes are dramatically contrasted in the stories of Thomas Betson, a fifteenth-century wool merchant, and Thomas Paycocke, an Essex clothier in the days of Henry VII. In addition to founding a new chantry—destined for destruction under the next Henry

—Thomas Paycocke ordered for himself a funeral that cost the equivalent of several thousand dollars in modern money, elaborately stipulating to his executors:

I will myne executors bestowe vpon my burying day, vij day and mounthe daye after this manner: At my buriall to have a tryntall of prests and to be at dirige, lawdis, and comendacons as many of them as may be purvcyed that day to serve the tryntall, and yf eny lack to make it vpp the vij^th daye. And at the Mounthe daye an oder tryntall to be purveyed hoole of myne executors and to kepe dirige, lawdis and commendacons as is afore reherssed, with llj high massis be note. oon of the holy gost, an other of owre lady, and an other of Requiem, both buriall, seuenth day and Mounthe daye.

He further specified that torches were to be used and that each of the twelve or more children were to hold tapers; the children were to be given eight pence each, and every man who held a torch, tuppence. Additional sums were alloted for meat and drink and two sermons.

Modest enough perhaps by comparison with the funeral of the Earl of Oxford, who had been heavily fined by Henry VII for an excessive display of power and wealth and at whose demise more than nine hundred black gowns were distributed, Paycocke's ambitiously programed rites give an indication of the growing preoccupation with prosperous-life-in-death. By contrast, Thomas Betson had requested simply in his will "the costs of my burying to be done not outrageously, but soberly and discreetly and in a mean [medium] manner, that it may be unto the worship and laud of Almighty God." Betson's attitude was not the general one, however. Even the poor, who accepted with remarkable docility the wretched way of living that was doled out to them during the feudal period, insisted on something better in the way of dying.

Efforts to discourage excessive expenditure were neither very decided nor popular. Reasons for that are not difficult to discern. The promise of a better life after death, which was given concrete assurance by a "good" funeral—with the corpse neatly dressed in a linen shroud, candles lighted at home and in the church, the proper attention for once being paid to the Willy Loman who was Everyman, the little feast

—had the desired effect of inducing people to accept a *status quo* that worked against them. Precisely the same situation exists today in much of Latin America and other areas where the feudal system prevails.

The clergy benefited from the arrangement since the church derived no small measure of revenue from the services at the time of death and from the Masses said thereafter to help the soul out of purgatory with all possible haste. The lords of the manors were also rewarded since they were entitled to the best possession of the departed. Merchants got their share from the proceedings through the sale of candles and whatever else of funerary paraphernalia the family was able to afford— draperies, clothing, mourning rings and other items for the attendants, and a costume for the dead.

The shroud, when one was used, was of linen, frequently loosened so that the body could emerge easily on resurrection day. Often a linen sheet was treated with wax or some other gummy substance to aid preservation. The widespread use of imported linen for shrouds and cerecloths worked such a hardship on the British paper industry and on the domestic woolen manufacturers that they succeeded in lobbying through a law called the "Burial in Woolen Act" in 1666, providing stiff penalties for using linen for corpses and coffins for any except plague victims. Judging from amending statutes passed in 1678 and subsequent years, however, which required relatives of any person being buried to make affidavits declaring that no linen had been used, the Burial in Woolen Act was about as effective as the Volstead Act.

Growing funeral displays during the late Middle Ages gave rise to the formation of burial clubs, an outgrowth of the trade guilds. Those clubs levied tariffs on the membership to pay for prayers, funeral services, candles, palls, and other things held necessary.

The Reformation in the sixteenth century checked for a short period sumptuous funerals, except among those of high rank—a concession designed to minimize protest where it really counted. New theological beliefs that rejected the conception of purgatory and the validity of prayers for the dead ended the custom of requiem masses. Vestments, candles, incense, and other items yielded to the puritanical desire for plainness.

But in spite of their contempt for the good things of this life, the Protestants continued the practice of public burial ceremonies. Church officials appointed themselves chief agents, as had been done earlier, to see that the rites were in order and that suitable burial places were maintained. The congregation was instructed to answer the tolling bells; men, women, and children organized themselves into a mourning procession that moved from the church to the cemetery singing hymns. Just as in earlier Christian services, the body became the focus of a sermon exhorting the faithful to note well the vanity of the things of this world. The funeral sermon was substituted for the mass, and, over the protests of many, such practices as the blessing of the dead and the carrying of a cross in the funeral procession were continued.

The new austerity program was not particularly successful, as both law and literature indicate. The rich were not, as usual, easy to legislate; and the poor felt entitled to what they considered at least one guarantee of their humanity. In 1580, the authorities of the city of Rye in Sussex decreed that no person who died within the town should be "chested" or coffined to their burial without a special license from the mayor. To make the decree stick, any carpenter or joiner who made a chest for any but a licensed person could be fined ten shillings for every coffin made. Occasionally a sop was thrown to the poor; in Scotland in 1598, for example, it was decreed that a "mort-cloth" like the pall customarily employed for royalty should be laid on the corpses of the poor.

By the end of the seventeenth century, funerals had become —for those who could afford them—bigger and better than they had been before the Reformation. Diarist John Evelyn described the trip he had made to Cornwall with the body of a woman of high degree; her embalmed body wrapped in lead was carried in a hearse with six horses, attended by two coaches with an equal number of horses to transport some thirty of her relatives and servants. "The corpse was ordered to be taken out of the hearse every night and decently placed in the house, with tapers about it." That funeral, Evelyn reported, cost not much less than one thousand pounds—a sum that must be multiplied by at least ten in order to arrive at today's equivalent.

In another section of his *Diary*, Evelyn described the funeral of a Mr. Cowley, whose corpse was conveyed from Wallingford House to Westminster Abbey "in a hearse with six horses and all funeral decency, near a hundred coaches of noblemen and persons of quality following." Even more extravagant were the rites accorded the dead wife of King Charles in 1695, in spite of her request that no expense be incurred at her funeral. Puckle reports that the fifty thousand pounds which were spent so drained the public treasury that the king's plan to buy all King Street, which led to Westminster, and to design it nobly had to be put aside.

The one force that was genuinely effective in cutting down European outlay for funerals was the Black Death, which for five centuries ravaged the continent.

The bubonic plague moved from China over the trade routes through India and first struck Europe with full fury in January, 1348, when three ships laden with spices and rats made port at Genoa. It made a mockery of the preoccupation with elaborate burial by turning all Europe into a charnel house. Within six months it had spread to England. And by the end of the century, it had claimed as victims 25 per cent of the entire population of Europe. In Germany, one of the countries that suffered least, the losses for 1348 were 1,244,434. In Italy, half the population died. The toll varied in England; in London "scarcely every tenth man survived," but 57,374 out of a population of 70,000 were plague victims in Norwich.

Accounts three centuries later offer more detailed descriptions of disposal practices. Johannes Nohl quotes a number of them in his fascinating chronicle of *The Black Death*. In a letter from Naples, written in 1656 by John Baptista Spinell and quoted in Nohl's book, some radical departures from conventional Christian burial are noted—including cremation. Although the "most aristocratic" were honored with a burial in the churches, 170,000 in that area had been unceremoniously dumped into huge trenches and buried. Another sixty

thousand were burned during the week of July 10. In spite of
the efforts to dispose of the corpses as quickly and hygienically
as possible, Spinell wrote: "Multitudes of dogs and cats
scamper through the streets, appeasing their hunger on the
corpses lying everywhere. . . . Those who are fortunate are
dragged with a rope around their necks to a field and burnt."

In another account, from Danzig, dated October 22, 1709,
the writer described the disposal practices for the forty thousand victims who had died within two months. "Day and
night the mournful bell is heard tolling, and in every street
one is met by coffins." Some of the coffins were carried, others
simply dragged along the street to the cemetery. The majority
of persons could not be accommodated by coffinmakers, however, and were simply placed in a grave—sometimes fifty together, piled one on another.

Two classical accounts of the Plague—those of Boccaccio,
whose father had been among the victims in 1348, and of
Daniel Defoe, whose *Journal of the Plague Year* is a remarkable tour de force based on records and eye-witness accounts
—describe graphically the extent to which funeral and burial
customs and rituals were modified by the terrible affliction.
Boccaccio reported that standard procedure in the fourteenth
century had been for the friends of a dead man to gather in
his house, along with close relatives, to mourn him; others
stood outside to pay respects. After the group had assembled,
the clergy arrived to lead the procession to the church; the
body was carried on the shoulders of the deceased's peers and
honored with singing and candlelight. As the plague spread
and the toll rose, such niceties were forgotten. The mourners
vanished or indulged in unseemly carousing; no longer were
the graves dug by friends, but by gravediggers who provided
the service for a price. The lights were extinguished, and the
clergymen simply placed the dead in the first vacant grave
they came across. For the economically less fortunate, rites
were even further minimized. Corpses were dragged out of
the houses by fearful members of the family and carted off
in batches to be placed in huge trenches "like merchandise in
the hold of a ship."

In England the same lack of ceremony characterized the

disposal of plague victims, with many desperate persons sewing themselves into shrouds as soon as they felt themselves ill—to insure for themselves that formality. Defoe wrote of carts going through the empty streets, where nothing could be heard except the cries of the dying, the bells tolling for those about to be buried, and the cart drivers crying: "Bring out your dead." In London, too, mourning, church services, funeral processions, and graveyard ceremonies were dispensed with as the heaps of bodies were flung indiscriminately into trenches, not infrequently the living with the dead. In the general cleaning that occurred after the plague had subsided, thousands of decomposed corpses of persons of all economic levels were found in their beds or lying on the floor.

The effect of the Black Death, as Nohl points out, was to produce a consciousness of spiritual equality and an awareness of more essential elements than position and power. "If prior to this the higher estimation of the great had been successfully sustained by the ostentatious show of their obsequies and the innumerable masses said for their souls, this deception now failed." And, of course, the American funeral is one of the most curious reflections of that standardizing disaster.

Chapter 4

The Undertaker Arrives

THE PROTESTANT REFORMATION and the later Puritan revolt achieved only short-lived reform so far as funerals were concerned. By the end of the seventeenth century, those who could afford it in England and America were sponsoring departing affairs as elaborate as those that previous religionists had known.

Churches, themselves, were fostering class distinctions in death between the elect and those predestined to occupy lower stations in the two kingdoms. A lucky few were permitted to rest inside the church, as John Milton was; most of the important and affluent were buried in places of honor in the churchyard—for a proper consideration. Those who could not afford burial fees were interred without a coffin in a part of the graveyard set aside for the poor. Heretics, criminals, sui cides, the eccentric poor, and other outsiders were not even allowed that dignity, but were buried beside the road or at a crossroads. (To protect themselves from their possibly vengeful spirits, the good citizens often weighted the body with stones or drove long stakes through the heart.)

In any event, funerals had become such status symbols by the end of the seventeenth century that in England "Friendly Societies," patterned after the medieval burial associations, had been organized to guarantee the members of lower economic and social levels a proper send-off. And the first professional undertakers had appeared on the scene to help less wealthy persons avoid the tremendous expense involved in providing coaches, hangings, and other funeral necessities.

The *Oxford Universal Dictionary* gives 1698 as the date the word *undertaker*, in the sense of one who makes a business carrying out arrangements of funerals, entered the language. *Undertaking*, meaning the business of a funeral undertaker, did not come into the language until 1850. That discrepancy is not surprising, however, when one understands that the undertaker was usually primarily engaged in some other occupation: carpentry, cabinetmaking, upholstering. Advertisements for the late seventeenth and early eighteenth century in England and America invariably list the other occupation first: "Mr. John Elphick, Wollen Draper, over against St. Michael's Church in Lewes, hath a good Hearse, a Velvet Pall, Mourning Cloaks, and Black hangings for Rooms to be Lett at Reasonable Rates." "George Smithson, Broker, Undertaker, and Sworn Appraiser. Opposite the Bull and Gate, Holbourn, London Buys and sells all sorts of Household Goods and at Reasonable Rate. NB. Funerals Performed."

The undertakers, needless to say, encouraged funerals to become more elaborate, and willingly provided items of various sorts that quickly became "necessaries." Bertram Puckle found in an old ledger a record of the cost of various items provided for an English funeral in 1824. That record, included in his *Funeral Customs*, contains forty-seven separate entries. Among the charges incurred for the interment of Miss Martha Harley are the following: Eleven shillings for "a strong coffin with white sattin lining and pillow; nine pounds, ten shillings, a mattress, three shillings, a mattress for the lid of same sattin; three pounds, two shillings, a white sattin sheet." Some of the more costly items were 66 pounds for four horsemen, 86 pounds, 12 shillings, 6 pence for a hearse and six horses; 22 pounds for a set of "best black Velvets" and a set of ostrich feathers; 132 pounds, 16 shillings, 6 pence for two coaches with four horses each; 174 pounds, 3 shillings for "expenses on the road and back." Dresses for the poles, turnpike fees, pages with wands, silk hatbands, gloves, silk scarves, and similar items were also included. Not finally was a charge of eighteen pounds, eighteen shillings for "Own Atendance & Assistans." That charge was levied in spite of the fact that the undertaker had realized a magnificent profit on the affair. His own costs had been 545 pounds, 9 shillings, 6 pence; his charge to the customer, 803 pounds, 11 shillings.

That profit was realized before undertaking officially became a primary business. It was helped to that status by the undertaker, who early realized the value of embalming, crude though that practice was—literally a thing of tar and sawdust, as Sir Richard Steele pointed out in 1701 in *The Funeral, or Grief à la Mode*. In that comedy, the perceptive social critic also noted sourly the tendency of the part-time undertaker to stage a profitably dramatic performance and to improve his own status by hiring mutes, mourners, liverymen, and assorted supernumeraries to swell the cast of his production.

In the eighteenth century, when costs became so great that Samuel Johnson had to closet himself to write *Rasselas, Prince of Abyssinia* to pay his mother's funeral bill, the growing preoccupation with death and elaborate obsequies gave rise to a whole school of "graveyard" poets. Many of them, particularly Robert Blair, an Edinburgh clergyman, had some salty things to say about the "ridiculous" and "unnecessary" display of the funerals in favor: "ridiculous," he specified, "except in the views of those who reap *pecuniary* advantage from them, and unnecessary respecting the dead, who are the principal subject and occasions of them."

Nevertheless, the funeral industry continued to flourish in England throughout the eighteenth and nineteenth centuries until at the time of Dickens it came into "its own" with feather-pages, outriders, mutes, wands, batons, elaborate hearses, gifts, mourning gear, funereal jewelry and gifts, and extravagantly catered wakes. In *Martin Chuzzlewit* there is a satirical exchange between Mr. Mould, the undertaker, and Mrs. Gamp:

"Why do people spend more money upon a death, Mrs. Gamp, than upon a birth?"

"Perhaps it is because an undertaker's charges come dearer

than a nurse's charges, sir," Mrs. Gamp replied practically.

In the United States during the same period the same progression had occurred. When the early "saints and strangers" arrived at Plymouth in 1620, they were of such fundamentalist cast that they regarded it heretical to celebrate either marriage—a clear weakness of the flesh—or burial with a religious ceremony. According to George F. Willison, their careful historian, "no prayers of any kind were said over the dead until the eighteenth century." The reason for that, of course, was their Protestant fear that it might lead to praying for the souls of the deceased, which in turn might lead to acceptance of the doctrine of purgatory.

Naturally, there was the problem of persuading people to relinquish the idea of a "nice" burial. Therefore, church officers permitted the deceased to be prepared for interment by family and friends in a coffin turned out by John Alden— of Priscilla fame—or Kenelm Winslow, the official coffin-maker. Followed by a crowd of mourners, the corpse was carried to Burial Hill on a bier covered with a black pall. The bier was carried by Indian and Negro slaves who were accompanied by honorary pallbearers who held the tassels for the "underbearers." Within a few years of their arrival, rites had become so elaborate that in 1633, Deacon-Doctor Fuller specified that his sister should mourn him in a pair of gloves valued at twelve shillings. The trade in funeral gloves grew so brisk, Willison reported in Saints and Strangers, that one Boston pastor collected 2940 pairs in thirty years, which he was able to sell for 1442 pounds—in today's currency perhaps $30,000. Other customary gifts to the pastor and pallbearers included white scarves and black-enameled gold funeral rings. Sometimes those gifts were presented to as many as a thousand mourners. This practice became such a financial burden that in 1721 Massachusetts passed a law regulating funerals; the law forbade the giving of scarves, gloves (except six pairs to the bearers and one pair to the minister), wine, rum, and rings.

In spite of the religious objections to funeral and burial rites, they were considered of such moment that in 1676, when Indian King Philip was betrayed and killed, he was denied burial.

Shortly after that, Governor Winslow, who died at fifty-three "after sore Pain with Gout and Griping," was honored with a forty pounds-sterling funeral, "the most elaborate yet seen at Plymouth." Most of the expenditure was for things other than religious, for it was not until 1697 that the first sermon for the dead was preached, by Pastor Wiswall over the body of John Alden's son, Jonathan, "with many misgivings and much lifting of eyebrows."

Extravagance continued despite a series of sumptuary laws that began in 1721. By the time Andrew Faneuil died in 1738, more than three thousand pairs of gloves were given away at his funeral and more than a thousand persons accompanied the cortege. According to that most explicit diarist, Samuel Sewall, the procedure ordinarily followed in the early eighteenth century involved the following: After death, neighbors —a nurse if the family had money—would wash and prepare the body, while the local coffinmaker measured and made a coffin from a type of wood commensurate with the social position of the deceased. (Those who could afford it might have metal decorations from England affixed to the coffin.) Relatives and friends nearby were summoned, who were repaid for their attendance with rings, scarves, gloves, and copies of the funeral sermon. When the family could afford it, the coffin was carried to the grave in a horse-drawn hearse. When it could not, slaves or hired hands did the heavy work while honorary bearers held the pall. Also, when it could be afforded, a sexton dug the grave, at which there was said a brief prayer before interment; then everyone left for the feasting.

The funeral feast, perhaps the most common of all obsequial ceremonies, was for many years the most costly and the most lively festive occasion in American colonial and frontier life. The custom of breaking bread with the departed for the last time is an ancient symbolic ritual that was adopted early in the Christian era because it filled certain practical needs. In addition to providing the "soul food" for the dead, funeral feasts also satisfied the living who had been summoned to view the body—a custom, Puckle points out, that was incumbent upon survivors to clear them of any suspicion of having been the cause of the funeral. Moreover, it was also a way of saluting the successor—a "thrift" that seemed reasonable to many, although Hamlet justifiably protested that "the funeral bak'd meats did coldly furnish forth the marriage tables." Family honor came to depend upon a good spread, one that catered heavily to the thirst and hunger of the living. Men of substance left handsome sums; poorer persons had to depend upon the generosity of friends and neighbors for a suitable farewell riot.

Funeral feasts in the Mediterranean Christian countries quickly regained the glory and grandeur of Greek and Roman prototypes; Irish wakes were legendary drinking bouts well into the twentieth century. Even the Victorian Englanders indulged lustily, for it continued custom through the nineteenth century for the sexton to announce at the foot of the grave that the burial would be followed by a binge at the local pub; and the dour Scots yielded to no one. According to W. M. Andrews' description of *Bygone Church Life in Scotland*, quoted in Puckle, "there was a lamentable amount of ale and whisky drinking before and after the funeral." Hospitable preliminaries (without water or ice) were followed by a religious service; that was succeeded by further eating and drinking, and finally the coffin was carried out of the house, "followed by all those who were sufficiently sober to walk straight."

Even the Puritans, that "most intolerant brood," as Hawthorne commented bitterly, allowed themselves free rein in funeral feasting, "the only class of scenes . . . in which our ancestors were wont to steep their tough old hearts in wine and strong drink and indulge in an outbreak of grisly jollity."

A glance at an early American funeral bill makes quite understandable why twentieth-century undertakers have ruled out funeral parties. In *Customs and Fashions in Old New England*, Alice M. Earle presented the following bill for the burial of David Porter of Hartford, who drowned in 1678:

By a pint of liquor for those who dived for him............................1s
By a quart of liquor for those who brot him home.........................2s
By two quarts of wine and one gallon of cyder
  to jury of inquest...5s

By 8 gallons and 3 quarts wine for funeral...........................£1.15s
By barrel cyder for funeral..16s
1 coffin..12s
Windeing sheet..18s

In New York and Virginia, where colonial life was livelier than in Connecticut, death was, too. Dutch funerals were more lavish, and the feasts that followed burials were understandably attended by adult males only, for the most part.

Virginians, whose gayer tastes were indulged in horse racing and elaborate wedding festivities, also regarded funerals as an occasion for merrymaking. As in New England, Habenstein's *History of American Funeral Directing* notes that "the consumption of liquor was enormous and likely to impoverish the decedent's estate." In America, the growing emphasis on political democracy had the curious effect of adding to the extravagance of Everyman's funeral, just as the concept of spiritual democracy had done earlier. Then, although it was clearly impossible for most to live like barons and knights and kings, the desire existed to die like them; and as nobles and royal persons had upgraded their funerals, so had the common people.

In America, it was clearly impossible for all persons to live equally; however, the feeling developed that it might be possible to die with reasonable approximation of equality. The funeral, since it occupies a relatively brief period and is a commonly shared experience, came to be regarded as the symbol of equal creation. In addition to the rights of life, liberty, and the pursuit of happiness—always ideals—people came to demand the unspoken right to a "good" funeral as tangible proof that the colonel's lady was, after all, no better than the wife of Mr. O'Grady. Nor was the colonel, himself, any better than Judy's husband.

That illogical but comprehensible attitude not only did serious damage to family finances, but had such disastrous effect on the public economy that by 1788 reminders were being issued in Massachusetts and other states that earlier sumptuary laws could not be disregarded as many other pre-Revolutionary measures had been. "To prevent excess and vain expense in mourning," police inspectors advertised in the

Massachusetts Sentinel that twenty-shilling fines would be imposed for giving away scarves, gloves, rings, rum, or any other spirituous liquor at a funeral—or before or after. Warning was also issued against wearing mourning clothing except for a black arm band for men and a black bonnet, gloves, ribbons, and a fan for women.

Between the American Revolution and the Civil War, which marked the beginning of funerary "big business" in the United States, a number of trends and events worked together with legal measures to curb excessive funeral costs. That was done with such success that during the Jacksonian era, the average cost was held to be about eight dollars.

The westward movement helped to bring about a mobility in American society unequaled anywhere in the civilized world. With relatives from the northeastern to the southwestern corners of the country and at stopping-off places along the Oregon and other "trails," family reunions became increasingly difficult to effect, even when a death in the family occurred. The rigors of frontier life, and not infrequently the desire to keep any demise secret from the Indians, made prompt and uncelebrated funerals imperative for many. Even those who could afford to indulge in the luxury of lying with their fathers were frequently denied the opportunity since the methods of preserving a corpse for a journey of any distance were exceedingly clumsy; "airtight" coffins were not, as a rule, airtight; and refrigeration was costly when it could be managed, since it involved frequent stops to repack the body in ice.

Also, pressures were removed; not the least of them was the what-will-the-neighbors-say? worry, which has always been a powerful motive for extravagance. Neighbors were, after all, responsible for the kind of funeral provided. And undertakers' associations and publicists had not yet come along to condition Americans that in matters funereal, at any rate, they should care very much about what unknowing and uncaring neighbors do say.

In cities, of course, things were different. Emphasis on elegance and luxury continued to grow, flouting civil law as well as religious doctrine. By the middle of the nineteenth century, one Connecticut cabinetmaker was proudly advertising that he had made "complete arrangements for the prosecution of the UNDERTAKING business in all its branches." Interested persons were invited to call at his coffin wareroom to see "full sets" of rosewood, mahogany, black walnut, cherry, and whitewood coffins, along with metallic airtight burial cases and caskets, also with silver trimmings.

Outside of the large population centers, simplicity and amateur activity were the general order—as many persons who grew up in small towns or farming communities still remember. In such places, well into the twentieth century, it was customary when a death occurred for the family to call in a friend to make the arrangements. He would either get some help and make the coffin himself or put in an order for one with a neighboring carpenter. At the house, women or men dressed the corpse and prepared it; women also prepared food for the guests who would come, while the men got the farm wagon cleaned to serve as hearse to the churchyard. When the sister of a woman I know died in a small town in Oregon in the 1940's, the community cleared a space in the old burial ground, dug the grave, decorated the cemetery with flowers, and several of the men carried the body to the place, with all of the neighbors following.

An interesting protest against the abandonment of this simple funeral ceremony was made by William Morris, the poet, inventor, medievalist, and craftsman, who planned the funeral he was given in 1896. The farm wagon that carried his unpolished coffin from Kelmscott was drawn by a single horse, led by a carter. "Wreathed by vines and strewn with the traditional willow boughs, this 'hearse' must have been a shock to many narrow minds," Puckle comments, "and the despair of the local undertaker." In twentieth-century America, William Carlos Williams' poem "Tract" envisions a similar leavetaking.

Undertakers, as such, did not acquire any prominence in America until the nineteenth century. There were some earlier professionals; the first was a London-born woman who set herself up in New York shortly before the Revolution as an upholsterer and undertaker in the English manner. According to Dr. Habenstein, who examined copies of all the extant American city directories from the eighteenth century and most of the directories for major cities from the first half of the nineteenth, the undertaker "as occupational specialist" first became important in this country in the first quarter of the nineteenth century. Previously the disposal of the dead had been managed by the church and family, the sexton, and the cabinetmaker. The cabinetmaker was particularly important; a number of the oldest establishments in the country today had their beginnings in a cabinetmaking shop. Another trade that was frequently combined with undertaking was livery stable keeping.

As cities grew and cemeteries became further removed, foot processions became difficult and tiresome. Moreover, they were quite out of keeping with the European niceties that were being imported along with glass, chic bonnets, and other elegance. One of the really swank features of English seventeenth- and eighteenth-century funerals had been the hearse drawn by six or eight horses—preferably black, after white had been set aside as a mourning color. Although many horses had originally been employed to carry the corpse as quickly as possible over impossible roads, the use of a large number became a matter of prestige for even very short distances. Livery proprietors, recognizing in the words of one of the most successful of their number "a sweet thing" when they saw it, were naturally interested in providing other paraphernalia and services.

Sextons, who were first classified as town officers, were natural candidates for the undertaking business since they had already realized a profit from their work of tolling the bell, digging the grave, and sometimes even laying out the corpse. They also had a clear advantage over other contenders since as town officers they controlled the permits to bury in churchyards and public cemeteries.

Although women, particularly nurses, had early performed a principal role in American funerals (they were not important participants in English funerals), they were relegated to a secondary place when undertaking became a specialized occupation. They have since, of course, come into their own;

a number of states have trade associations made up entirely of women undertakers.

At any rate, by the time the Civil War broke out the undertaker was plying his trade in most of the sizable cities— "laying out" the corpse, furnishing the drapes and other décor for the house of mourning, providing the coffin, helping with vital records, transporting the body from house or church to the cemetery—taking charge of all the material needs, usually under the direction of a clergyman.

In casting about for ways to make their occupation a profitable one, the new group of "specialists" in mid-nineteenth-century America and England was confronted with some basic problems. Lacking well-preserved corpses so that rites could be extended to cover more than a very brief period, the undertakers were forced to focus their money-making on simple merchandising of caskets and goods. That, from their point of view, was not adequate. Selling burial plots could also be a rewarding activity, but generally the churches and municipalities controlled those. Elaborate mourning gear had been ruled out by law and convention, and even such customs as giving mourning rings and gloves and other mementoes came to be regarded as old-fashioned. These were problems indeed. But all of them were solved by the Civil War.

Chapter 5

The Underground War Effort

WARS HAVE ALWAYS PROVIDED persons of a certain ethical bent impressive opportunities to enrich themselves at the public expense. The Civil War, which has euphemistically been described as "the last gentlemen's war," enabled many in this country to transform the once reasonably haphazard occupation of sutlery into the science of profiteering. Behind every romantic Henry Fleming, north and south, was a realistic entrepreneur less concerned with red badges of courage than with the folding green emblems of personal prosperity. That nation-shattering conflict "emancipated" American businessmen along with the Negro slaves, offering them unprecedented chances to turn a quick and shady profit and later, through the Fourteenth Amendment, giving their corporate identities unique freedom from control by state and local governments.

During the terrible years of Chancellorsville, Shiloh, Gettysburg, Fredericksburg, and Bull Run, businessmen made extraordinary demands and received extraordinary concessions. Railroads carrying soldiers to battle in freight and cattle cars asked and received first-class fares for their patriotic services; munitions dealers sold discarded Army rifles to the government for great gain—one shrewd merchant-politician peddled to the North for twenty-two dollars each some outmoded and dangerous Army carbines that he had picked up a few months earlier for two dollars apiece. Wormy biscuits and contaminated foodstuffs for the brave boys in blue and gray commanded luxury-fare prices. In one horse-trading deal the Union Army paid $58,000 plus $10,000 transportation for a thousand horses; on delivery, 485 of them had to be discarded because they were either diseased or worthless. A legislative committee published a carefully documented three-thousand-page report of frauds that occurred during President Lincoln's first year in office.

Anyone, it appears, with anything to sell—and many with nothing—headed for Washington to obtain a government contract. Seeing an opportunity to turn the dead as well as the living to a profit, hundreds in the funeral trades stormed the capital. Coffinmakers, cemetery owners, surgeons and specialists plying the new "art" of embalming, railroad lobbyists, undertakers—all demanded to know what could be more patriotic, what could do more for troop morale and national morale than shipping the bodies of the dead soldiers back home for burial. What, indeed? Surely the government could see to it that the right thing was done. The government did, thereby helping to set the pattern for the American funeral with all its ostentation and commercialism.

A number of trends and events that had occurred made the war years the desirable time to strike. Experiments in chemical embalming that had been going on since 1840 when Dr. Richard Harlan published his translation of Gannal's *History of Embalming* on his return from a European tour had been successful enough to make feasible the idea of preserving corpses for an extended period; coffinmaking was becoming a profitable urban trade for some manufacturers rather than being merely a sideline for a carpenter or cabinetmaker; undertaking in 1850 was classified as a specialized occupation.

It was in that year, too, that a precedent for government action along these lines had been established when Congress appropriated ten thousand dollars to provide a "suitable resting place" for the officers and men who had died in the Mexican War of 1846-1847. The following year, a few acres of land had been acquired in Mexico City for the first American national cemetery, and the bodies of 750 "unknown" troops were recovered from the ditches that had been hastily dug after the battles of Chapultepec and Churubusco, where they had been buried beneath a single granite shaft.

In principle, no step could have been more logical than to bury the war dead where they fell. That idea was revived in 1862, when Congress authorized the President to acquire land for military cemeteries within the United States; appropriately, it was decided to use the sites of major battles for that purpose. Two years later the first official Graves Registration Unit was set up, charged with making positive identification of the Federal soldiers who had been killed so that they could be reinterred in national cemeteries. However, since grief and bereavement are characterized by the sufferer's rejection of logic, relatives of the dead soldiers began to insist that their dead be shipped home. Their importunings, encouraged and made possible by the growing industry, were recognized—in spite of no provision having been made for such procedure and although positive identification had been obtained for only about half of those who died on the battlefields.

Governmental accession to family wishes was both a triumph and a challenge to the new chemical embalmers, who descended on Washington and the battle areas in swarms. Here, if ever, was a golden opportunity to perfect the still imperfect process of embalming that had come from France and England, where it was growing in practice. Some crude efforts at preserving corspes had been made earlier in the United States: filling the body cavity with charcoal after evisceration, wrapping it in cloths soaked in alum or wax, and sometimes pickling corpses in alcoholic beverages—as Lord Nelson had been returned from Trafalgar. Iceboxes and cooling boards had also enabled bodies to be transported considerable distances.

The chemists, physicians, anatomists, and others, skilled and unskilled alike, who had already realized that chemical embalming opened broad new vistas, were understandably in a fine frenzy. And after having been treated to the spectacle of a number of preserved "cases" publicly displayed in some of Washington's undertaking shops, the people responded with equal enthusiasm. So great became the demand that lack of knowledge or chemistry was no stumbling block at all. W. H. Devore of Pittsburgh, who had secured the government contract for embalming and burying all bodies from camps and hospitals located in his area and who emerged from the war in prosperous condition, told his colleagues in an article in *The Casket* in 1895 that "a multitude of opportunities were presented for experiment." In addition to the supply of dead soldiers, many private persons behind the lines were willing to offer up their deceased for a go at it, as undertakers cried their superiority in ads such as "Bodies Embalmed by Us Never Turn Black." Added sanction was given when Lincoln's son Willie was embalmed—and still later, Lincoln, himself. The cost for the privilege of being an experimental subject ran high—one hundred dollars or more for embalming a Union soldier with less than three dollars' worth of chemicals. But it so quickly became a mark of prestige that it became the thing to have done among social leaders, diplomats, and the everyones who were anyones in Washington.

Embalmers quickly found themselves in great vogue, because many undertakers who had government contracts were faced after every battle with a need for assistance to enable them to get the corpse to its destination. Moreover, any undertaker who could offer the additional service of embalming was assured of clients. Among the first to offer the new service was Joseph Gawler, whose great-grandsons are still burying Washington's dead. Gawler's principal trade was cabinetmaking; his new business, founded in 1850, flourished so heartily during the Civil War that it moved into the home in 1870 that had served as General Winfield Scott's headquarters. As with many other establishments founded then, it continued to flourish; in 1961 his descendants announced the construction of a new million-dollar-plus establishment in Washington, complete with employees' lounge, minister's room, a sizable chapel, and seven "State Rooms" of varying sizes among the many divisions in the three-story "home."

To a large degree, of course, all successful undertakers operating in the country during the past century have owed thanks to the early practitioners, who developed the basic method of the arterial injection of embalming fluids and who broke down public resistance to mutilation of the body in the pagan manner by shrewd salesmanship and a willingness to gladly teach. Most famous of the pioneers was Dr. Thomas Holmes, a Brooklyn inventor, surgeon, salesman, and manufacturer who boasted that he had amassed a fortune of almost half a million dollars in the Washington embalming business during the Civil War. He lost it, and eventually retired to Brooklyn in something less than glory to turn out root beer extract. More representative of the educator-salesmen was "Professor" Clarke, a road salesman for the White Water Valley Coffin Company of Indiana. In the course of his travels, Clarke bought some embalming fluid from one of the early inventors and got some instructions in its use. Impressed by the possibilities the new "art" offered to undertakers and seeing in it a chance to turn a profit, he persuaded a staff member of a medical college in Cincinnati to institute a course in embalming, thereby establishing the basis of mortuary education. Within the first year, Clarke's Cincinnati School of Embalming, as it became known, graduated, from ten different classes in that city and in Philadelphia, Boston, and New York, 122 "professionals." The training, chiefly in embalming, but also in lining and trimming caskets, funeral conduct, and "practical undertaking," took a week to complete.

Although many new techniques have been developed in the embalming process and students at the various colleges are required to have a knowledge of the fundamentals of chemistry and anatomy, basically the skill is a simple one that could be mastered within a few weeks by anyone of even modest intelligence and a tolerance toward corpses. Embalming is actually the only specific skill required in the undertaking business, whose leaders like to consider themselves professionals. It is, of course, not necessary to possess even that training to set up a business as a mortician in most places.

The railroads were the first segment of the transportation industry to benefit from the new practice of embalming. However, so close and so essential has been the link between both that embalming continues to be legally mandatory for any body shipped by common carrier—a tradition that has completely ignored advances made in refrigeration.

Although some of the initial efforts were so unsatisfactory that railroad companies complained to General Grant about the offensive condition of bodies being shipped north, the transportation industry quickly recognized the impressive possibilities for additional revenue. If one soldier en route to camp or to a battle zone in a cattle car would be charged to the government as a first-class fare, what would it not be worth to transport his body? What the traffic would bear turned out to be quite a bit of money—now, as it was then. Even today, when railroads no longer boast openly of themselves as a "third house" in state legislatures, the rates for shipping bodies are extremely high.

Two can travel more cheaply than one—provided one is dead. For example, as late as May, 1962, when I checked two major railroads in Los Angeles to ascertain that discrepancies between the fares for the living and the dead still existed, the following rates were quoted. The price for sending an unescorted body from Los Angeles to Dallas on the Santa Fe Railroad was given as $112.98; the price of sending an escorted body was $56.49, plus a first-class fare for the escort of $50.60. (Perhaps that fare was lower on the theory that the dining car and other services would realize a profit from the quick.) On the Union Pacific Railroad, the cost of sending an unescorted body to Kansas City was $67.86 multiplied by two; the cost of sending an escorted body was $67.86, plus whatever fare the escort preferred to buy—pullman or coach.

Railroads are not the only mediums to impose high charges. All transportation companies find shipping bodies profitable. For example, the cost of shipping furniture, books, and other items air freight from Los Angeles to Boston in May, 1962, was $20.45 for each one hundred pounds. To send a well-preserved body by air freight cost $51.13 for every one hundred pounds—a cost that becomes a considerable item when a massive hardwood casket is added to the weight of the body. Often a vault weights the bill further.

Rates seem even more disproportionate when sea travel is involved. A glance at the current files of the various tariff conferences which regulate rates for cargo indicates how heavily persons are penalized for carrying out a last request or fulfilling an emotional obligation. The cost of shipping a corpse from Mediterranean ports, as cited in Tariff Number 32, approved in 1962, amounts to $605; an urn of ashes, $544. To send a body from Brazil to the United States costs $440—exactly the sum that would be charged a passenger who eats, sleeps, uses facilities and services, and who is not stowed away with the cargo. By comparison, the cost of sending live animals is $94.75 each, if accompanied, and $122.25, if unaccompanied. According to Tariff Number 31, 1961, made at a Japanese-American conference, the cost of sending a body to or from a Japanese-American port is $631.50. To send a package of individual human ashes costs $252.75. By comparison, the cost of sending a *ton* of meat and bone was set at $28.50, dry animal meat at $33 a ton, and tea dust at $36.75 to $40.25 a ton.

For a brief period, even streetcars did quite well in the funeral trade. The short-lived vogue began in Atchison, Kansas, when the street railway company offered for hire to the principal cemetery on the line a car ornately decorated in black and gold to carry the corpse, the casket, the undertaker, and pallbearers. In Chicago and Cleveland they were also used during the first part of this century.

Today, some of the principal beneficiaries of the lavish funeral practices are the major car manufacturers and special body makers, who offered their 1962 "road beauties" with the announcement that "a new era has dawned to impart solemnity and dignity to the funeral procession." Service cars, ambulances, limousines, flower cars, and the traditional hearses, now coaches, have become expensive items of equipment for morticians. Built-in obsolescence operates in this area with a vengeance. Although a top-grade, air-conditioned hearse may cost as much as $16,000 and an equivalent limousine up to $11,000, "no self-respecting mortician in a city like ours could afford to keep them more than two years," a Los Angeles undertaker said recently.

According to this undertaker, after two years the "big city" merchants sell all their professional motor vehicles to undertakers in smaller cities, where the competition is less vigorous and where the latest model is not the absolute measure of success. In another two or three years, the hearse, ambulance, car, and other items are resold to undertakers in "small towns." After that? Well, currently they are considered a best buy among high school and college students. And some of them make their way across the border, where even very ancient models are regarded with esteem in little towns, and some not so little towns. In Cuernavaca, Mexico, during the 1940's and 1950's, one of the most noticeable vehicles was a hearse of rare vintage, its heavy, carved wooden draping painted grey; across the front it bore proudly in white letters: *"Quo Vadis?"*

A high fashion note in funeral equipage was also struck during the Civil War in this country, during and after which a "style change" became as characteristic of hearses as of women's dresses.

Originally a hearse was a simple iron framework to which spikes were attached so that candles could be impaled on them. This harrow-shaped candelabrum became more ornate during the Middle Ages and Renaissance until it finally came to resemble a many-gabled structure without walls that surrounded the hearse. On anniversaries and special days, it was draped with an elaborate pall, suggesting a canopied bed.

When carriages came into vogue to carry the body to the cemetery, they adopted the spikes, the heavy draping, and the plumes. The ornate funeral car that carried the body of the Duke of Wellington to his grave in 1852 is cited by Puckle as "a good example of the transitional stage between the hearse erected in the church and the sort of traveling shop window to display the handiwork of the undertaker" that was characteristic of nineteenth- and early twentieth-century hearses. A huge superstructure, heavily decorated and modeled after his ship, the *Victory*, was mounted on a large wagon. On the "deck" of the ship was the coffin, topped with his hat and other insignia. Four high baroque columns supported a draped canopy that sheltered the coffin and which bore a crest of tall plumes.

Most persons in England and America had to do with less,

although carriage makers in those and other countries began to introduce innovations—scrimshaw curtains, metal columns, fancy scrollwork, plumes, emblems, urns, and other luxuries —that would provide the plebes with one stylish ride. Less successful than modern automotive manufacturers, who have been able to effect a demand for an annual model change, the carriage makers had to content themselves with a fifteen-year cycle, Habenstein has reported. However, that was compensated for to some extent by diversification: small, white children's hearses became standard equipment for undertakers in major United States cities during the last quarter of the nineteenth century in addition to the elaborately ornamented black "funeral cars" that were considered *de rigueur* for carting off any adult of social pretensions—or of none.

Then, as now, the cost for a vehicle likely to attract new business was heavy. A New Orleans undertaker paid five thousand dollars in 1893 for a hearse that had been a center of interest at the Chicago World's Fair that year. Weighing more than a ton, it was a profusion of gold lamps, fringes, tassels, and flying angels; massive carvings in high relief depicted scenes from the Crucifixion, the Nativity, and the Ascension. Such lavish offerings made undertakers somewhat reluctant to accept auto hearses during the first decade of the twentieth century when they made their appearance. The same attitude prompted the protest in 1957 of the army's converting from caisson funerals to motorized hearses.

But the horseless carriage was destined to become as much a part of the American way of death as the American way of life. By mid-century, the vehicles temptingly depicted for undertakers on entire pages in color in the industry's trade journals were lavish enough to satisfy even gangster taste in such matters. In a society which measures morality in trade names, even the humblest car owner was assured that he would embark on his last voyage in a "good" car—a car that was a "standard of the world" or a reasonable facsimile.

Undertakers, well aware of the value of an elegant hearse and limousines in attracting new business, but squirming under the heavy costs, have recently made some effort to cut back their vehicle expenses by eliminating ambulances. In a series of letters debating possession of ambulances that appeared recently in a trade journal, one writer boasted proudly that he and some of his noncompetitive colleagues had "forced" another colleague to abandon his. Hearse and limousine rental services are now becoming more common in larger cities; a number of undertakers consider it more profitable to rent the equipment they need at about thirty dollars a vehicle for a service than to suffer the heavy depreciation involved.

Auto manufacturers and body makers are spending large sums to discourage such defection. In 1962, one of the largest —featuring four series of vehicles regally entitled *Royale, Crown Royale, Sovereign,* and *Crown Sovereign*—offered "the man who wants an added touch of elegance" more than fifty models to choose from, with more than five hundred different interior color and fabric combinations. Another, inviting undertakers to "enhance your leadership," described his line of hearses and ambulances as "symbols of distinction in your profession." Interchangeable religious symbols and ambulance crosses and the initials of the mortuary or mortician were added allurements to buy. Cadillacs are in such demand as status symbols that the 1961 pre-annual convention issue of one of the largest trade journals in the undertaking industry allocated "positions of eminence" on its cover to Thomas Glidden, president of the National Funeral Directors Association, and Robert Longhurst, Chief of the Cadillac Commercial Division, "Mr. Cadillac."

Undeniably, the prestige of being hauled along the freeway in a luxury vehicle, which creates a serious, growing traffic hazard, is very attractive to many persons. Not all, unfortunately, have resolved the problem as satisfactorily as an oil-rich Oklahoma Indian who some years ago made his indulgence in final grandeur a "lifetime" investment. For years he was driven through the streets of Oklahoma City lying in great state in the back of a handsome hearse. Barbara Hutton's son, whose tastes were not developed in a ten-cent store, uses his "fishtail" hearse to carry his water sports equipment around southern California.

The Civil War was kindest of all to the coffin manufacturers, who seized the opportunity to become the principal architects of the modern American funeral.

In many cultures in which earth burial is the primary form of disposal, the coffin is an important status symbol. It has been since 2500 B.C., the period of the XIth Dynasty in Egypt. The first were massive rectangles covered with hieroglyphic inscriptions that gave full accounts of the inhabitants' family trees and contained prayers and magical texts that would help to impress the powers of the underworld. Gradually, the coffins assumed anthropoid shape—a reversal of the evolution in America—with each bearing a carefully painted likeness of the occupant. Often the nobles found that no less than three would do honor to them properly, the outermost serving as a sarcophagus, the innermost being a representational casing heavily decorated with gold and jewels.

The Japanese and Chinese cultures, until recently, placed great emphasis on elaborate coffins. The most significant gift a dutiful Chinese son could make to his parents was a handsome coffin, which was then kept on prominent display in the house until the time came for it to be occupied. Evidence of status, not sentiment, counted; the coffin was often a principal determinant of the prosperity of the son as well as his willingness to honor his father and mother. Made usually of fine hardwoods, it was modeled according to rules prescribed for various social ranks: the highest dignitaries were entitled to an eight-inch-thick outer shell and a four-inch-thick inner coffin. Students, who were regarded highly in China, were entitled to a six-inch outer shell. Chinese children fared less well; according to accounts quoted in Puckle, they were simply wrapped up in cheap stuff and set outside to be picked up with the rest of the refuse. Japanese coffins, equally elaborate, were more closely associated with religion; a customary form was a temple, heavily carved and beautifully ornamented with mountings of precious metal and with silken hangings.

In keeping with their belief that all things of this world were vanity, vanity, and that the penitential period of decomposition should be accelerated rather than decayed, the early Hebrews buried their dead without coffins. The poor were laid in a shallow trench, with earth heaped over them; the rich were placed in natural caves or in sepulchers fashioned in rock.

Joseph, who—as Mann emphasizes in *Joseph in Egypt*—became "a child of Egypt . . . sharing in her outlandish practices," set precedent for later religionists with his relatively elaborate burial, embalmed and "chested." Although for centuries persons of the Jewish religion insisted on very simple coffins, usually of pine or of the boards of the table from which they had "served the poor," during the last century in the United States the coffin has come to acquire for them the significance of a status symbol. One southern manufacturing firm has achieved nationwide acceptance of a special orthodox casket. The casket is made of solid wood, with no metal hinges, handles, or other fittings; the individual sections are held together with wooden dowels, and the hinges are made of wood fastened with catgut pins. The casket, quite contrary to the principle of spiritual democracy, comes in eight different grades, "from a pauper's model through the most elaborate."

Although the early Christians also eschewed caskets and other items of pagan funerary ostentation, coffins relatively soon came to be in great demand among the poor as well as the rich. It became such a drain in England that laws were passed prohibiting "chested" burial; most of the laws were disregarded, and when the colonists arrived in the United States they brought with them a tradition of the use of coffins. The Dutch and other settlers readily incorporated it into their practices.

During the seventeenth and eighteenth centuries, however, a coffin was an inexpensive item, often of home manufacture. That is in sharp contrast to the post-Civil War period, when the coffin became the largest single item of expense; even today the coffin determines, almost exclusively, the price of the funeral. The early practice that continued for centuries in many parts of the country is described in William Faulkner's moving and grotesquely humorous account of Addie Bundren's burial in *As I Lay Dying*. All through the long day of her dying and into the night that followed, Cash, her carpenter son, worked with a jeweler's preciseness to fashion the hexagonal, narrow coffin, which was tapered at the head and foot in the older fashion.

As long as the coffinmaking was a matter for family or nearby carpenter and as long as its period of show was brief, the receptacle continued to occupy a minor place. Food, liquor, transportation, garb, gifts were the major expenses. In the bill for the funeral of Miss Martha Harley in 1824, presented in Puckle's book, only 11 pounds and 11 shillings of the 803 pounds, 11 shillings total were spent on the coffin. In seventeenth-, eighteenth-, and early nineteenth-century America the same was true. A minor item in the burial of David Porter in 1678 was the twelve shilling coffin. Within the last century, however, the focus has shifted so far that persons wishing to discuss costs with an undertaker in the United States are simply led into a "selection room," where they are allowed to make a choice. The price tag on the coffin is the base price of the funeral.

On the basis of the evidence they gathered from directories, funeral bills, and printed advertisements, Habenstein and Lamers regard the growth of coffin shops and warehouses as "possibly one of the most significant developments" in the nineteenth-century funeral business. Westward expansion encouraged the spread of shops that were concerned exclusively with the manufacture of coffins. This was a trend toward specialization that was increasingly evident in other businesses as well. The cabinetmaker who had turned out an item on demand began to realize that it would be more profitable for him to manufacture a number of items to display so that he could create a demand. As with other goods, when coffins became a matter of comparison and contrast, the purchasers began to indulge in their desire for status and willingly succumbed to the suggestion that "just this once nothing but the best will do."

Competition among coffinmakers quickly became enthusiastic, prompting them to ludicrous lengths. By the end of the nineteenth century dozens of patents had been granted for a wide variety of coffins and caskets and burial cases in materials as diverse as stone, iron, hydraulic cement, vulcanized rubber, potter's clay, papier-mâché, zinc, glass, and even celluloid. In shape they ranged from simple rectangles and hexagons to anthropoid horrors with a glass plate to permit the face of the "inner man" to be seen. One brief "wonder" was equipped with a towering "all weather" warning device that would enable an occupant who had been buried too soon to signal for help. The fear of being buried alive was profound in the nineteenth-century United States, which had been terrorized by "The Fall of the House of Usher" and other weird Gothic tales. That fear has also been common in other cultures. In Germany, it was the custom for some time to leave bodies in mortuary chambers until putrefaction set in; a bell rope was placed in the hands of the corpse and officials were required to make periodic checks. In 1896, the Association for the Prevention of Premature Burial was founded in England to insure members against being buried alive; arrangements were made by the society with various medical specialists who would "scientifically" certify that death had occurred after conducting a series of tests specified by the association.

An important function of the wake in every country, aside from its value in allowing friends and relatives to see that the deceased had not met his end by foul means, has been that such an extended watch insures that the departed has indeed departed. That fear in the United States was great, and was largely responsible for the popularity of embalming. In places where such techniques are not employed, a *coup de grâce* is often widely favored. For example, a friend who attended the funeral of an upper middle class woman in Mexico City in 1962 reported that just before the procession was to leave the funeral parlor for the cemetery, a doctor arrived to pierce the woman's heart with a long needle. "That precaution is not taken by everyone," my friend was told, "although most want the guarantee that the deceased will not revive in the grave."

Other fears were seized upon by the coffin manufacturers as profitable for exploitation, including the fear that the body will be corrupted by its underground stay—a curious consideration for those who accept the religious doctrine that the dust shall and must return to the dust. A turning point in the coffin industry and the funeral industry dates back, therefore, to 1848 when Almond D. Fisk introduced a metallic burial case guaranteed to prevent putrefaction. By 1850, it was being widely advertised in glowing testimonials signed by men of the stature of Jefferson Davis, Henry Clay, Daniel Webster, and other political leaders. The ensuing demand resulted in the establishment of a new type of manufacturing company—with standardized mass production and widespread distribution— which signaled the end of the small coffin shop. By 1889, there were 194 factories in profitable operation. Their importance cannot be minimized since their owners played an important role in shaping public attitudes as well as policy within the industry.

Another fear that had important consequences was the anxiety that death was an end; persons were happy to accept literally the spiritual metaphor that death is a short sleep after which we wake eternally. The coffin was thus turned into a bed—or a couch; as the industry has been pleased to insist—padded with velvet mattresses and silken pillows to insure a luxurious rest. During a recent visit to an undertaking establishment, we were urged to admire the "comfort" of some of the more expensive models in the display room. "This makes resting as easy as a hospital bed," our host glowed proudly. Right he was. When he turned a little crank, the mattress was elevated at one end; another turn deftly lowered it.

Utility as first was stressed: protection of the body against water, protection of the living against infection, and preservation of the body for transportation and extended rites. Gradually, however, coffins came to be considered art objects. The American "aesthetic" of the late nineteenth century took over. And that taste, which manifested itself in such designs for the living as the "cardboard house," padded and bustled clothing, and glum parlors weighted with overstuffed furniture and decorated with mezzotints and antimacassars, outdid itself in designs for the dead: baroque tombs, elaborate hearses, sumptuous coffins.

The artistic aspects of the funeral were aided in mid-century when an enterprising manufacturer hit upon the idea of replacing the tapered coffins and figure-revealing burial cases with a rectangular casket. The new *casket*, with its splendid connotations of jewels and precious goods, minimized its relationship with practical usage and emphasized display and extravagance —a point not lost on other manufacturers. One of the most enterprising of these innovators was Samuel Stein, an Austrian cabinetmaker who set himself up in business in Rochester, New York, in 1850 to turn out showcases for local merchants. Casting about for ways to expand his operations, he hit upon the idea of offering an adaptation of his display case as a casket. Although the "showcase" was doomed to failure because of its acute revelation of contents, he found the field profitable enough to continue experiments—first replacing the glass sides with wood and then covering them with cloth. The modified showcase made a formal public debut at the funeral of the famous New York *Herald* editor, James Gordon Bennett, in 1872. According to a report in the rival *Sun,* it was a sensation. The casket, "remarkable for its elegance," was made of hardwood covered with Lyons velvet, with eight solid silver handles representing two hands clutching eight-inch rods. The lid of French crystal glass was constructed in two sections, secured with two heavy locks and draped with more velvet. The casket was framed in a silver molding guaranteed "to survive the lapse of ages." And the inside was, if anything, even more splendid; it was "upholstered with white satin, silk, and Venetian lace, heavy silken tassels dropping from each corner."

Fired by the heady publicity, Stein decided to make use of the Philadelphia Centennial four years later to attract further attention. He leased space in one of the main exhibition halls for a display, but objections of neighboring exhibitors to the lugubrious offering resulted in revocation of his lease. Undaunted and convinced of the need for shrewd merchandising methods, Stein constructed a building nearby and took advantage of the site to demonstrate what the good death could mean. His venture was remarkably successful in stimulating the buying impulse among those who couldn't afford to succumb to it as well as among those who could. General Grant, for example, was buried in a lavish "Style E State" model Stein casket nine years later. By 1890, when Stein's company merged with the even larger National Casket Company, it was producing six hundred caskets a week and had opened up a valuable new field—outside boxes of hardwood to protect the costly inner caskets from wear and tear underground.

Inspired by his example and aware of the importance of lively selling methods, other manufacturers were hard at work. Within a decade after the Civil War, drummers were swarming over the countryside, offering undertakers advice and assistance, instructing them in the "science" of embalming, and providing them with catalogues that showed a variety of models in a wide choice of materials and colors—black, white, blue, lavender, gray—for "immediate delivery" from the factory. In larger cities, showrooms were hired to display the caskets, and every effort was made to associate them with elegance. At first the caskets were named simply for the men who designed them, but the trade rapidly became aware of the value of such grandly delusionary nomenclature as "The Monarch," "The Grand Duke," "The Princess," "The State," "The Dauphin." Religious associations were introduced: "The Calvary," "The Star of David." More recently, the patriotic note has been injected, in keeping with the new effort to create a favorable public acceptance for the "American way of death." Recent offerings have been "The Williamsburg," "The Valley Forge," and "The Patriot."

Realizing the importance of training the retailers since ultimately the success of the manufacturers depended upon them, the makers put aside their competitive activities long enough to set up trade papers through whose columns the undertakers could be indoctrinated and instructed. If the individual entrepreneurs could be organized into a cohesive union—a trade association—life could be made more profitable for the manufacturers. Since volume was obviously limited by the death rate, the way to fame and fortune lay through having the retailers sell more expensive caskets.

The first of the papers was *The Undertaker*, a monthly first published by Henry E. Taylor, a funeral goods manufacturer of New York. Describing itself with macabre humor as a paper "dedicated to the interests of the undertaker and to the discussion of grave matters," the periodical quickly changed its name to *Sunnyside*. Some years later it merged with *The*

Casket, which has been considered the most pretentious of the trade journals of the nineteenth century. The latter, subsidized chiefly by the Stein Casket Company, ingratiated itself with the trade in short order. At first distributed free of charge, the publication went all out to woo a following. Saluting its readers as "men of means, intelligence, taste, and refinement; reading and thinking men, who have elevated their profession," it then proceeded to enlighten them editorially on a number of essential matters, including the desirability of buying Stein caskets.

Many others followed. By 1960, there were at least nine journals of recognized standing and, in spite of the obviously limited circulation possibilities, several others had recently been established. Although the trend has been toward independent ownership, the journals have continued to reflect the attitudes of the casket and hearse companies, which are still impressive supporters through advertising. And the pattern set in the earliest periodicals has continued, despite changes in format and production. Flattering salutes to the "distinguished professionals" and helpful hints ("Don't overlook those puncture gaps") are interspersed with social notes from all over: "Mrs. ———— and daughter Laurie of ———— Funeral Home took delivery of a Pontiac Superior Consort funeral coach at Kosciusco, Mississippi, and drove it back home. The trip was a lark." Editorials and features about individual mortuaries, designed to instill in readers the proper attitude toward their job of selling funerals and funeral goods, provide more serious instruction. Readers are carefully schooled about the stand to take on various matters from pending legislature to answering criticisms leveled at any and all. To a large degree the journals have made so harmonious the relations between manufacturers and retailers that the interests of both now seem indistinguishable, eliminating almost entirely the former protests that undertakers used to raise against what was once held to be "the coffin trust."

Thanks to the trade journals' careful sponsorship of trade associations, the many small businessmen have been molded into what might reasonably be described as "organization men." The coffin manufacturers and the makers of other goods may largely credit themselves with that accomplishment. Like producers in a number of other fields, they realized early that a trade association provided the quickest and surest way of bringing into line persons who were serving their interests; a trade association offers a remarkable medium for shaping attitudes and broadens the base for obtaining favorable legislation. Moreover, if the organizers are the suppliers, they have a powerful weapon for obtaining compliance; undertakers who reject the policies set up by manufacturers have frequently not only suffered whatever humiliation might be entailed in being expelled from an organization of their peers, but actually have been imperiled in many cases by having sources of supply closed to them.

It is not surprising that the columns of the first trade journal, which was published by the coffin industry, were wide open to what some historians have been moved to label politely "the associational impulse." And when the first national convention of undertakers was held in June, 1882, during which the National Funeral Directors Association was established (under another name), the coffinmakers and an embalming fluid company generously provided the complimentary banquet.

The National Funeral Directors Association and other trade associations have helped the industry to establish such a rigid framework for competition that it has successfully managed to defy all laws of supply and demand, diminishing returns, and other classical economic concepts. In spite of an overabundance of suppliers—the number of coffin manufacturers almost doubled between 1925 and 1950—and such an overabundance of distributors (a spokesman for the industry said in 1950 that two thousand undertakers could take care of all the business in the country, although 24,000 were operating), casket costs and the cost of funerals have continued to soar. An average casket cost an undertaker about $10 in 1889, $52 in 1925, and $150 in 1950. During those years the price of funerals continued to rise proportionately since according to the simple system of "cost accounting" recommended to the morticians by a number of coffin industry spokesmen the way to determine the total cost of a funeral is to multiply the cost of the casket "by five or six."

That fanciful system of economics would not be possible if undertakers had not been so thoroughly schooled that many of them feel it would be heresy to question the principles on which their practices are based. Have not the associational leaders insisted time and again that the questioners are wicked subverters of the American way? It is not surprising then that in the *History of American Funeral Directing,* Habenstein and Lamers assert that: "so closely are the funeral directors and manufacturers of morticians' goods related in the total complex of funeral services that the economic features of one group can hardly be discussed without describing in the same breath the like features of the other."

Chapter 6

Merchants of Mortality

IN MANY CULTURES, death and the subsequent mourning and disposal rites have been purely nonprofit affairs, undertaken by members of the family, by friends, by fellow sectarians, by tribal associates. Such practices are by no means limited to primitive societies: the Greeks held to that way for centuries; Jewish tradition placed the obligation on relatives; early Christians felt that the death of one involved all members of the religious community. One interesting holdout against commercialized death exists today in the United States. The Friends Meeting in Yellow Springs, Ohio, sponsors a plan of disposal that involves only volunteer services. When a death occurs, a committee of Friends prepares the body, arranges the legal and business details, and finally takes the body to the crematorium. At a later date, a memorial service is held.

Generally, however, when nonprofit undertaking is the order of death, economics, as well as religious beliefs and social traditions, plays a determining role. For that reason, in Mexico and other transitional countries highly commercialized and nonprofit final arrangements are both popular. In the larger cities, among the upper class and with persons of the growing middle class, funerals and burials have acquired gringo-like, businesslike overtones, with mortuary establishments offering customary services, although embalming is not customary. In the poorer barrios of the cities and in villages and small towns, death and disposal are still amateur activities. When someone dies, all the friends and relatives and neighbors are alerted to come at once so that the proper formalities can be observed within the twenty-four hours before interment takes place.

These people arrive with gifts of food, drink, candles, cigarettes, and money; in some sections, careful accounting is made so that the contributions can be returned at the proper time to the last tortilla and the exact measure of pulque. The women set about preparations at home: making the fires, organizing the menu, washing and dressing the corpse, and arranging it on the floor on a mat so that it may be "viewed" in the required manner. The men then go to the church to arrange for burial, often stopping at the churchyard to dig the grave. When they return, the fiesta begins in earnest. Later in the day, after everyone has eaten and drunk and sung songs and told stories, the body is rolled in the mat or put into a coffin and carried to the cemetery by the frequently unsteady mourning procession. Children's funerals are gay affairs—to everyone except the parents—with a band to play the way to the cemetery and skyrockets set off to light the *angelitos* a path to heaven.

Wherever the death rate is high, funerals have become important social occasions; wherever life is sorry and full of misery, they are often hailed as a welcome relief to be celebrated in the grand manner. Persons in the United States still affected by such cultural conditioning have become ideal victims for exploiters—prizes eagerly sought by merchants of mortality. Not long ago, for example, I witnessed the funeral of a young Chinese father and wage earner that could only have had a crushing effect on the finances of the family he left behind. In addition to the ornate casket, proudly displayed, and the cortege, which included about twenty hired limousines and flower cars, one of which featured a two-by-three-foot photograph of the deceased framed in white blossoms, the procession also featured an eighteen-piece marching band— occidentals wearing orange jackets and military hats—that preceded the cortege to the cemetery through the heavy traffic near downtown Los Angeles. Death as a profitable activity is not a new concept, although it has reached new heights in the United States in the twentieth century. "Dismal Traders," as Bertram Puckle calls them in his informative and entertaining *Funeral Customs*, have played a part in many cultures.

Although Judaism frowned upon ostentation and emphasized mourning, the rigid requirements governing the period of prayer and lamentation gave rise to professional mourners, who have continued to ply their trade into our own time. A friend has as one of the most vivid memories of the Jewish community she grew up in in Poland the spectacle of a group of hired mourners at the funeral of a relative. "We children were terrified," she recalls, "to see those women in their reddish wigs and torn clothing crying and wailing in the house of our uncle."

The Egyptians, of course, whose civilization centered around the cult of the dead, found that the elaborate rites and practices that grew up around funerals and burials were quite unwieldy. Egyptian arrangements became so complicated that five different groups of occupational specialists were concerned with embalming alone: painters, dissectors, apothecaries, surgeons, and physicians or priests, in addition to professional mourners, coffinmakers, and the assortment of others involved in building the elaborate tombs.

Although the Greeks kept even their most lavish funerals free from commercialism, their Roman successors decided that prestige and prolonged rites required special assistance and consequently specialized workers. In addition to the head undertaker, the *libitinarius*, the Roman industry also included embalmers, the *pollinctores*, the *designator*, master of ceremonies and director of the funeral procession, and the *praeco* or crier, who summoned friends, relatives, and associates to the funeral. In addition, there were musicians, jesters, torchbearers, and actors, all of whom took part in the lavish procession. Hired mourners were employed for proper sound effects. Curiously enough, the social status of all funeral workers was very low as long as they practiced their trade, although if they resigned they could participate in Roman political life, and even stand for high office.

Christianity, for a while at least, resulted in the divorce of commerce and funeral rites. The simple ceremonies were carried out as acts of charity by members of the religious community working under the direction of the clergy. Even grave-digging was a service voluntarily rendered. Within a few centuries, however, the delegation of the death duties to persons who saw in them a chance to earn money began to occur. And it was not long before the rites of the Romans and the Egyptians began to supplant the simple obsequies that characterized the typically Christian funeral.

Since a coffin and an embalmed, or well-preserved corpse are the essential items in the funeral industry as we know it, the rise of the industry's merchant princes was long delayed. Generally, what profits were to be made were spread around an assortment of persons. Most of them were primarily of another trade: butcher, baker, candlestick maker, jeweler, clothier, stonemason, carpenter, glover. There were, however, a few exceptions.

Among the first professionals in the European funeral industry were the functionaries of the medieval burial clubs and guilds. In order to assure those in the lower classes a departure that would do credit to them, the members of the working classes organized themselves into associations and contributed regularly a sum that would provide each member with the items held necessary for a suitable send-off: prayers, masses, palls, candles, and—for members of the richer clubs—coffins and shrouds. A turnout of a proper size was guaranteed by the requirement that each attend the others' funerals. Group activities became so extensive that some of the duties had to be delegated to persons who were willing to make it a means of earning a livelihood. One of them was the "bidder," who announced the death of a member and bade all others to attend by rapping on the doors of their houses with the door-key of the deceased. Another roamed the streets with his bell on the day of the funeral, calling all listeners to go to church. On the anniversary, he made a second round of the town urging hearers to pray for the soul of the departed.

The tolling of the bell, which dates back to Roman funeral practices, became a symbol of death in western Europe. "And therefore never send to know for whom . . ." admonished John

Donne in his famous "no man is an island" sermon. One of the most terrifying moments in *Macbeth* occurs when the Thane of Cawdor, his courage screwed to the sticking-place, prepares to murder Duncan: ". . . the bell invites me." In the nineteenth century, Poe described the shivering fright experienced at the "melancholy menace" of the funeral bells. And in twentieth-century Brittany the quaint custom of tolling the bell was perpetuated by old men and women from an almshouse, whose steady tolling during their circuit of the town was interrupted by two orphans crying the name of the person who had died and urging others to pray for his soul.

Among the other early professionals were gravediggers during the terrible years of the plague. For the most part, they were liberated convicts and galley slaves; no one else would willingly undertake such service. Called "Monatti" in Italy, a name that appropriately reflects the solitude in which they were forced to live, they were called "ravens" in France and "Mortus" in Russia. In his impressive history of *The Black Death*, Johannes Nohl tells of the atrocities committed by medieval undertakers. The Monatti entered the houses of the healthy and took men, women, and children off to the plague hospital if the residents refused them money. Although they were legally authorized to act, many got into the business who were not. Indeed, it became such a profitable occupation that scores of young men of the criminal class turned to it: "They fastened bells to their feet and moved about the city as if they were Monatti . . . robbed, violated, and blackmailed to their hearts' content." Several times in Milan in the fourteenth century the Monatti and the unlicensed gravediggers met in the same house and engaged in bloody conflicts.

Among others who made death and burial their single occupation have been succeeding generations of ghouls. Grave despoiling was a vocation in vogue among the Egyptians before 2500 B.C. It was so common in Western society by the time of the Renaissance that Shakespeare, a serene spirit if ever one existed, prepared for his tomb an admonition that represents a stylistic falling off:

> Good friend, for Jesu's sake forbear
> To dig the dust enclosed heare;

Bleste be the man that spares these stones,
And curst be he that moves my bones.

Motives for desecration have been various. Religious and social upheavals, science, and political actions have all played a part at one time or another. During the Elizabethan period, graves of the Catholics were destroyed and ransacked in England; Republicans at the time of the French Revolution looted graveyards to obtain lead coffins which were melted down for bullets. In our own time, the Arabs have ransacked the Mount of Olives Cemetery at Jerusalem, using the markers and tombstones as paving stones.

Grave-robbing was widespread in the early nineteenth century, when the "resurrection men" opened up a traffic with anatomists, who needed cadavers for their work. When scandalized religious groups and frightened citizens began to set up watches at cemeteries to prevent further robbery, the ghouls turned to the living. Most notorious of the "resurrection men" were Burke and Hare, who were convicted at Edinburgh in 1828 for the murder of sixteen persons. None of the earlier activities, however, can be compared in scope and viciousness with those of the Nazi ghouls, who systematically despoiled the corpses of their six million victims before sending them to the huge gas ovens or heaping the bodies in trenches.

One of the most remarkable and by all odds the most sympathetic professional in the death and burial business was the "sin eater," who derived his sole income from taking upon himself the moral trespasses of the newly departed. According to Puckle, a sin eater was seen plying his trade as late as 1825 by a professor at Presbyterian College in Wales. This curious and pitiful scapegoat lived an isolated life, avoided by the villagers as an associate of evil spirits, until a death occurred. Then he was summoned to the house where the corpse lay. The survivors handed to the sin eater *over* the corpse a loaf of bread and a bowl of beer, which he was required to consume on the spot. After he had thus symbolically taken to himself the weaknesses of the dead flesh, the bowl and platter from which he had eaten were burned and the sin-eating scapegoat was paid his fee. The going rate for that extraordinary service was sixpence in 1825.

A distinguishing feature of all those professionals, with the exception of the Egyptians, was their unacceptability to the society in which they lived and practiced their trade. As long as persons involved in the death and burial rites have been associated with religious institutions or were performing family and friendly offices, they have held no special status as undertakers. Once they purified themselves after contact with the dead, they were permitted to enjoy all the social privileges again. However, when persons have worked at funeral and burial tasks for profit they have invariably been relegated to an inferior position in the social order, attracting to themselves all of the fear and loathing of death, all the resentment and rebellion against it.

Smarting keenly at the low esteem in which they were held in spite of their growing influence during and after the Civil War, in the 1870's the undertakers—like doctors and veterinarians and dentists, among others—became aware of the importance of acquiring a "professional" status in the best sense. For that reason, they rejected the notion of becoming part of "a grand undertakers' union" and fell in with the suggestion of organizing themselves into a more dignified "association."

Social status was one motive for becoming associated. Another motive was the need to minimize competition, particularly in such states as New York, Michigan, and Pennsylvania, where there were so many establishments that the death rate permitted an average of only 60 to 77 deaths per mortician a year. (In other areas, fewer were attracted to the trade, and the national average—87—was much higher.) Obviously, a hard-pressed undertaker whose livelihood was at stake could respond only wholeheartedly to such stirring speeches as those made at the National Association meeting in 1884 demanding immediate steps be taken to curb the jobbers, drummers, "embalming-fluid fiends" and the "thousand and one other frauds that hang on to and suck the very life blood out of this profession."

Since the undertakers' association would work in conjunction with others already set up among casket manufacturers, cemetery superintendents, and even baggage agents, the whole industry could be tightly organized. It would, therefore, be possible to see that justice was done to those already practicing—at whatever expense to the public might be considered necessary. In a blueprint for action in 1886, an early association president stressed the importance of such things as working to secure favorable legislation to exclude all but those considered "fit," having the state regulate the burial of the dead, adopting a "code of ethics," getting the National Burial Case Association to guard against funeral reform and getting crematories erected (all of which aims the associations have nobly achieved). It is of overwhelming importance, he emphasized, "for us to act and talk as though our competitors were gentlemen; if we gain professional fame it will be by us as individuals leading pure, upright, professional lives."

The stress on purity, uprightness, professionalism, and—above all—solidarity was given seventy-five years later by Wilber M. Krieger, managing director of the National Selected Morticians and director of the National Foundation of Funeral Service at the California convention in 1961: "Always remember this, that whenever you cuss the other funeral director, you're tarring yourself with the same stick because you, too, are a funeral director. . . . If we can keep a solid front in our dealings with the public we can create the finest public relations that anybody ever dreamed about."

As a result of this organizational image imposed upon them from without and of an inner desire to be considered a person of consequence—a Somebody who is no pariah—the undertakers have carefully cultivated the social role of impeccable mediocrity, adopting such mannerisms as would give the illusion of *soundness*. Like bankers and brokers, undertakers have found it all important to win a reputation for respectability—for ultrarespectability. Not knowledge, but appearance is all. This point has been impressed upon them to such extent that the undertaker—with his pale, sober mien, his somber dress, including the ubiquitous black suit, his carefully cultivated stock of euphemisms, his restraint about indulgence in customary vices, and his guarded ostentatiousness, as expressed by his deep-seated appreciation of the "right" address, the "right" car, the "right" clubs, and the "right" views—is often an anachronistic figure.

To be sure, during the last two decades and particularly in the urban centers some have moved away from the nineteenth century and are conforming to new standards of respectability. Pallor is giving way to lamp-nurtured sun tans; pin-striped suits are becoming mildly fashionable. Some have even daringly substituted sports cars for the customary black "solid" varieties, indulge in Martinis and evenings on the town. A few have lately entered partisan politics. Those in larger cities, of course, can afford to be less observant of the rules of behavior than the undertaker in a small community who is on duty twenty-four hours a day. However, even in larger cities there are those who feel that the old way is the best way—or the safest. Not long ago, we met the owner of one of the largest mortuaries in Los Angeles, a genuinely quaint figure in that city where costume is a matter of whim. His black suit, black tie, and black shoes and socks were relieved by a highly starched white shirt and about three inches of white handkerchief in a breast pocket. During the entire conversation he continued to wear a pair of the white cotton gloves that were a symbol of the trade for decades.

In the manner of the new convert who is invariably more sectarian than the head of the church he has joined, the modern American undertaker is paying for historical sins of the trade by being more proper than anyone else. He is the joiner par excellence. His face, carefully prepared to meet the faces that he meets, is visible at club luncheons on Monday, Tuesday, Wednesday, and all the rest of the days of the week. In three highly typical obituary notices that ran in one of the trade journals in August, 1961, most of the space was devoted to lists of the organizations to which the deceased undertakers belonged. Wilmer W. Snyder of Buffalo, who had operated a funeral home in that city for forty-eight years, was past president of the West Side Kiwanis and of the Businessmen's Association, past grand master of Mispah Lodge, Free and Accepted Masons, and past grand master of Erie District 3, Independent Order of Odd Fellows. Gilbert S. Millspaugh of Walden, New York, was described as "a member of almost every civic and service organization in Walden." He also served as deacon and elder of the First Reformed Church of Walden, was a trustee of the Walden Savings Bank, and served on the Board of Education. Jack Marshall of Tilden, Nebraska, was cited as "prominent" in the Elks, Odd Fellows, Shrine, and other Masonic organizations. He had served as president of the Tilden Lions Club and the Tilden Commercial Club, president of the Nebraska Funeral Directors Association, and president of the National Funeral Directors Association. One of the largest funeral establishments in Los Angeles, which boasted of almost eight hundred services a year in 1961, stresses in trade advertising such connections as: the National Association of Approved Morticians, National Funeral Directors Association, California Funeral Directors Association, Kiwanis, Sertoma, and American Legion.

Such enthusiasm for joining cannot be considered merely the promptings of the herd instinct. Membership in fraternal and service organizations, still as impressive proof of social acceptance as it was in the days of George Babbitt, is useful in obtaining new business. Membership in trade groups also has its useful aspects: it provides some kind of certification of ability to outsiders and is helpful in acquiring clients. Moreover, it is a defense against "them"—meaning these days practically everyone outside the funeral industry—and it is also an appropriate avenue for social release since the many conventions, while perhaps lacking in the flamboyance of an American Legion gathering, nonetheless offer occasions to enjoy the bright lights and the customary indulgences among friends.

For the most part, the general surrender to the associational impulse has made the mortician a fairly dull person. Whatever benefits the numerous organizations have bestowed upon him financially and socially, they have cost him spontaneity, individuality, creativity. Conformity is inevitably the price of associated existence, and conformity means the surrender of personal identity.

To talk to one undertaker is to talk to hundreds, since they have all acquired a vocabulary designed chiefly to permit them to indulge in ritualistic communication in the office and out. The attitudes of the group leaders are the attitudes of the followers: the leaders' views are their views. And the wages of the sin of departing from group ways is expulsion and ostracism. That was brought to widespread public attention most recently in May, 1961, when Nicholas Daphne, who had paid his dues to the California Funeral Directors Association (C.F.D.A.), had his membership revoked along with that of another California undertaker and was denied admission to the hall in Santa Monica where the convention was being held. The reason given for the action against Mr. Daphne was that he had violated the code of ethics adopted the year before placing restrictions on price advertising and on making agreements with special groups.

Since a number of C.F.D.A. leaders also advertise prices, the move was obviously taken as a countermeasure against the California funeral cooperatives with one of which Mr. Daphne had contracted to provide simple funerals for as little as $150 to $210, including embalming. The association had "suggested" a rock-bottom price of $450.

C.F.D.A. President C. Emory Taylor insisted that the purpose of the code was "to foster and perpetuate high ethical standards for those within the funeral service profession in California." Mr. Daphne insisted on his right to operate as an independent businessman, to provide goods and services at a price that would yield what he considered a reasonable profit. Anxious to prevent the revolt from spreading, the C.F.D.A. board of directors went so far as to bar Mr. Daphne from the exhibit hall where he would see and possibly order the equipment and merchandising being displayed, as *Mortuary Management* conceded in an editorial, by "the people whose exhibit space money makes the convention possible."

In a rather startling gesture of defiance, Mr. Daphne and his wife paraded in front of the convention hall for three days —pickets without portfolio. The affair was so enthusiastically covered by press, radio, television, and magazine reporters that the industry began to have serious second thoughts about the public revelation of "professional economics." Warning sourly that "Nick now wears a halo around his head as the saviour of the poor, down-trodden public," an industry spokesman cautioned members against becoming involved in discussions of funeral costs: "You have as much chance to win as you do in a crooked dice game." And he further warned against passing rules or regulations that can be "misinterpreted by outsiders as indicative of a move toward raising or maintaining high prices of funerals."

In spite of the very powerful weapons they wield, national, state, and local associations have had some rather startling encounters with maverick morticians in recent years and have had some sore blows dealt to their dignity. One of the thorniest of the independent undertakers was the late W. W. Chambers, founder of a highly successful Washington, D. C., funeral operation, whose merchandising methods at one point included bus placards offering special rates for the next thirty days. Testifying before a Congressional committee in 1948 against a proposal to license undertakers, Mr. Chambers, who had conducted five White House funerals, offered such interesting items of fact and opinion that the committee room became the most popular place in town for a brief period. "This business is a mighty sweet racket," he commented with disarming candor. He had left his livery business to enter it because it had the other "beat a mile."

Mr. Chambers' son, W. W. Chambers, Jr., also caused a furor in 1961, when he told the reporter for a national magazine that it was his opinion that the average funeral is too expensive. He reported that he could make a profit on anything over $400, a figure that included all the luxuries of embalming, cosmetology, open-casket displays, and other assorted items. Other trade spokesmen set it far higher, at $650 and more. A spokesman for the Los Angeles morticians said early in 1962 that the minimum price was $461. What makes the financial statements more confusing is that many undertakers are providing complete funerals for about $150 to $200 to cooperative groups. And although they may be "loss leaders"—if they can be obtained at all—other undertakers advertise very much lower prices. During the summer of 1962, two of the largest operators in Los Angeles had plastered the city with ads reading "For Undertaking Utter-McKinley Understands— from $100" and "Forest Lawn—Undertaking $145."

Thorniest of all insiders, perhaps, has been Forest Lawn's

"Builder." Hubert Eaton, or Dr. Eaton (since he insists upon his honorary title), has been engaged in active combat with California's morticians in court and out since, after going broke in the Nevada mining fields, he stood on a hillside on the outskirts of Los Angeles early in the century, surveyed the cemetery he had been hired to manage, and realized that he had finally struck pay dirt.

Half a century later, Eaton, who is the son of a Baptist minister, told a biographer that he had been "called" to revolutionize the funeral industry. Many of the undertakers, publicly as well as privately, describe his having entered the business in more irreverent terms. But whether he was divinely inspired or just pushed into the business by his spectacular failure, Eaton brought with him the personality, background, training, and experience that enabled him to promote a nondescript burial ground into one of the major tourist attractions in California and to amass a private fortune of heroic proportions. A tall, grey-eyed, thin-lipped young man from Missouri, Hubert Eaton quickly established himself as an illusionist without peer—and that in an area boasting Cecil B. De Mille.

Listing his own accomplishments with great frankness, Eaton considers the major steps in his success story the inauguration of such "firsts" as setting up trust plans, consolidating all forms of interment under one management, and establishing a mortuary within a cemetery. Perhaps these were important, but Eaton's greatest success was his ability to persuade hundreds of thousands of persons that a cemetery was not a cemetery, but—in the essentially blasphemous phrase of his celebrator, Bruce Barton—"a first step up toward Heaven." And Eaton was in possession of the tread.

According to Mrs. Adela Rogers St. Johns, whose fulsome and thoroughly approved biography of Eaton is a best seller at Forest Lawn, the "Builder" learned the basics of sales psychology at William Jewell College, where he more formally studied chemistry. As manager of the basketball team, he boosted failing attendance by doubling the price of admission. Hubert knew then, Mrs. St. Johns says, that one way of making the public pay was "to make it expensive." He had an opportunity to put that theory into practice when he and his cousin Joe Eaton staked out a claim during the outbreak of gold fever in Nevada in 1907. Hubert went east and managed to raise almost a million dollars to develop it. Although the mine proved to be a dud, he had gained valuable experience in selling an intangible: in return for the promise of easy money, people had been eager to surrender coin of the realm. What would they not do later in exchange for the promise of immortal mortality that the Forest Lawn sales campaigns touted?

Like all successful promoters, Eaton had also acquired an appreciation of a good front and an attractive package persuasively offered. And he continued with rich sureness to believe that God was determined he should become a wealthy man, undaunted by the fact that his prayers for a rich strike in Nevada had not been answered. Like other skillful sales persons in various enterprises, Eaton has had no hesitancy about associating his activities with God's will and generally advertising himself as a true believer. He has spent a vast sum to acquire religious paintings, statues, and other art objects. Currently his search is for a "smiling Christ." To give sanctity to his business, he has built a series of churches within the walls of Forest Lawn. He has been somewhat less than frank, however, about his celebration of Moses; in building the Mt. Sinai cemetery, his organization took refuge behind a fictitious name.

He has, however, made a determined effort to associate himself and his chain of cemetery-mortuaries with motherhood, celebrated in scores of statues. He has also drawn into his enterprises the "right" element in the community. Among the members of Forest Lawn's "Council of Regents" have been bankers, investment brokers, Hollywood stars, and such notables as former United States Vice-President Charles Dawes and the University of Southern California's Chancellor Rufus von KleinSmid, all of whom have been required to tog themselves out on state occasions in red robes and mortarboards "as part of the pageantry Eaton loves and believes in."

Underground movie stars have also been put to work for him; to lie next to a corpse of a cinema luminary is considered such an honor that the places bring premium returns to Forest

Lawn. More recently, he and the organization have been exploiting patriotism. Forest Lawn's newest section and one of the most expensive is the "Court of Freedom," where within easy distance of a mosaic of the signing of the Declaration of Independence it is possible to be buried in such style that one Los Angeles doctor recently paid $85,000 for a crypt for himself.

Dr. Eaton's more creative salesmanship was balanced from the first by a shrewd regard for practicality. When he arrived at Forest Lawn, he carried with him a "Before Need" sales plan with which he had become acquainted in St. Louis, where it had been based on the notion that cemetery lots could be sold for investment purposes to persons of a speculative bent who lacked enough capital to acquire larger parcels of real estate. That aspect is still being utilized by his salesmen, who point out readily that a particular piece of "property" that retailed for $595 in 1953 was worth $1690 by 1961. Within a year of his arrival in California, the "Before Need" plan—now common among cemetery owners—had enabled Eaton and his sales crew to boost business at Forest Lawn by 250 per cent.

Meantime, the American Securities Company which he had helped to organize as a first step—the company which has been "the foundation and backbone of what was to be its affiliate, the Forest Lawn Company," his biographer says—had become a solvent financial institution. A few years later it was so solvent that it enabled him to defy the Forest Lawn board of directors and to secure a financial interest in the cemetery and complete control of its operation.

Within the framework of the American Securities Company, Eaton established an insurance company, which became a major source of income, and later the Forest Lawn Trust Plan. That operation was designed to permit persons too old to apply for life insurance to purchase bonds that were guaranteed for face value *at any time—when applied on purchases at Forest Lawn!* There are now several million dollars in those trusts, which are said to average about seven hundred dollars each. Although they pay only a 3 per cent return, a salesman who recently attempted to persuade me to buy one advised that it would be "a good idea" to allow the interest to accumulate so that possible inflation would not devalue the type of casket and other goods it was designed to cover.

To provide a more attractive package for the intangibles Forest Lawn was selling, Dr. Eaton and his wife began a series of what one art critic has called "art scavenging" expeditions to Europe to buy statuary and other items that would enhance the grounds and help to bring in revenue for such livelier services as weddings and christenings. Here, too, the economics were of stunning simplicity. When the Eatons arrived home with their art by the ton—nudes, angels, mothers, family groups, and other assorted pieces of sculpture—they were put on display in the cemetery along with a little sign advising shoppers that they could be purchased "as a private memorial" and moved to different locations *within* the park. As a *Playboy* writer pointed out in Madison Avenue parlance governing television and radio inner communication, an Eaton statue on display is a "sustaining" memorial; when sold and moved to another location, it becomes a "sponsored" memorial. Needless to say, prices of plots near the choicest bits of sculpture are affected by the art moved into their vicinity.

Tireless in his zeal to make a cemetery operation a big thing, Eaton decided early that it would be more profitable to consolidate all forms of interment under one management and one overhead; up to that time, ground burial, mausoleum entombment, and crypts for "cremains" had been separate provinces. Consolidation, he has pointed out, gave Forest Lawn "a tremendous sales advantage" over competitors. Even more daring—and fantastically profitable—was his establishment of a mortuary within the cemetery. The decision to do that, he told the National Sales Executives Club in 1955, when he accepted their top award, "brought legal and political worlds crashing about our heads."

Although Eaton had issued warnings of his expansionist tendencies as early as 1929 in a speech before the American Cemetery Association, it was not until December 20, 1932, that he collided head-on with the morticians. That was the date of Forest Lawn's application to the California State Board for a license to operate a mortuary. According to St.

Johns' biography, Eaton and his legal advisor had expected some trouble, but the application set off a "smoldering fuse. The enemy, composed of the California State Funeral Directors Association, and the National one as well, closed ranks and began shooting from the hip." The Glendale City Council, obliging as ever to the owner of one of its leading businesses, rejected a proposal that the city be required to issue a permit to construct a mortuary. That decision enabled Eaton to comply with the State Board's ruling that when it finally considered the application the mortuary should be ready for operation, with all supplies on hand.

Eaton got started on a $150,000 building when the next blow fell. Assembly Bill 1044, introduced in January, ruled out mortuaries within the confines of a cemetery and prevented cemeteries from investing perpetual care funds in income-producing real estate—another profitable source of income for Forest Lawn. The battle this time was not in Glendale, with its obliging city officials. Nor was it in Rome, where Pope Pius XI, at the request of King Victor Emmanuel III, at the request of the Ministry of Arts acceded to Eaton's request that St. Peter-in-Chains be closed for a day to permit workmen to make a replica of Michelangelo's "Moses." Dr. Eaton said later that Moses was responsible for the request having been granted, although some of his more worldly agents are reported to have admitted having spread a little money around Rome on cocktail parties and on contributions to "worthy causes."

This time the battle was in Sacramento, where the undertaking associations also had influence—as Bill 1044 testified—and where a lobby was on hand to see that the influence continued. According to Forest Lawn spokesmen, one dollar of the price of every casket sold in the United States for a year went into a legislative fund to help fight the plan.

On January 26, 1933, Forest Lawn placed an order with a national casket company which had its headquarters in Portland, Oregon, after Dr. Eaton had been refused a supply by local casketmakers and Los Angeles representatives of the large national concerns. The company said that the order would be filled, but a month later the president is reported to have told Eaton's office that if he did fill the order he would be "boycotted by every funeral director in the U. S." In March, expectedly, the morticians who made up the State Board handed down an adverse decision on the grounds that the mortuary at Forest Lawn did not have a specific address and location devoted exclusively to the business of funeral direction and that it was not in accordance with the law. Since the only "law" prohibiting mortuaries within cemeteries was the assembly bill, Eaton and his attorney took the decision to the California Court of Appeals the next day.

Although the bill was passed by the assembly two months later, it was vetoed in the state senate, thanks to the shrewd work of Forest Lawn advocates in the state capital. Shortly after, the Third District Court of Appeals issued a mandate to the State Board that a license be issued by October 7, 1933. The State Board delayed, during which time the National Funeral Directors Association asked the National Recovery Administration to insert a clause in the business codes they were drawing up to prohibit Forest Lawn from engaging in the package deal it was already advertising. The advertisements ("One Telephone Call Does Everything") appeared although the license had yet to be issued. Eaton, who by this time, thanks to his Council of Regents and to Forest Lawn's offer of investment opportunities, had a considerable amount of the economic and political power of California concentrated behind him, went to Washington to confer with the National Recovery Administration's General Hugh Johnson. The National Funeral Directors Association request was turned down, and in December, 1933, the State Board finally awarded Forest Lawn the license to operate a mortuary.

Although many undertakers consider him the "Cadillac of the trade," for association leaders Eaton has all the charm of an armored tank. After almost a year of public wrangling between Forest Lawn and the Los Angeles funeral directors' group as a result of the former's advertising "Undertaking $95," the affair was settled out of court in the summer of 1961. The differences "have been amicably resolved," announced Eaton's nephew, Frederick Llewellyn. According to *Mortuary Management*, the funeral directors had secured "some concessions for this action." Shortly after the suit was dropped, at least one concession was made public: new Forest Lawn billboards appeared stating "Undertaking $145." That advertisement continued to appear on billboards for at least a year, although in the early summer of 1962 one of his salesmen said that it was "misleading."

The success of Dr. Eaton's free-wheeling methods of selling has inspired many tradesmen to turn over a new leaf. "We've been behind the times," one mortician noted, resolving to introduce what he considered art and culture into his operation. Meantime, others have settled for installing swimming pools and entertaining the organization men, junior and senior, in order to attract "high-class trade." Almost to a man, cemetery owners are following his lead, hiring sales crews to tout "Before Need" plans, setting about their grounds pieces of questionable sculpture, forbidding tombstones, and building chapels and mortuaries. "Forest Lawn is a nice place to be buried—if you like circuses," one cemetery owner in a Los Angeles suburb told us with fine disdain. Then, he added wistfully, "Most people do. You've got to hand it to Hubert Eaton." A number of persons have—including authors Evelyn Waugh and Aldous Huxley—for his apparently boundless vulgarity and his ability to profit by all that is snobbish and base in humanity as well as all that is decent and commendable. He is the fine artist of the American undertaking industry, the *crowned* prince of merchandising, in extreme.

Chapter 7

The Happier Hunting Grounds

THE CONCEPT OF A CEMETERY as a private enterprise operated for personal gain is a relatively unusual one, associated chiefly with the United States for the past century. In other cultures that have practiced inhumation, when special areas have been designated as disposal sites they have been maintained and directed for the most part by the religious institutions or by such social institutions as family, tribe, community, or state.

In spite of the fact that many cultures have preferred cremation, water burial, aerial exposure, and other forms of disposal, the earth is really, as Puckle has pointed out, "one vast burial ground." For the belief has existed for thousands of years, as it does very explicitly today among some Australian tribes, that the spirits of those persons whose bodies went unburied wander about the earth, intent upon harming the living who have denied them life beyond the grave. The Chaldeans, Assyrian-Babylonians, Greeks and Romans, Jews and Christians, Germans and Egyptians, primitive tribal hunters who have never developed community existence—civilized and uncivilized alike—all have been preoccupied, chiefly through fear but also with love and respect, with a desire to provide a final "home" for the dead.

Among early peoples, provision of a grave was the obligation of the family. Sometimes the survivors simply turned over the family dwelling to the corpse and moved on; sometimes, as in Melanesia and other parts of the South Pacific, they erected temporary huts over the grave in which the closest of kin lived for a few months to pacify the spirit below. In Europe and other places, limestone caves afforded shelter for the living and sepulchers for the dead. Typically, Jewish burial was in a cave, although some persons were interred on a part of their estate that was considered too remote for contaminating the living. The concern for sanitation was shared by the ancient Egyptians and Chinese, who used dry burial as a protective measure against the plague. Bodies heavily shrouded in coarse cloth were laid upon beds of charcoal under six or more feet of sand in a place where they could decompose slowly and safely.

The ancient Gauls and Britons had their chalk tombs; shafts were sunk deep into the soft material and when the cut had been filled with bodies a tree was planted on top and another common grave was opened. Roman catacombs served the Christians for burial and worship. Among some groups the place of burial was sacred ground; the early Germanic people, the Christians, and the Indians in many parts of Latin America constructed temples and churches beside the bones of their saints and warriors. Among others, the place of burial was a place of danger and defilement. Roman, Jewish, and other cultures had such horror of the dead that they willingly observed an original law of the Twelve Tables: "Let there be no burial or cremation in the city." The Mount of Olives Cemetery at Jerusalem and the tombs along the great avenues leading out from Rome are evidence of that.

Although Roman custom regarding burial was upheld in Roman law restated in the fourth century prohibiting interment in cities or the presence of coffins, urns, sarcophagi, and other possible sources of infection, the ban was not easy to enforce after Christianity began to take hold. Insisting on their rightful due once this vale of tears had been traversed, lesser persons demanded a church burial inside the walls of the town like those accorded to the saintly and the rich. That became so common by the ninth century that Charlemagne issued edicts reviving Roman law.

Churchyards had been added to overcrowded churches as places of burial in 752, as being suitable for all except heretics, suicides, and others beyond the pale who might cause harm or contaminate the corpses of the good and the true. Both became such serious problems that by the sixteenth century Archbishop Latimer was protesting the state of St. Paul's churchyard in London as the cause of "much sickness and disease," and a century later John Evelyn was equally wroth about the churches having been transformed into "charnel houses."

Although some small private and public plots had existed for families or members of special groups, burial was, by and large, a church monopoly throughout Europe and in much of America until the nineteenth century. Secularization then resulted largely as a consequence of the concern with the separation of the functions of church and state and the growing interest in public health and sanitation. Following the example of France, which had rigidly proscribed burial within city walls after some disastrous epidemics, in 1806 the New York City Board of Health urged the removal of all graveyards within the city proper and recommended that the cemeteries be made public works.

The first important new suburban cemetery was not a public park but mutually owned Mount Auburn Cemetery on the outskirts of Cambridge. That place established a number of dominant trends in American cemetery development. Inspired by Dr. Jacob Bigelow, who had protested for years the public health hazards of church vault and churchyard burial, a group of prominent Bostonians—including Daniel Webster, Edward Everett, and Supreme Court Chief Justice Joseph Story— obtained authorization in 1831 for the Massachusetts Horticultural Society to dedicate a valuable tract of land it had been given for experimental purposes for a rural cemetery. The cemetery, it had been decided with Yankee acumen, would be operated as a business, not a charity. In return for their investments, the owners received burial plots. Continued care of the place would be insured by selling burial rights and other services to other families and individuals. That was so successful that Mount Auburn's care fund totals in the millions today.

The place was beautifully maintained, owners were encouraged to put up elaborate monuments and memorials, and prominent space was given to prominent persons. Many—perhaps most—Bostonians of consequence are buried there, including Mary Baker Eddy, founder of the Christian Science Church, who eliminated the word *death* from the vocabulary of millions of Americans. The broad avenues and curving roads encouraged people to scramble for a good address; the basic pattern for the familiar American subdivision was set. More important immediately, Mount Auburn Cemetery established the major lines of development cemeteries were to take —at considerable cost to the reposers and, as some cemetery owners have so quaintly identified them, the "waiting ones."

According to James Worley, executive vice-president of the American Cemetery Association, it was from the Mount Auburn idea that five types of cemetery corporations developed in this country: large mutually owned cemeteries, particularly in the Northeast and Midwest; profit cemeteries, especially in the South and West; church cemeteries maintained by the congregation; cooperative cemeteries set up by lodges and other organizations; and municipal cemeteries. "But each and every one of these cemeteries, regardless of the type of corporation," Mr. Worley has held, "was and must continue to be dedicated to the same fundamental cause and the use of sound business methods."

In many European countries and in some areas of Latin America, the state or local government operates the burial ground as a public service, supported principally by the taxpayers—and in some instances by a surtax on the users. One rather extraordinary system is that employed in Uruguay, where five years after a body has been buried relatives are required to go to the cemetery, extract the bones from the large casket in which the body has been decomposing, repack them in a smaller casket, and store them in an assigned niche. The fee for the privilege of doing that a few years ago was fifty pesos—about a month's wage for a domestic worker at the time.

Although many states and municipalities as well as the federal government established public cemeteries in this country during the nineteenth and early twentieth century, strong pressures to curb that trend have been brought to bear whenever a necessary public work has been proposed. Cemeteries for the public are protested as "socialistic," although potter's fields for indigents are welcomed as necessary. That attitude among cemetery owners is not to be wondered at, since the Mount Auburn venture early established just how profitable even a "nonprofit" cemetery could be. Within a few years after its inauguration, Laurel Hill in Pennsylvania was established, Green-Wood in New York, and scores of others. Some of the first leaders moved to consolidate their favorable economic position by having a Rural Cemetery Act passed by the New York State Legislature in 1847. That act, which set a precedent followed in other states to the gratitude of later entrepreneurs, gave lavish tax concessions and unusual powers to the cemetery associations.

Churches, which have always enjoyed remarkable freedom from mundane tax worries about their profitable secular enterprises as well as their religious enterprises, continued to provide denominational and sanctified resting places for their members. But whatever the spiritual aspects of church cemeteries, most of them have been managed in a businesslike way. Prices for choice locations in most church burial grounds compare very favorably with those in private-profit cemeteries, in California at any rate. The equality promised each soul is certainly not very visible in the graveyard; if riches cannot buy admission to heaven, money speaks very loudly indeed in obtaining a preferred place for the body to rest. One of the dreariest sights in almost any church-operated cemetery is the potter's field section where the poor are interred, a sorry reminder of that first of the line established with the thirty pieces of silver Judas returned to high priests.

Some churches turned the management of the cemetery over to vestrymen, deacons, and other lay members; some have established rigid price schedules that clergymen have easily been able to follow. In some cases, however, the clergy simply washed their hands of the matter. According to the American Cemetery Association, one church cemetery, Spring Hill, founded in Nashville in 1787, was "enthusiastically turned over to a family in the congregation in the 1880's to run on a profit basis."

Lodges and other organizations whose members found themselves priced out of cemeteries in their areas or who were excluded because of religious, racial, or nationality distinctions established their own cemeteries. Among the first genuinely cooperative groups in this country were the burial organizations of the "land people." Jewish immigrants from various European countries banded together on the basis of the community of their origin and bought cemetery lots scattered widely in Manhattan, Long Island, and Brooklyn, and were thus buried, if not with the fathers, with brothers and townsmen. Negro cemeteries are common throughout the South and West. Orientals, Latins, and other groups long held socially unacceptable in California had to rely on church cemeteries or public places for burial.

Federal, state, and municipal cemeteries have been unsegregated for the most part. Public cemeteries in Los Angeles and Santa Monica have been made interesting and colorful with Buddhist shrines and tombstones inscribed with lovely Chinese characters identifying, with a dignity and respect they were infrequently accorded in life, the occupants of the graves.

Unfortunately, much of what was memorable or human about cemeteries has been banished in the interests of efficiency, economy, and cemetery aesthetics. Markers, which cut down maintenance costs, have replaced the tombstones and headstones which make a number of early graveyards interesting places to visit with their elaborate or frank or frequently humorous epitaphs:

> Soon ripe
> Soon rotten
> Soon gone
> But not forgotten

or:

Old Thomas Mulvaney lies here,
His mouth ran from ear to ear,
Reader, tread lightly on this wonder,
For if he yawns, you're going to thunder.

or simply, on the tomb of a six-year-old:

She was an amiable child.

In his *Stories on Stone*, Charles L. Wallis has amassed a collection of such immortalizing epitaphs that constitute a special form of folk art worth preserving. William Faulkner's acute insight into Southern character is revealed in the first of his brilliant novels about the Sartoris clan in the scene in the cemetery, where Miss Jenny inspects the fresh grave of young Bayard Sartoris after having gone to the Negro burying-ground beyond the cemetery proper "to see if they fixed Simon all right." Contrasting the simple inscription on Bayard's tombstone with the other "pagan symbols" of Sartoris vainglory "and the carven gestures of it in enduring stone," she notes with due wryness the elaborate monument of the old Colonel John Sartoris—identified as soldier, statesman, citizen of the world. Beneath his name was the inscription:

For man's enlightenment he lived
By man's ingratitude he died
Pause here, son of sorrow; remember death.

The inscription, Faulkner recounts, had caused "some furore" on the part of the murderer's family, who had made formal protest. The Colonel's son, old Bayard, had complied with popular opinion and caused the second line to be chiseled out; but he had his revenge in a line he added beneath it: "Fell at the hand of ———— Redlaw, Sept. 4, 1876."

A visit to a cemetery in Mexico is to feel the pulse of humanity. Because the people there have acknowledged death and accept it as a part of life, cemeteries reflect the real joy of living. One of the most colorful fiestas is that held on our Halloween, when families of the dead go to shower their graves with calendulas and the bright marigold-like "flower of death," to light candles, and to picnic extravagantly for the delight of the "little angels" and the older dear departeds. Their efforts to make the place bright enough to delight the most artistic of the spirits of the dead give creativity and character to their own lives. In Mexico there is also acceptance. A talented Negro musician I met there some years ago explained very simply his determination to stay on: "If I go home and die, I'll be shoved off in a corner of some cemetery. Here I can be buried with the rest of the folks."

Segregation, an element of snob appeal, has been an important selling point in many private cemeteries. Publicly operated cemeteries, particularly national cemeteries, have been refreshingly free from that. No one has questioned a dead man's race, religion, or national origin when he was to be buried in Arlington or any of the other ninety-seven cemeteries operated by the government. Although, legally, private cemeteries in many places have been compelled to desegregate, many in California where such a law is in effect either evade it entirely or set aside special areas for members of minority groups on the novel theory that "they'll be happier among their own people."

Discrimination, of course, also operates in reverse. Catholics and Jews, for example, may be buried only in Catholic and Jewish cemeteries respectively, although even among those groups the desire for prestige and a swank address has caused some defection. Practicing Catholics are required by church law to be buried in "sanctified" ground, and sanctification is the specific duty of a bishop. However, one Los Angeles owner of a nondenominational cemetery told us that several Catholic persons had been buried in his cemetery in good order.

The Forest Lawn cemetery chain stirred up a hornet's nest in Jewish circles in southern California after publication in the Los Angeles *Daily Journal* of a certificate to do business under a fictitious name. The certificate revealed that the widely advertised new "Jewish" cemetery in the city, Mount Sinai Memorial-Park, was owned and operated by the Forest Lawn Memorial-Park Association. In a dramatic feature story in the *B'nai B'rith Messenger*, January 13, 1961, readers were treated to the spectacle of a copy of the certificate and a reproduction of an envelope with the Forest Lawn logotype and slogan. "When you, as a purchaser of a Mt. Sinai Memorial-Park plot," the caption warned severely, "have correspondence with the cemetery, you may expect to have your Jewish sensitivities outraged by the invitation to visit the Crucifixion." The article, intent on dispelling secrecy about ownership of Mt. Sinai, also contained opinions from the Rabbinical Assembly of America, the Rabbinical Council, the Union of Orthodox Rabbis, and other authoritative sources. All were agreed that according to Halachic law in the Talmud, burial in soil which may be reclaimed by the original non-Jewish owner "is absolutely forbidden . . . lest the transgression be committed of eventual removal and desecration of the remains."

Other churches and individuals have exhibited strong preference for apartheid. A special section of one Los Angeles cemetery has been set aside for members of the Mormon Church. Some individuals of various persuasions have gone to great lengths to insure themselves a satisfactorily aloof burial place. The new Greek Orthodox Church in Los Angeles, which has been compared favorably in opulence and majesty with St. Sophia's in Istanbul, is matched on a miniature scale in splendor by the adjacent tomb that Spyros Skouras, chief patron of the edifice, had constructed for himself and his family.

The desire to possess in death all the things that have often been denied in life—brilliant and notable associates, a good address, the best of everything wordly, and also that proximity to religion that required too much effort to make a lively struggle for—has enabled cemetery owners and operators to profit. Those themes, those "advantages" have been stressed since the cemetery superintendents and proprietors first banded together in a trade association in 1887; they have been stressed to such effect that public cemeteries have become almost synonymous in people's minds with potter's fields. That public relations, or "educational" campaign has been matched with vigorous lobbying in state legislative centers and in city and county zoning board anterooms to obtain impressive concessions for private profit cemeteries.

This country had an opportunity during the nineteenth century to obtain a cemetery system that would function as a worthwhile public service. That was in 1850, after the Mexican War. The cemetery that was built in Mexico City, the first of a series, is a handsome place, although when I visited it in 1950 no one had been buried there for more than twenty years, so strong had become the feeling about a "good" private address.

Cemetery owners as well as morticians have played an important role in having dead troops brought home for reburial since the Civil War. Well aware that it is an ill war that blows no possibility of great gain to the trade, the various associations were better prepared to realize greater gains by the time of the Spanish-American War. A newly-organized Quartermaster Burial Corps, staffed with civilian undertakers and assistants, accepted the responsibility of exhuming and returning the bodies of American troops from Cuban soil to the United States. Three years later, the mortuary-cemetery trade had the situation even more closely under control in the Philippines.

World War I was also a profitable episode, although there was still room for improvement, the trade realized. When the next of kin of fallen troops were polled, 46,520 voted to have the dead returned for another burial on this side of the Atlantic; 31,591 voted to leave them in United States military cemeteries that had been set up on or near European battlefields.

By the end of World War II, results of the continuing educational program and of incessant lobbying for a larger share of business were apparent. Of the 171,000 casketed remains returned to the United States at the request of relatives (three-fifths of the total deaths), 80 per cent were buried in private plots and only 20 per cent in national cemeteries.

Families of the dead were given no opportunity for choice during the Korean conflict. Although large military cemeteries had been established in Korea, it was decided that they were to be temporary burial places; all the dead troops would be returned to the United States. By sheerest good fortune it was found that a surprisingly large number of embalmers in grades from private to major were among the ranks in the Far East command, and civilian embalmers and technical specialists were recruited in sufficient number to finish the job.

There were less than one hundred national cemeteries by 1955 —a very modest number, indeed, to cope with the millions of former servicemen eligible to use them. In March, 1962, a Congressional subcommittee charged with solving the problem of burial space in the ninety-eight national cemeteries heard testimony from Army officials that added to their concern: "It is conservatively estimated that more than forty million persons are legally entitled to burial in national cemeteries," a spokesman said. Chairman of the subcommittee, Representative J. T. Rutherford of Texas, said that his group had fifty-two bills before it to provide for the creation of new cemeteries or the expansion of present ones. However, he added, "in the absence of a national policy, it is difficult if not impossible to consider these bills on their respective merits." Often they were located so far from major centers of population that the eligible found it impractical to use them if they had wished. For example, the closest national cemetery to Los Angeles is at Point Loma, almost 150 miles away. Transportation of the body by a mortician would be quite costly, and some families would reject the idea of a person's being buried so far from home. Moreover, since the Veterans Administration has turned over to morticians the right as well as the responsibility for making all the arrangements, not many are buried there from Los Angeles.

A city that can afford to turn over more than three hundred acres of prime land to a baseball operation—as Los Angeles did—might well be able to dedicate a lesser amount of land for a public cemetery or a national cemetery. Such a proposal would collide with private interests, of course. As a matter of fact, pressure has been consistently exerted to cut back the service that the county does offer, so obviously and so humiliatingly a charity that few would care to receive it even if they were eligible. The Los Angeles County Cemetery, reserved for indigents, has not interred bodies since 1922. Instead, corpses sent there have been cremated, a practice that is regarded with such distaste by some religious groups, including the Jews, Catholics, Mormons, and Christian Scientists, that bodies known to belong to those denominations that are county charges are turned over to religious charities for burial. Catholic poor are buried in a church cemetery in the county, for which the county pays thirty dollars a grave space. Jewish poor are buried in one of the Jewish cemeteries in Los Angeles at no cost to the county. Other agencies also accept the task of providing burial places for their members. Although 11,809 persons were buried in the Los Angeles County Cemetery from 1896 to 1922, when the practice was discontinued in favor of cremation, so much space remains of the nine acres it occupies that an adjacent private cemetery recently petitioned to acquire public land, and the director of the Real Estate Management Department of the county government recommended that five and one-tenth acres of the cemetery land be declared "excess property."

Actually, a cemetery is one of the favored forms of land investment these days, offering the promise of infinite riches in little room. Even an acre, if strategically located, can bring in a healthy revenue, a number of city land owners have found. With traditional single burial, at least eighteen hundred to two thousand bodies can be accommodated in a single acre. Today, however, most cemeteries are selling the idea of two-decker graves, which means that at least four thousand bodies can be accommodated in one acre. The principle, rejected by Jewish tradition, but widely accepted now, is very simple: initial burial is simply deeper, so that another casket can be interred on top. Some cemeteries, including Forest Lawn, interested in profitable ways to utilize space are able to cram a much larger number of bodies together by the simple expedient of peeling off a top layer of earth about eight feet deep and laying a concrete pad, with shallow dividers marking off spaces for a series of coffins. A second pouring makes another series of cells on top of the first. An upper and lower are sold as "companion crypts," although a body is obviously just as companionable with the next upper or next lower. When one of the partner-owners dies, the concrete that forms the "ceiling" of the lower cell is chopped away, the coffin inserted, more cement poured, and the top is ready for occupancy. By having only brief concrete divider walls separate two graves from adjacent "companions," it is possible to accommodate many thousands of coffins in a single acre of ground.

An even more popular and profitable way of utilizing space is the mausoleum concept for above-ground entombment. An adaptation of the apartment building principle, a structure is built to house successive layers of occupants—six, eight, or ten compartments high and almost any number wide. This way dozens of bodies can be buried using only a few square feet of ground. Since cemeteries receive special tax privileges (on unoccupied ground they pay only the low taxes imposed on undeveloped land, and when a space is sold it is taken off the tax rolls forever) it is not hard to see how profitable a few acres can be, even when competition is keen.

An interesting revelation of cemetery business practices came to light in California in December, 1962, when the District Court of Appeal ordered a group of shareholders in Crestlawn Memorial Park in Riverside to dissolve a stock sale through which the leader of the group and his family, the court said, attempted illegally to seize control of the $500,000 cemetery association and its growing assets.

Crestlawn, a 360-acre cemetery and mausoleum in Riverside County, is considered "the brain child" of two salesmen who in 1952 sold stock in the cemetery association and raised $200,000 to purchase the land and do the original development work. They also sold a number of conditional sales contracts for burial plots and services.

The young corporation ran into financial difficulties in a short time, and some shares of its five-dollar par value common stock and ninety-five dollar par value 6 per cent cumulative preferred stock were bought up from "distressed investors" by an Oceanside financier. By 1956, he and members of his group had a majority of preferred stock and were able to take over management of the corporation from the majority of common stockholders. According to the district court ruling, the Oceanside financier and his group immediately set about revising the stock issuance provisions, the balance sheet, and the by-laws "with the conspiratorial intention of fraudulently gaining permanent control of the cemetery operation at the expense of the common shareholders." A first step, the records show, was their application to the state commissioner of corporations for a permit to sell another ten thousand shares of common stock, although they concealed from the commissioner, the court ruled, the fact that they unlawfully intended to gain permanent control through the proposal to sell the new common stock only to the preferred shareholders within the group. If the stock transaction had been completed, the court noted, it would have given the financier and his group complete control.

Where the possibility of rich rewards exists, the temptation to indulge in financial manipulation is often great.

In the winter and spring of 1962, George Burleigh, president of the Los Angeles Funeral Society, and members of the society's space committee made a survey of thirty-one cemeteries in the Los Angeles area. They were concerned chiefly with establishing minimum prices for plots, crypts, and niches for urns of ashes. The range of prices in the lowest bracket offered by the cemeteries was extraordinary: space of precisely the same size in least expensive sections of the cemeteries ranged from $100 to $550; the least expensive crypts offered by the cemeteries varied from $388 to $1200; tiny niches sold at minimum prices of $45 to $205. Differences in the upper price ranges were even more remarkable; there, anything is the limit. The tomb of Irving Thalberg in Forest Lawn has been valued at $800,000. Clark Gable's final resting place is on a scale considered appropriate for one the movie magazines styled the "king" of screen stars, and even that of a man of seemingly modest taste like Joe E. Brown is extraordinarily expensive. According to one Forest Lawn salesman, this represents an investment of "at least $100,000."

Location and reputation for elegance figure importantly in the price structure of a cemetery. For example, one Catholic cemetery (all are church operated) in the Los Angeles area sells crypts at a beginning price of $1200. Another cemetery of the same denomination sells them at a starting price of $880. Plots in both start at about $100 above the average for the area: $336. That, it should be remembered, is the average of the lowest prices offered by all Los Angeles cemeteries, including those in areas serving persons in the very lowest income brackets. The starting price in many cemeteries is very much higher than that. A third sells plots starting well below the area average—only $200—and still another undertakes to bury the indigent for only $30. Prices in Protestant and Jewish cemeteries are equally varied, and those in nondenominational cemeteries fluctuate more widely.

Location and reputation, generally governing factors, are not always the determinants. Mr. Burleigh's committee found that one cemetery well within the city limits, one which boasts the bodies of a number of top-ranking movie stars—a big selling point in Los Angeles—was a "best buy" for crypts. They ranged from $388 to $696 if purchased before need so that a 20 per cent discount could be realized. Ground burial prices there, however, ran well above the local average.

One of the more unusual cemeteries in the Los Angeles area is Woodlawn in Santa Monica. A municipally-operated cemetery, it draws clients from a wide area. It is not entirely a public service since persons unable to pay are rejected and sent to the county facility. The price of ground burial there is $285, including the plot, endowment care, opening and closing the grave (a major item), a concrete box to protect the coffin, and a flower container. The price of double interment in the new two-decker arrangement is $406, including the two spaces, endowment care, opening and closing the grave twice, two concrete boxes, and a flower container. Space may be purchased in advance for ten dollars down and ten dollars a month, with *no* interest or carrying charges. That is an important consideration since the 6 or more per cent that many cemeteries charge for installment buying adds healthy sums to the bill. Moreover, unoccupied graves may be returned to the cemetery at any time and the complete purchase price will be refunded. This extraordinary offer is matched nowhere else, to my knowledge. Since land is what most cemeteries traffic in, the last thing they wish to acquire is land, particularly from persons who have been talked into buying plots at a price high enough to cover a salesman's large commission.

According to Ivy L. Griffin, a former army officer who is the Woodlawn manager, the cemetery is more than a self-supporting venture for the city. It is not permitted to advertise; nevertheless, about seven hundred burials take place there each year. Moreover, Woodlawn also puts $3.20 per square foot into an endowment care fund, although the state law requires only $0.65 per square foot. In spite of these things, it turns into the city a net profit of thirty thousand dollars a year. "We couldn't get as much tax from the land, even if homes were built here," Mr. Griffin pointed out. The cemetery could realize a greater profit by increasing prices to the area's average and by instituting some of the other popular "businesslike" practices, but it has been regarded as a public service since the land—part of the old Carrillo Ranch—was taken over by the city for taxes in 1915. (At that time, the cost of six graves was ten dollars.) When Actor Leo Carrillo died several years ago, he was buried there with his ancestors.

Since Hubert Eaton obtained his license to operate a mortuary within the cemetery grounds, a number of others have followed suit. Many have also adopted the practice of outlawing tombstones and aboveground monuments in favor of flush markers, thus becoming "memorial parks" and cutting their maintenance costs by about 40 per cent. Many have introduced gift shops, flower shops, crematoriums, and other adjuncts and have so branched out in their operations that they are currently regarded by morticians as one of the six principal challenges (i.e. enemies), along with protesting clergymen, inquisitive federal investigators, and funeral reform societies.

It is not surprising, therefore, that land already dedicated to cemetery use commands a high price; shrewd investors are scouting the suburbs these days for even small cemeteries for sale. One very handsome newly developed cemetery about a hundred miles from Los Angeles is owned by a certified public accountant with a keen awareness of investment possibilities. Cemetery land within city limits is becoming increasingly difficult to obtain. But it can be done. In January, 1963, Groucho, Harpo, and Gummo Marx petitioned the Los Angeles Regional Planning Commission to rezone 105 acres they owned in Altadena for a cemetery. Although Hubert Eaton's application to start an annex of Forest Lawn in the Hollywood Hills was bitterly fought by some powerful persons in the community, including the former publisher of the *Hollywood Citizen-News*, he managed that coup skillfully. Zoning officials capitulated to his request partly because by the time they were called upon to render a final decision, the Forest Lawn organization had already buried six bodies in the tract.

The memory of the Hollywood Hills and the later Cypress affairs was fresh in the minds of many West Covina residents in 1961 when word leaked out that a huge tract in the suburb that had been bought under an individual's name six months earlier was really owned by Forest Lawn, which had already filed rezoning requests with the Los Angeles Regional Planning Commission. Property owners called a meeting, raised ten thousand dollars within four minutes to fight the cemetery, and set up a round-the-clock vigil over the eleven-hundred-acre tract acquired at a cost of more than one and a half million dollars. During the day, some housewives stationed themselves with binoculars to make sure that no bodies were buried, while others patrolled the area on horseback and in cars. At night, their husbands took over with the aid of huge searchlights.

The extraordinarily lively battle continued through the summer of 1962 in court and out. Both Forest Lawn and the protesting residents attempted to incorporate cities so that their several wishes would be served; zoning hearings had wide attendance; charges and countercharges of political manipulation and disreputable practices were flung back and forth in the local press. By mid-1962, many of the residents were still fighting furiously, but others were declaring wistfully that it looked like a losing game. "We just don't have the resources to cope with Forest Lawn," one leader told me sadly. Trade journals were, predictably, betting on Forest Lawn.

The original cemetery in Glendale on the outskirts of Los Angeles is hailed by the American Cemetery Association as the prototype of memorial parks. And members speak wistfully of the vision and enterprise of "the Builder." Seeming less a place than an advertising dream, Forest Lawn's chief contribution to the burial industry has been to achieve that "death conditioning" described in *Brave New World*—without the chocolate éclairs. Adela Rogers St. Johns' biographical account, which frequently reads like a parody of Aldous Huxley's *After Many a Summer* and Evelyn Waugh's *The Loved One* and continually gives the reader the illusion of having been whirled in a cotton candy machine with Dr. Eaton, advances the notion that it is really a "modern miracle of faith."

In *First Step up toward Heaven,* on sale at the busy cemetery gift shop along with an assortment of items many of which are aptly categorized in the colorful cant of pitchmen as "slum," she gives a detailed account of some of the more speakable episodes in its development under such chapter headings as: "Destiny Takes a Hand," "Tombstones Must Go," and "The Duck Baby Comes to Forest Lawn."

The latter is of singular interest since it describes Eaton's first fumbling excursion into the art world, an excursion that was destined to translate the cemetery into an outdoor design for living worthy of southern California in the years of Our Ford and Mary Pickford. The object he set his heart on, which later became the source of a wrangle between himself and the cemetery directors, was a bronze statue of a child that had attracted some attention among art-illiterates at the Pan-Pacific International Exposition in San Francisco in 1915. According to Mrs. St. Johns, Eaton won the day and that "veritable Shirley Temple among statues" was installed with great fanfare in the cemetery.

The "duck baby" was such a success that more statues were put in, ponds were dug and filled, flowers and trees were planted, and swans and earlier singing birds were installed on the premises. From there, he moved easily into the religious sphere. An important part of the cemetery cult in this country, as in many others, had been its association with the various churches; Eaton brilliantly turned the tables and started his operation in reverse by ordering installed in his secular grounds a replica of Stoke Poges, whose churchyard had inspired one of the most famous poems in the English language. It was a master stroke. Everybody, well, certainly anybody with pretensions to what Forest Lawn considers *culture,* had read Thomas Gray's "Elegy Written in a Country Churchyard." Moreover, it had just the sort of Old World charm and historic tradition that would offer maximum appeal in Los Angeles—particularly when equipped with a stained glass window depicting a tree of life and with gardens installed on both sides of the nave, well stocked with canaries guaranteed to sing when the organ started to play.

The Little Church of the Flowers was a huge success, and it

opened up a new and eminently profitable vista to "the Builder." The names of Cora Gregory Willis and Archie Milton Howes may not be familiar to most persons, but at Forest Lawn they have been immortalized as heralders of another of the frequent "modern miracles" that have occurred in genuinely astonishing numbers and with the genuinely astonishing consequence of enriching the man who seems to have spent a good deal of time praying for them. They were the first couple married in Forest Lawn Cemetery—in a ceremony that started such a rage that within a few decades fifty thousand other couples had followed suit. Indeed, in a few years it was necessary to install another church in order to cope with the waiting crowds—this time, a replica of the Wee Kirk o' the Heather, where Robert Burns' Annie Laurie was buried. Business boomed, with a pipe organ grinding out "Maxwelton's braes are bonnie. . . ."

A few years ago, Dr. Eaton told National Sales Executives, Inc., in a speech of thanks for their Management Award that one of his most important decisions had been to use historical art as "a silent salesman. . . . I brought home only famous things surrounded by traditional happenings and stories to fire people's interest and imagination, and these have great *natural sales power.*"

Replicas of Michelangelo's *Moses* and *Day* and *Night* went up. *David* arrived and was given a fig leaf to make his presence suitable for a place in the Forest Lawn sun. The two most widely-touted art works are the stained glass version of Leonardo da Vinci's *Last Supper,* and Jan Styka's *Crucifixion,* a 196-foot-long painting, which had been found in a Chicago storage house wrapped around a telephone pole after having been rejected by the Chicago Art Institute at the end of a curious journey from Poland to the United States. The painting has been housed in a building "frame" worth one and a half million dollars.

Styka occupies a niche in the Forest Lawn Memorial Court of Honor, an effort to create an American version of Westminster Abbey. Thus far, other "immortals" entombed there include Gutzon Borglum, the sculptor; Robert Millikan, Nobel prize winning physicist, and Carrie Jacobs-Bond, who is said to have written many of "our best beloved songs."

Most recently, the cemetery has turned its attention to patriotism as a sure-fire silent salesman. Two of the newest projects are Freedom Court in the cemetery, where a huge mosaic of the Declaration of Independence has been installed to lure prospective occupants, and Forest Lawn Foundation Writing Awards. Although some of the educational institutions in southern California have declined to participate, University of Redlands, Claremont Men's College, Occidental College, Loyola University of Los Angeles, and Pepperdine College encourage their students to participate in the yearly essay writing contest. With something less than gratitude after a conducted tour of the place and dinner in the mausoleum, a young participant who writes a column called "Wryly" in the Claremont student paper last year protested that the topics they were given to write on were "so hopelessly slanted that we never could have straightened them out."

It is not to be wondered that "the Builder" is the envy and admiration of advertising men and cemetery owners alike. For the latter, Hubert Eaton's main headquarters and the branches he has established are "the standard." Most of them can and do wistfully quote the impressive statistics given in the 386-page *Art Guide to Forest Lawn*: 300 "superbly landscaped acres," 100,000 shrubs, 370 stained glass windows, 7 open courts and many walled and unwalled "gardens of fame," 8 miles of winding road with curbs, 80 miles of underground piping, 800 to 900 employees, many of whom have stayed the three years required for membership in the Forest Lawn "family" (and who were recently given the right—by court order— to organize themselves into a union after several had been dismissed for trying that); and 28 buildings, including the Hall of Crucifixion, the Museum, a mortuary built to withstand an earthquake, three churches, a host of profitable business enterprises, and the Mausoleum noted in the *Britannica*. What other cemetery owner can boast such accomplishments? With the help of the American Cemetery Association, which styles itself a "forum for new ideas as well as the exchange of technical information to keep cemeteries soundly managed and financed," members can hope, however. The Association takes pride that the largest and most prosperous cemeteries in the country are working through it "to publicize their ideas and hold up standards to be used in developing and improving cemeteries in the future."

That quite a few cemeteries have, unfortunately, no constructive ideas and no standards, has been made perfectly clear in a number of publications, including one put out by the Association of Better Business Bureaus, Inc., which concluded with a warning in bold-faced type: "Before You Invest—Investigate!" In that cautionary pamphlet a number of dodges and unscrupulous practices approaching downright thievery were revealed. Some of the advice was not particularly helpful since few citizens have the knowledge or time to investigate carefully the structure of cemetery organizations or to look closely into the backgrounds of the promoters. However, a number of pertinent points were raised, and a number of illustrative case histories were included. Persons thinking of buying lots were advised to shop about; salesmen for one venture in Iowa consistently told prospective buyers that the least expensive six-grave lot in a nearby cemetery cost $535, although that was actually the price for the most expensive. Establishing complete price was also held to be important since grave opening and closing, liners and vaults, markers, and other items may bring initial costs up greatly.

Promises have often been meaningless. For example, in Detroit, salesmen offered complete prepaid funerals, when actually all their company had for sale was a casket plus a "promise" that any funeral director would conduct the funeral for an additional sum of money such as $250. "Before need" plans and package deals have often been extremely costly. The Better Business Bureau pamphlet emphasized that often it is wise to deposit the money for the package merchandise in the bank where it will draw interest and may be withdrawn in case of an emergency. Moreover, it reminded, an investment of three hundred dollars in United States bonds will earn one hundred dollars in ten years. By paying three hundred dollars for merchandise that may not be needed for ten years, it is possible to lose one hundred dollars in interest.

A Forest Lawn salesman who called on us not long ago inadvertently made some interesting revelations about cemetery finances in regard to package deals. Although billboards all over the city advertised "Forest Lawn Undertaking—$145," he said that in order to arrange for undertaking service in the "Before Need" plan $500 is the minimum price that can be paid. In addition, another $450 is recommended—including $25 for the minister, $50 for flowers, $100 for a marker, and $85 for opening and closing the grave—although that is about as "incidental" as a coffin. Assuming that a young couple bought companion crypts for $874—the price and style recommended to us as "reasonable"—and bought the minimum funeral for each, plus only $200 for each in "incidentals," the immediate cost, including an $18 trust fee for each, would be $2310. That sum could be paid for over a period of more than five years at the rate of $27.76 a month—to provide a service that might not be needed for thirty years, or forty, or fifty years. Although the money deposited in the trust would draw 3 per cent interest —a very low rate—the salesman pointed out that it would be wise to allow the interest to accumulate. "You could even add to the amount from time to time," he suggested, "so that you can maintain the quality of the casket and the service."

And Forest Lawn has a splendid reputation in the industry! In making arrangements with that company, after all, there is more than a reasonable guarantee that it will be operating when demand is made for the goods to be delivered. That is frequently not the case: in many instances promoters have bought sizable tracts of land, cleared a portion, put up a few "works of art," buried a few bodies at bargain rates or without cost in order to get things going, and set a sales crew to work. When the land was sufficiently mined, the promoter and his crew simply decamped.

Like the undertakers, the cemetery operators have generally gone to great lengths to identify themselves and their activities with our most cherished values. In a brochure put out by the American Cemetery Association, *Remembering through the Ages*, which bears on its cover a photograph of a host of golden daffodils in the best romantic tradition, Executive Vice-President James Worley identifies Abraham as "the man who fathered the concept of one God . . . [and who] is also the father of our concept of burial and memorialization." Any good cemetery manager or salesman, therefore, Mr. Worley suggests, will treat a buyer as the Hittites treated Abraham. Buyers are to be appealed to to react like Abraham, who knew that his property "had to be acquired in a sound business way" and who was "well aware of the value of selecting proper burial and memorial ground far in advance of need."

Moving from the religious to the patriotic motif, Mr. Worley concluded his exhortation to buy with a story about Communist troops in Manchuria, who did not bury the Japanese civilians they evicted, but dumped their bodies into the river below and fired at them. That offense, he ended his account of the genuinely distasteful incident, "illustrates the deep cleavage that exists between the free and Communist systems. It also implies clearly the vital purposes of cemeteries in our society."

Although some prospective buyers may have difficulty in following Mr. Worley's logic, the sentiments are easily grasped and are, of course, above reproach.

And that sales presentation has much to recommend it in comparison with the brash talks of other salesmen. In Los Angeles some of them have been so insistent and so favored that for several months in 1962 Matt Weinstock's popular local column in the Los Angeles *Times* featured some of the more exotic approaches. One woman reported that her day had been spoiled by a salesman who had told her bluntly that his organization would "get" her eventually, and it would be sensible for her to surrender the money now. Another salesman told a housewife that he was calling in behalf of a colleague who had spoken with her before. His friend had "passed on," he said delicately, and he was carrying on his burden.

Another salesman called a Los Angeles publicist to persuade him to buy a lot. He was undaunted when the publicist said he owned one in a midtown burial ground: "In that case, we'll take yours in trade." But when the publicist asked for the "Blue Book" on the lot, in typical Los Angeles used-car parlance, the salesman hedged: "Well, in that area with the smog and traffic noises and all, it isn't worth much."

The need for a decent burial has been considered a moral obligation since long before Creon caused the doom of his whole family by refusing to permit anyone, upon pain of death, to give burial to the body of Polynices—a decree which flouted the most sacred duty of a family and which was ignored by Polynices' sister, Antigone. However, just why a group of businessmen feel that they are defending America's freedom by selling cemetery lots is rather perplexing. So is Mr. Worley's insistence that "soundly managed and publicly appreciated and supported cemeteries manifest our devotion to liberty and proclaim the strength of our ideas."

Perhaps the real measure of devotion to liberty and strength of ideas might be far better gained by a trip to the quiet acres of Arlington National Cemetery to salute the unpretentious and unpretending who lie there under the simple memorials.

Chapter 8

The Critics and the Necrocrats

THE ASSOCIATED EFFORTS of the "necrocrats" to associate themselves with the sacred and the sublime have been extraordinarily successful in discouraging protest. Even the bravest social critics and commentators have been reluctant to be accused of attacking motherhood, nature, God, art, patriotism, and all the other important values with which lavish funerals have been equated by the trade.

Understandably, many publishers have neglected criticism of the "American way" in funerals, fearful of violating their readers' taboos or distressed by the possibility of losing the accounts of some of their best advertisers. For the undertakers, although perhaps no more sensitive than many other entrepreneurs about having some of the sordid dealings of some members of the trade held up to public view, have reacted in what can only be considered a paranoid manner to published comments.

In 1961, for example, when the *Saturday Evening Post* ran a less than laudatory article entitled "Can You Afford to Die?" the trade journals roared angrily for months, encouraging readers to cancel subscriptions to the offending journal and to write letters to the editor protesting the lack of "fair-mindedness." Dire warnings about the probable fate of the *Post* were printed to soothe readers. *Collier's,* it was pointed out, had once published an article uncomplimentary to some aspects of the funeral industry, and that magazine is no more. Similar disaster had overtaken *Coronet.* To help bring about a new demise, encouragement to fight was offered: "The degree of abasement earned by the *Saturday Evening Post,"* one journal editorialized wildly, "is only matched by the degree of nobility encountered in the attitudes of the funeral service operators."

When several radio and television broadcasters in Los Angeles invited members of the Los Angeles Funeral Society to appear on their programs, they received excited calls and letters of protest from individual morticians and association representatives. Shortly after television commentator Tom Franklin announced his intention to interview representatives of the cooperative group working to obtain funeral reform in December, 1961, he received an "undercover and confidential" report that had been compiled by a private investigator at the request of a segment of the trade. In the report, members of the funeral co-ops were described as "zealous, left-wing, pseudo-intellectuals who are intent on destroying the faith which the general public has for years placed in the funeral directors and morticians of the United States." According to Mr. Franklin, the report contained "some interesting—if not libelous—conclusions." Leading members in the San Francisco group, he added, are linked in the report with Communist-front causes and described as "unscrupulous, vindictive, sabotaging radicals."

When confronted with a possible reaction of such violence, many newspapers and magazines and radio and television leaders have preferred to back away from the subject. A few years ago, a reporter on a Los Angeles newspaper who had compiled some interesting information about bait advertising and other unethical practices was told that the paper "could not afford to involve itself." Not all reacted so violently. The Camelback Funeral Home in Phoenix, Arizona ran in its advertisements in the Arizona *Republic* copies of the *Post* blurb announcing the article with a caption: "Yes, Mr. Editor, you are so right." The establishment also offered free copies of "this important article," and asserted that it had been successful in giving the people in the Phoenix area a "high standard dignified service at a realistic cost."

In March, 1962, United States District Court Judge Harry C. Westover denied modification of a two-year prison sentence he had imposed upon a California mortician for overcharging the government. He appended to his denial a comment about the pressure that had been applied to have him modify his original sentence: "In all the years I have been on the federal bench," Judge Westover told the convicted man's attorney, "I have never received so many letters. Some of them were voluntary, but I'm sure many were solicited."

In spite of the associated pressures, a number of studies—both fictional and factual—have appeared since Mark Twain took a sharp swing at the profiteers. During the 1920's and since, they have become increasingly vitriolic. That has been due partly to the fearlessness of such editors as Henry L. Mencken. Partly it has been the result of the excesses of that decade which culminated in the funerals of gangsters and such Hollywood personalities as Rudolph Valentino. That idol of the screen was laid to rest in a Hollywood mausoleum in a silver casket only after a saturnalia of sentimentality in New York that had mounted troopers struggling for several days and nights to maintain some semblance of order outside the Gold Room of Campbell's Funeral Church, where the body was being exhibited in full evening dress.

One of the most brilliant articles of the late Elmer Davis, who wrote regularly in the twenties for *The New York Times*, has survived only because of Mencken's delight during his years as editor of the *American Mercury* in excoriating cherished American idiocies. In a customary wry plea for reasonable behavior, Davis discussed the wonders and the follies of funeral folkways in a piece called "The Mortician," which set the pattern for all later articles. Taking deftly satirical swipes at the industry's desire for respectability—the replacement of conventional terms like "undertaker" with what industry leaders considered a "less gruesome and repulsive" title like "mortician"—Davis also concerned himself with the extraordinary economics of the industry. At the National Funeral Directors Association convention in 1926, he pointed out, it had been "roundly declared" that the 24,000 undertakers in the country ought to be cut down to 10,000. "The best ten thousand of the lot could do good jobs and make a comfortable living without overcharges." He chided the public as well as members of the trade for the excesses. Often, he pointed out, they were belated apologies for "the tabulated meannesses of the last ten or twenty or forty years." The average rosewood casket, he conjectured correctly, is bought in reparation "for countless snarls across the breakfast table." Davis also exposed to public view the esoteric sense of humor of the traders when they happily met together in convention sessions. He listed the dishes served at the concluding banquet of an Indiana undertakers' meeting: Blood Solvent, Embalmer's Delight, Whipped Plaster of Paris, Carbohydrate Compound, Face Cosmetics with Cold Cream Dressing, Cavity Filler, and similar delicacies. The menu provides cause for real mourning that Sinclair Lewis had not painted a full-length portrait of the George Babbitt Mortuary.

Fortunately, a number of talented writers from Wolfe to Salinger have helped to create an awareness of the vulgarity and crudeness and exploitative practices of "the American way of death." In one of the most memorable chapters in *Look Homeward, Angel,* Thomas Wolfe described the visit of Eugene and Luke to Horse Hines' "parlor" after the death of their brother Ben. At first touched by the "awful mysteries" of death and impressed by the ritualistic air of the undertaker, they acceded to his choice of casket: "It's a good buy. She'll give you value for every dollar you put into it." Horse let the boys have the $450 casket for $375 "out of respect for the family." The climax of the scene occurred when Hines led the boys into another room to show them his creation: "the poor stuffed crow, with its pathetic barbering and its neat buttons" that was once the beloved Ben. Having taken a stick of rouge and touched the cheeks of the corpse, Horse congratulated himself with a slow wonder: "That's art, boys!" Eugene collapsed in a fit of hysterical laughter—a tribute to the lost, dead brother.

An infinitely more bitter view of the profession is taken by J. D. Salinger in *The Catcher in the Rye,* one of the most distinguished pieces of social criticism of the past few decades. The contrast in tone is matched by the contrast between Horse Hines and his little parlor and Mr. Ossenburger, the big-business mortician, and his chain of undertaking establishments. Invited to survey the wing of the dormitory named for him and to hear the student body render a cheer for him at the first football game of the year, Mr. Ossenburger was ultimately saluted by being asked to make a speech to the students during chapel. In the approved hearty manner, the mortician began his speech with some fifty "corny jokes." After having thus established himself as a right type, he urged the students to follow his example and talk to God everywhere they happened to be. He, himself, Mr. Ossenburger declared, talked to Jesus "even when he was driving his car." That, of course, was too much for Holden, who visualized the sanctimonious business-man "shifting into first gear and asking Jesus to send him a few more stiffs."

Even in the clearly fictional works there has been an uncomfortable amount of fact. The Happier Hunting Grounds, the Beverly Pantheon, Whispering Glades Memorial Park, Jo Stoyte, Mr. Joyboy, the "Dreamer" are not idle imaginings of fanciful minds. The reality is, if anything, more taxing to the imagination.

Since man's attitudes about and reactions to birth and death and love are the stuff of which literature is made in every genre, it is not surprising that funerals and burials have been brought into sharp focus. James Agee's *A Death in the Family* is minutely preoccupied with the details of both. One of the more memorable characterizations in that novel is the dismal study of Jay's alcoholic brother, Ralph, who immediately volunteered his services as undertaker when he was told of the death, for which he was partially responsible; he wanted "to try to make up for it."

Perhaps the most frightening brief portrait of a profiteer is William Faulkner's description of Mr. Lovelady in "That Evening Sun." In a single paragraph, Faulkner revealed the misery and meanness of a segment of southern Negro life in his sketch of the "short, dirty man" who made the rounds of the cabins and kitchens on Saturday morning to collect the fifteen-cent installments for "the coffin money." Mr. Lovelady has been replaced by more affluent successors, Negro as well as white, for the compulsion is strong among the members of many minority groups to make sure that death will accord the dignity and significance that have been denied in life.

Faulkner's more detailed study, *As I Lay Dying,* is a richly tragicomic account of the pilgrimage of the Bundren family through fire and flood to bury Addie with "her own people" in Jefferson forty miles away. The book, which begins on the day of the mother's death with her son making for her inspection a beautifully-beveled coffin and ends on the day of her burial with her widower introducing to the remaining children the new Mrs. Bundren, is a moving and memorable picture of human pride and love and folly and stupidity.

Needless to say, such literary light shed upon the dark corners of American funeral practices has been of genuine disservice to the undertaking industry, which prefers to have the blinds of illusion fully drawn. Actually, the funeral literature was extremely important in the revolt which broke out among many literate persons. But then, reading often has hazardous consequences.

Literary criticism has given sharp and memorable utterance to the growing sense of protest among the clergy that their functions had been usurped by tradesmen and that basic religious tenets had been sacrificed to "the American way" of profiteering paganism. More than one clergyman facing an intelligent congregation has felt himself moved to deliver a sermon under such a title as "Keeping Up with the Pharaohs." However, partly because religious reform in this matter also carried implications of social reform and partly because religious teachings have frequently offered imperfect consolation for the overwhelming fact of death, many clergymen kept their misgivings to themselves—like Falstaff timorously or reasonably regarding discretion as "the better part of valour." Those who were hardy enough to speak out were often vigorously challenged.

An excellent indication of the violence with which reform measures have been attacked was given by Rev. Hugh Stevenson Tigner in the *Christian Century* in 1938 in an account of the events touched off in Middletown, New York, in 1937, when the Ministers Association outlined a set of procedures for funerals that were designed to return the functions to the church. The clergymen had sensibly decided to act together, since as one of Mr. Tigner's colleagues pointed out: "It would have been suicide for one of us to have done this alone." The principal reason for the rebellion was not the economic aspect of current funeral practices, but the esthetic and moral aspects. However, Mr. Tigner conceded, the ministers "were irked at seeing a small empire of business interests fattening on death." Although no criticism or objection had been voiced by anyone who attended the churches on the day the reforms were advocated, Mr. Tigner said, when they were published two months later and received wide attention in the eastern press, "the town buzzed as I never knew a town to buzz. . . . The nature of the response was bitterly hostile." According to Mr. Tigner's report, the local undertakers turned the affair over to the regional association and out-of-town clergymen were called in to conduct funerals "whenever the family would allow it." The undertakers, he continued, were not the only persons protesting the program of reform. The general business community in Middletown regarded the action of the ministerial group "as bordering upon subversion." There were loud cries of "Why don't they [the ministers] preach the gospel and leave people's business alone?" Mr. Tigner explained the reasoning as follows: "Any existing and clearly unforbidden business is sacred. A thing may be morally reprehensible, but that is merely an unpractical argument against it. If it is a legitimate business, that gives it absolute authority . . . churches are expected to function in whatever system secular interests provide."

In spite of the hostile reaction in Middletown, a number of other clergymen persisted in speaking up as funerals continued to become more lavish and as the funeral directors increasingly usurped the functions and prerogatives of the clergy, who had come to be regarded as hired hands giving a traditional note to proceedings.

At first, of course, clergymen had been understandably pleased at the growing attention given to funerals. America has been from the first a secular nation; even at the beginning of its history, there were more "strangers" than "saints," and the number of persons without declared church affiliation was always greater than the number with until as recently as 1950. Funerals of elaborate proportions were, clergymen reasoned, a way of focusing attention on death and the meaning of life and, consequently, religion. To their general consternation, the funerals had just the reverse effect, since the measure of the undertaker's art came to be the degree of lifelikeness of the body. Embalming and skillful manipulation of the muscles of the body enhanced that illusion of a relaxed and rested air, and the corpse was frequently provided with telephones, pipes, toys, books, and other activity symbols of more vital days. The reputation of one Los Angeles funeral establishment was set by one of its embalmers who could make almost any child assume the pose traditionally associated with the infant Jesus.

Cosmetology became as important in undertaking "preparation rooms" as in movie studios, with beauticians summoned on occasion to give the corpse a permanent or water wave or otherwise adjust the hair. Barbering had always been done by a male attendant, but mortuary colleges began to emphasize the importance of cosmetology courses for all students. In special cases outside help is invited. One of the principal functionaries as well as a chief mourner at the funeral of Marilyn Monroe in the summer of 1962 was her studio hairdresser. His artistry was commended in several obituary notices, which reported that thanks to the careful hairstyling and post mortem application of cosmetics the film star looked ten years younger as a corpse than she had before she took the overdose of drugs that resulted in her death.

Funeral directors, sympathizing with the fear and revulsion most persons experience at the sight of a corpse and eager to provide a properly lively setting for the bodies that came to them often from tiny apartments, began to expand and elaborate upon their simple parlors. Within a generation, they had become funeral "homes" in actuality, with bedrooms where the corpse was often carefully arranged on a king-size or four-poster bed for viewing by friends and family before it was put into a coffin and brought into a kind of drawing room to receive less intimate visitors. To be equally accommodating to the clergy, one funeral establishment after another began to construct chapels of varying size and degrees of elegance as another adjunct. Today, many of them boast what is held to be this "necessary" feature.

Having ruled out the home as the center of mourning activities was one thing; substituting secular chapels for religious edifices was quite another matter. Clergymen began to worry openly. In 1944, *Newsweek* magazine reprinted a protest which had been published in the bulletin of the Federal Council of Churches in America. On the basis of a United States Department of Commerce survey, Council spokesmen estimated that in 1942 more than half a billion dollars had been spent for funeral and burial services and goods. That was only $18,000,000 less than the sum spent for tuition at private schools, colleges, and universities throughout the country. It was only $159,000,000 less than all the money spent in gifts and bequests to all organized religions during the same year. The *American Funeral Director* retorted that the figures were meaningless; during the year, Americans spent $618,500,000 for tobacco products and $404,800,000 for beauty parlor services. However, as Dr. LeRoy Bowman commented in *The American Funeral* on the controversy, it must be taken into account that the money spent for the luxuries served a population of over 131,000,000 individuals, whereas the nearly half a billion dollars spent for funerals served for three days the immediate families of only the 1,500,000 who had died.

The Middletown group was joined by other groups, encouraged by the response received throughout the country to reports of the growing concern on the part of national organizations. Throughout the Middle West reform activity was particularly strong. In Cleveland and other places, societies were organized to encourage simple funerals. In 1953, the parish social relations committee of the Holy Trinity Episcopal Church in Oxford, Ohio, made a study of "the increasing secular encroachment on the marriage and burial practices in the United States." The recommendations to eliminate many of the services performed by the undertaker at the undertaking establishment were approved by more than 85 per cent of the congregation. According to an article by A. L. Kershaw about the committee's work published a year later in *The Pastor*, many letters had poured in as a result of the publicity received; some were accounts of distressing personal experiences endured by the writers on funeral occasions, some were from funeral directors reporting that steps had been taken toward reform, some were from furiously protesting funeral directors and national association leaders, including "some virtually irrational statements."

Two Congregational clergymen and professors of religion, Dr. Paul E. Irion and Dr. Everett W. MacNair, summed up the position of many clergymen interested in funeral reform in the "Christian Burial" issue of *Social Action* in April, 1959; their articles have frequently been reprinted and widely circulated. Stressing the importance of the spiritual values of the funeral, they emphasized that the purpose of the funeral is not indulgence in hostilities or irrational extravagance. It is to turn man's attention "to the resources divine and human which are available for the strengthening and stabilizing of his life."

Although there has not been universal agreement among all Protestant clergymen interested in reform, most have agreed that costly funerals are irrelevant. All are of the opinion that a clergyman should be consulted when a church member's funeral is being planned and that the service should be conducted by him. Many think that the burial service should take place within two days, making embalming unnecessary. Some feel that cremation should be encouraged as "the most logical answer" to the problem of an exploding population that is making increased demands upon city land.

A reasonably typical pattern for Protestant funeral reform was drawn up by the Social Action Committee of the First Congregational Church, Royal Oak, Michigan, in a widely-distributed flier entitled "Suggestions Concerning Christian Funerals." Following a brief introduction that stresses the idea that a funeral—a Christian funeral—emphasizes the spiritual aspect of death "by turning our thoughts toward God and the continuing life of the spirit," these suggestions are made:

1. When death comes, call your minister. Look to him for counseling not only regarding spiritual matters, but in connection with some of the practical details of the funeral.
2. Think seriously of holding the funeral service in the church. There is no rental or clergy fee for church members.

3. Costly caskets and expensive floral displays are not necessary for the expression of sorrow and affection. Gifts to medical research, libraries, charitable and educational organzations, and the church make significant and lasting memorials.

4. In order to keep the funeral as spirit-centered as possible, consider: (1) having the casket closed before the service begins or (2) having a private burial and cremation followed by a memorial service in a church.

5. If there is a graveside service, consider keeping it as simple and private as possible, perhaps having only intimate friends and members of the family present.

Among the most vigorous, perhaps, of all Protestant groups has been the Unitarian Church. For many years, the Laymen's League has served as a clearing house for church societies and cooperative groups and has actively sponsored the movement to end lavish and opulent practices.

Protest was slower in growing among Catholic and Jewish clergymen since the rites and activities were more clearly fixed in a traditional pattern. However, during the past decade, in many Catholic countries voices have been raised. In 1961, Archbishop Sebastian Baggio, Apostolic Delegate to Canada, in a letter to the Funeral Directors Association, said that because the cost of dying is "getting all out of proportion, it might be well for the Association to make an 'agonizing reappraisal' not only of price structures, but also of pagan customs and trappings that have crept into the industry." Moreover, he continued, ". . . contemporary English distinguishes between that which is inexpensive and that which is cheap, in the sense of being vulgar. . . . There is no loss in dignity because of poverty. Thus, for a poor man to choose an inexpensive funeral (if and when such is available) for a loved one is eminently dignified, for it is in keeping with faith, reason, and common sense.

"When a poor man attempts to make a lavish display—with all the modern trappings of questionable taste—that is obviously beyond his means, it is then that he suffers a loss of dignity and has put on an expensive show that has been cheap and vulgar."

As one might imagine, the funeral directors have responded with nervous alarm to any attempt to impose what they call "church dictation of funerals." In an editorial under that title that appeared in the March, 1962, issue of *Casket and Sunnyside*, a resolution being considered by the United Conservative Synagogues of America to revise the whole conduct of Jewish funerals was called "more than an idle threat." The editorial warned: "This attempt by the church to force dictation of funeral service from the top down is far more than just a threat to one particular branch of funeral service. [Jewish undertakers have their own national association.] Numerous individual Protestant Churches either have endorsed the memorial society movement or at least have advocated very inexpensive funerals. This attitude also has met favor in certain portions of the Catholic Church.

"Thus, it would not be surprising if one or more of the great church bodies in the Christian faith adopted or attempted to adopt such a resolution. Then, the fat would really be in the fire."

By way of reassurance and encouragement to keep fighting, the editorial then pointed out that the Jewish Funeral Directors of America, through its board of governors, had appointed a committee to find out who is responsible for the resolution among the conservative rabbis, "what their gripes really are," and what can be done "to improve clergy relations and thus maintain the status quo of Jewish funerals." Reminding readers of the importance of associating with their clergymen to prevent such an effort from getting under way in their communities, the editorial wound up with the startling conclusion that "you may be told in various instances that a funeral is a religious experience and that funeral services therefore belong in a church. In such cases, remind your clergyman that there can be as much religious manifestation in a funeral chapel as in any other chapel. The word of God is in man's heart rather than in the walls of a church or synagogue."

Leaders of the funeral industry have undeniably become disturbed and distressed by the growing criticism among clergymen of all major denominations, and the more perceptive of them have come to realize the impossibility of branding all opponents as "pseudo-intellectuals" or "subversives" or "left wingers." In order to explore basic differences and to try to bring about some kind of working agreement, they have recently been supplementing money set aside for public relations campaigns with funds for research.

In 1958, for example, the board of governors of the National Funeral Directors Association of the United States, Inc., (N.F.D.A.), made a grant to Dr. Robert L. Fulton, a Los Angeles State College professor of sociology, to "investigate in a systematic way" the nature and extent of charges made in and out of the pulpit by clergymen about the commercial and pagan nature of the American funeral.

Dr. Fulton sent out a detailed questionnaire to 1,990 clergymen, representing every church in the country with a membership of half a million or more. That number was reduced to 1,802, chiefly because of the almost total failure of Negro churches to participate in the study. In the final processing, 627 questionnaires were tabulated and analyzed—202 replies from Catholic clergymen, 389 from Protestant ministers, and 36 from Jewish rabbis.

Dr. Fulton's findings were first made public at the N.F.D.A. convention in St. Louis in October, 1959. After discussing in great detail the social and personal attributes of the clergymen, the economic level of the congregation, the place of the funeral, and the differences in attitude among clerics of various persuasions, he revealed the core of the study in a sentence: "Fifty-one per cent of the Protestant ministers and forty-one per cent of the Catholic priests of the sample believed that the funeral director exploits or takes advantage of a family's grief in selling funeral services." That extraordinarily high number was somewhat modified by qualifications such as "infrequently" or "sometimes," which were appended to the answer by some clergymen. However, even if they were removed from the list, there was left a hard core of 23 per cent of both the Catholic and Protestant clergy who asserted without reservation of any kind the belief that "the funeral director takes advantage of his position for personal gain." In considering those findings, it is also important to note that although many clergymen said they did not know what a fair price for a funeral would be, there was a tendency among Protestant clerics to consider a funeral of seven hundred dollars or less as "reasonable."

Analyzing his study in some detail for members of his own

profession in an article, "The Clergyman and the Funeral Director: A Study in Role Conflict" in *Social Forces,* May, 1961, Dr. Fulton reiterated much that had already become public knowledge: the fear among clergymen that emphasis on bodily remains results in a lack of attention to the spiritual meaning of death; the protest against paganism and ostentatious waste. The article also discussed at great length other factors that Dr. Fulton, who is currently working on another grant from the N.F.D.A., considers significant and which reflect less creditably upon the clergy; the undertaker's "relative" attitude toward all funerals and his growing status at the expense of the clergy.

It seems, Dr. Fulton pointed out, that in making his services available to persons of various faiths and in relating all funerals in an apparent effort to establish the claim of equal sanctity the undertaker "leaves himself open to the charge of paganism." Not only do his words and actions give the impression of questioning the sanctity of one rite—and consequently one church—over another, but "by his presence at the funeral service, he appears to threaten the very efficacy or value of the rite itself." Moreover, he added, clergymen, particularly Protestant clergymen who have lost status relative to other more handsomely rewarded professional men, find it "galling personally" as well as contrary to the tenets of their faith to have the undertaker, who was yesterday a lowly tradesman or sexton, taking complete charge of the funeral and even offering the service in his own chapel.

Curiously enough, 98 per cent of both the Protestant and Catholic clergy polled indicated that they were not in favor of funeral arrangements being handled by representatives of government agencies. Indeed, one clergyman printed in the space provided for an answer to the question: "Hell, no!" Yet in most European countries the churches have worked closely with the state to provide meaningful low-cost funerals. In such countries as France, Catholic clerics have taken a vigorous role in seeking to obtain even simpler and more economical funerals; their counterparts in the United States have not expressed the same concern about the cost aspects.

The morticians have countered clerical criticism with a four-pronged attack of their own: they have employed sociologists and psychologists to determine motivation in depth and to help shape their educational campaigns; they have attempted on the one hand to conciliate and appease the clergy and on the other to attack all opponents as "un-American" and "self-seeking." Meanwhile, they have continued, of course, to consolidate their own position as keepers of the keys to the hereafter by strengthening the link between the things of Caesar and the things of God, chiefly by constructing bigger and more impressive chapels. One new mortuary in a Utah community—a fairly representative mortuary in a fairly representative city—has a chapel with a basic seating capacity of two hundred. But two large rooms on the side of the chapel can be opened up to make the chapel large enough to accommodate 650. During services in the secular chapels, undertakers' assistants patrol the center aisle with the formality and gravity of deacons, and the "altars" where the caskets lie have grown very baroque. Many churches are having an increasingly hard time providing quarters as elegant for a final—or even an earlier—religious rite. More than fifty thousand weddings, for example, have been solemnized in Forest Lawn's churches, and other cemeteries are making efforts to attract to their new chapels the marriage trade as well as the carriage trade.

Some large-scale efforts have been made to soothe the growing friction and to bring about a state of peaceful co-existence. The N.F.D.A. representatives have worked in cooperation with Rev. Paul Irion, Rev. William Clyde Donald III, Dr. Edward N. Jackson, and Dr. Eric Lindemann; "they have long studied the clergy-funeral director problem and have endeavored to create better relationships," a trade journal reported in 1961. A few years before, Earl T. Newcomer of Kansas City, Missouri, who publishes *Profitable Mortuary Methods*, made a speaking tour of Indiana to create good will among the clergy. His presentation, "The Public Needs Both of Us," was published as a booklet, and various segments of the trade sent out copies in large numbers to ministers, bankers, and lawyers in other parts of the country. In Minnesota, the executive secretary of the Minnesota Funeral Directors Association collaborated with Robert C. Slater of the University of Minnesota in preparing a pamphlet about the "clergy relations program" in that state. Inviting other clergymen to enjoy the fine results of cooperation, it has been published by the N.F.D.A. under the title "A Program for Sharing."

When it has not been possible to enter into peaceful cooperation with clergymen, the funeral directors have attacked them head on. An article entitled "Pastors Seek Hand in Arranging Funeral Rites" in the *Lutheran Companion* drew a biting retort from Lloyd H. Vandervoort of the Williams Funeral Home in Canfield, Ohio. In an answer that appeared in the May, 1961, issue of the church publication, Mr. Vandervoort—who is a member of his church council and was an accredited delegate to the Augustana Synodical Conference in Seattle—demanded why it should be necessary to have the clergy determine the point of "lavishness" when a parishioner purchases a funeral. "Would these pastors presume to help outfit a nursery, select a bridal gown, or plan a honeymoon?" he asked with marvelous irrelevance.

National leaders have also pressed the attack, often in terms that indicate they have profited greatly by the findings of sociologists and psychologists who have worked with them to explore the motives and motivations of their opponents. They have emphasized that clergymen resent their "loss of status" and have suggested that they are as much concerned with material things as any funeral director.

In a speech delivered at the California undertaking convention in 1961, W. M. Krieger, managing director of the National Foundation of Funeral Service and director of National Selected Morticians, Inc., managed deftly to imply that clerical protest is both un-American and materialistic. Calling demands for simplicity and less extravagance "the European theological approach" to funeral service, Mr. Krieger said ringingly: "It is being expounded very largely by the younger clergy, those who are just coming out of our seminaries. Why? Because the clergy are using this kind of an approach to help build bigger and better churches."

Apparently discouraged to some extent in their attempt to work out a truly harmonious "program for sharing" with the clergy, the industry has been expressing itself in a somewhat more violent manner recently. In 1962, an editorial in a powerful trade organ accused the clergy of being power hungry and materialistic and of encroaching on human freedom in "a bureaucratic and sinister way." A stirring call to arms was issued: "Shall control of funeral service be left to the dictatorial orders of the uninformed or self-seeking members of the clergy? Or shall the American people have the right to bury their dead with dignity and after their own conscience in keeping with their financial needs?" The continuing struggle is a lively one and well worth watching.

Chapter 9

The Economics of Necrolatry

CRITICISM OF THE BIZARRE economics and the financially destructive aspects of funerals have come from many sources since Mark Twain made a sharp protest in *Life on the Mississippi*. When a child of one of Twain's Negro acquaintances died—a man who had never earned more than four hundred dollars a year—the father was charged twenty-six dollars for a plain wooden coffin. "It would have cost less than four," Twain noted witheringly, "if it had been built to put something useful into."

In the 1920's, the literary men, welfare workers, and clergymen who had been opposed chiefly to the vulgarity and paganism of the morticians' practices began to cast a cold eye particularly on the cruel exploitation of the urban poor. One of the pioneers was Rev. Quincy L. Dowd, whose *Funeral Management and Costs: A World Survey of Burial and Cremation*, published by the University of Chicago Press in 1921, took sharp issue with the economics—or lack of economy—prevalent in United States funeral customs. Foolish and costly excesses in this country were contrasted with more restrained practices in Europe, where public provisions had long existed and where the disposal of the dead has been regarded as a necessary public service for many years. Mr. Dowd's personal observation of the staggering effects of undertaking bills on many low income families had persuaded him of the need to speak out. Social workers in increasing numbers joined the chorus of protest since they, more readily than others, had accumulated concrete evidence with which to condemn the preposterous abstractions advanced by the trade about "signs of respect" and "necessary outlets for grief."

Touched by the misery he had witnessed in the Chicago slums, Graham Taylor mourned the exploitation of settlement clients in 1930 in a book called *Pioneering on Social Frontiers*. In it, he pointed out the "pathos" of funeral customs which confer after death the only distinction that is ever accorded the recipient. And he scored the cruelty of preying upon willing victims: "The living need protection from being sacrificed for the dead by the extravagant indulgence of their grief, as well as by the exactions of custom, the pride of benefit orders, and by the wasteful if not extortionate toll laid upon the bereaved by the unscrupulous funeral trades." Frequently, he said indignantly, "nothing is left to meet the immediate needs of the widow and dependent children."

Puckle had noted the same folly among the British poor in 1926, when he pointed out that in the slums an admirable opportunity was offered—thanks to the fierce pride of the poor, their fanatical insistence on "suitable" obsequies, and the readiness of money lenders to encourage them "at a penny a week interest on the shilling"—for one to see how generously these foolish notions were catered to.

An elderly woman I know, one of the first social workers at the Grand Street Settlement House in New York, still becomes excited at the way of death among her clients of thirty and forty years ago. One of the most memorable "cases" was an Italian family of three generations trying to encompass the necessaries of life within the bounds of a fifty-dollar-a-month welfare allotment and whatever odd jobs the social worker was able to find for the father and several of the older children in the job-scarce depression years.

When the grandmother died, she was invited to the funeral. "It was incredible," my friend told me. The center of interest in the two tenement rooms the family occupied on the lower

East Side was a gleaming coffin lined with satin and white velvet. Candles shed a soft glow on the corpse, neatly arranged
and wearing a new dress and veil for the viewing. The affair
went on for several days, with much wine and food served to
seemingly everyone who had ever known her and many who
had not. "But when I looked at her feet, I really got mad," the
social worker remembered the scene indignantly thirty years
later. "The price tag still clinging to the new black shoes she
had on read '$35.' My God, can you imagine it? Wearing $35
shoes to the grave when the kids were going to school with
paper in the soles of theirs."

During the jazz age the most important of the criticisms
made, because it was the most objective, most comprehensive,
and from a most unexpected source, was John C. Gebhart's
study of funeral costs, published in 1928. That study, financed
by an initial grant of $24,000, later supplemented, by the Me-
tropolitan Life Insurance Company, was a remarkably fair and
inclusive one. It was conducted under an Advisory Committee
on Burial Survey made up of forty-one social workers, econo-
mists, educators, attorneys, psychiatrists, research workers,
clergymen representing the three major religious groups in the
country, and six undertakers.

The groundwork for the report, Gebhart acknowledged,
had been done by a number of groups seeking to stimulate
funeral reform: the Burial Reform Association, which had
made a two-year study from 1894 to 1896 which had concluded with a recommendation for simplicity in burial practices; the New York Charity Organization, which coupled its
appeal for simpler funerals in 1905 with an accusation against
unscrupulous undertakers; the Chicago City Club; and the
Chicago Council of Social Agencies, which provided alarming
figures about high costs. In his study, Gebhart used principally
four sources: estate settlements in the courts, industrial policy
holders of the Metropolitan Life Insurance Company, the
United States Veterans Bureau, and the New York Board of
Child Welfare.

The 15,000 funeral bills he studied indicated how severely
survivors were penalized, particularly in the lower income
groups. A study of estate settlements in New York, Brooklyn,

Chicago, and Pittsburgh revealed that the average price of funerals for estates under $1000 ate up about 62 per cent of the total, averaging between $350 and $372. Estates valued at between $1000 and $5000 showed funeral bills that ranged from $484 (averaging 15 per cent of the gross estate) in Brooklyn to $541 (23.7 per cent of the net estate) in New York County.

The most startling findings were those revealed by a study of the funeral costs of policyholders of industrial insurance. Gebhart found that the average price of the 7,871 adult funerals he considered from that source was $363. The average amount of insurance carried was $308. That left an average balance for the workingman's family to meet—with the principal wage earner gone—of $55. Average funeral prices in eleven of eighteen states were greater than the insurance carried by as much as 64 per cent of the families. Gebhart concluded his study on a gloomy note, pointing out that "as long as the public is ignorant of what funeral service and merchandise should cost and as long as manufacturers, through shortsighted policy, encourage new members to enter the undertaking business to make it possible for inefficient and superfluous ones to continue, there is little hope of lowering funeral prices to the public or correcting the flagrant abuses that now exist."

He was right, of course. The Metropolitan Life Insurance Company, which had sponsored the study, was so concerned about the findings that it ordered its agents never to reveal to undertakers how much insurance the bereaved family had. That the measure was not outstandingly successful is not surprising. Without education, survivors have been easy and willing victims. To indicate to what extent the more things change the more they are the same, a union business agent in California told a group last year that he would never again tell an undertaker the amount of insurance held by a dead worker. "I thought they were asking to find out how much they could reasonably charge," he said. "Instead, I found that they were charging up to the very last cent the family got, and then some."

In 1961, a study of intestate estates in Dane County, Wisconsin, having a value of less than $2000 showed that during the previous eight years funeral expenses had averaged about

53 per cent of the gross estate. In 1962, the Los Angeles Public Administrator's office said that a "standard" undertaking allowance of $500 is made in handling the estates of persons who die intestate leaving $1500 or less.

Labor and management have continued to investigate and to register protest, since it has been no secret that union death benefits and state compensation have been gobbled up by enterprising undertakers who have concerned themselves with doing the "right thing" by the Loved Ones—leaving the Waiting Ones frequently waiting for relief checks so that the family could eat.

A dramatic incentive to action was the Centralia mine disaster in Illinois in 1947. Although the average price for a "standard" adult funeral service was less than $450 in the country that year, the families of the 111 dead miners were charged an average of $732 per funeral. Some of the local undertakers charged the miners' widows up to $1178.50. Charges for identical services and caskets varied by several hundred dollars, it was reported. Reason: some of the miners had larger union welfare death benefits than others.

Four years later, the United Auto Workers made a detailed study of funeral costs of all Ford Motor Company pensioners who had died in 1950. The study showed that the average funeral expenses were more than eight hundred dollars. The average life insurance benefit amounted to thirteen hundred dollars.

In a pamphlet written by Allan Earnshaw Backman, executive vice-president of the National Better Business Bureau, which was published by the Council on Consumer Information in 1956, a table of figures indicates how bravely the funeral industry had forged ahead during the decade between 1944 and 1954 in spite of protests and vigorous efforts to stem excesses. In 1945, 61.7 per cent of all funerals were priced at less than $500, and only 2.9 per cent at more than $1000. Eight years later, only 32.4 per cent cost less than $500, and 12.4 per cent cost more than $1000. Nationally, by 1955 only 26.3 per cent of all funerals were priced at less than $500. By 1960, only 22 per cent were below that figure.

According to the Federated Funeral Directors of America, the average selling price for an adult standard funeral service in the nation in 1944 was $380.34; by 1955, it had risen to $643.16. A survey by another organization in 1960 showed that the average cost had increased to $708. Those figures, of course, do not include expenses for the vault, clothing, cemetery and flowers, the honorarium for the clergyman, and additional transportation charges.

The costs have to be scrutinized with great care since it is difficult to arrive at an "average" price because the "average" cost includes charity cases and because prices fluctuate so wildly from one area to another and from one establishment to another. Moreover, it must be remembered that the figures have been compiled by the industry, and it is exceedingly difficult for an outsider to get specific information.

Why the costs should have so spiraled is a matter for real head-shaking among those trained in more traditional patterns of economic thought. For one thing, the demand has not increased appreciably, thanks to extraordinary gains made in medical and other sciences. In 1940, with a population of 131,000,000, there were 1,417,000 deaths in the nation; in 1960, with a population of almost 178,500,000, there were only 1,702,000 deaths. Yet in that time the amount of money annually expended on funerals rose from about one-half billion to almost two billion dollars. Moreover, that slight increase in demand was offset by the larger number of suppliers; during the past two decades increasing numbers have entered the undertaking business, lured by the promise of prosperity equal to that evident in most establishments. The oversupply of funeral homes has been a serious economic problem for many years. In 1888, the average number of funerals available to each mortician on the basis of the death rate was 95; that had dropped to 84 by 1913, and reached a low point of 48 in 1930. By 1940, the number had risen again to about 62 funerals a year, and in 1949 it dropped slightly to 57; it has remained relatively stable since.

In 1927, a spokesman for the N.F.D.A. told members of the trade and reporters that the 24,000 funeral homes should be cut down to 10,000. That number, he estimated, could make a comfortable living without overcharging. Even more startling was the assertion by W. M. Krieger to Dr. LeRoy

Bowman, in an interview in September, 1950: "There are too many firms in this business .... 2000 firms could do all the business in America." There were then almost 25,000 undertaking parlors.

The number of establishments has increased since then. It is conceivable that undertaking establishments could offer reasonably priced funerals if each received an average share of the business. W. W. Chambers, Jr., owner of a Washington funeral home, told a reporter in 1961 that a four-hundred-dollar funeral would return a "fair profit" to a mortician. In that year, William C. Cowan, president of the Los Angeles County Funeral Directors Association, said that $461 was the "break even" price. And a study made by Funeral Service Facts and Figures of 1960 costs concluded that undertakers realized a profit of only $54.50 from the $708 average funeral. What makes all those figures very bewildering is that Mr. Chambers' establishment conducts about 2500 funerals a year, and among the members of the Los Angeles County trade group is an institution that advertises itself as one of the world's largest. Yet morticians working in Los Angeles and in other areas with memorial societies and funeral cooperatives have been able to provide funerals at minimum prices of one hundred dollars to two hundred dollars and realize a profit. None of them is in the "giant" category, although one might expect that morticians with only a modest volume would have to charge more to realize the same profit since overhead on any establishment is relatively high.

Even a "Mom and Pop" establishment has certain fixed expenses that must be met: the salaries of a varying number of employees, adequate stocks of goods, advertising costs, expensive equipment, and the construction and upkeep of a building handsome enough to reassure clients. Not the least of the fixed expenses are the dues that must be paid to trade associations: three hundred dollars is the yearly assessment of one group; others are even higher.

Of all expenses, many consider the last the "most necessary." That is not to be wondered at, because the trade associations have worked financial marvels to insure that income will be received by the largest possible number of operators, including the 61 per cent who receive fewer than one hundred "cases" a year. Since the trade associations closely reflect the desires and interests of the manufacturers of coffins, vehicles, and other funeral goods, they have worked overtime to insure the largest possible number of outlets for their goods, however detrimental to the ultimate consumers that might be.

The trade organizations have, consequently, viewed as a principal problem competition in the form of lowered prices. Obviously, without the elimination of that competition, marginal operators would have fallen by the wayside. (Incidentally, the marginal operators—the number receiving fewer than fifty funerals a year—constitute about 43 per cent of the members of the profession.)

They have accomplished the solution through the use of price "floors," which association members have been exhorted and threatened to maintain. In the case of smaller operators, violation has resulted in expulsion from the group and in institution of a boycott that makes it impossible for them to buy coffins and other paraphernalia. When that has been ineffectual, civil suits have been instituted seeking injunctions to prevent morticians from advertising low prices. Since licensing powers in the states are almost totally in the hands of leading morticians invited to serve on the state boards, there has been additional incentive to conform to "approved" practices.

Of recent years, however, the price floors have shown signs of weakening. Nicholas Daphne's expulsion from the California Funeral Directors Association, chiefly for working with the Bay Area funeral cooperative to provide funerals for members for a minimum of $150, did not deter him from continuing his activities. Indeed, response to the publicity the affair received was so favorable that his business increased.

The suit brought against Forest Lawn by the Los Angeles County Funeral Directors on December 24, 1961, seeking injunctive relief from the former's billboard and newspaper advertising campaign that featured ninety-dollar prices, was something less than a notable success. Although Forest Lawn and the trade group announced a few months later that they had "resolved their differences harmoniously" out of court, Forest Lawn simply instituted another billboard and newspaper advertising campaign featuring "Undertaking—$145." The association had requested a $350 minimum. Another huge competitor immediately undercut that, proclaiming from scores of billboards and bus placards that "Utter McKinley Understands—from $100."

Recently, several of the trade journals have begun to concede the impossibility of maintaining price floors. However, they will probably not be abandoned for a long time since larger businesses are eager to perpetuate a system that permits them to receive astronomical profits. The $750 "average" a small establishment received in 1961 for each of the twenty or thirty or forty funerals it managed to obtain spelled survival. It spelled genuine affluence to those establishments that received a thousand or more. "We'd be crazy to try to buck the associational policy," one large undertaker said frankly. "We'd be cutting our own throats."

Under the novel system of economics introduced by funeral trade groups—although not unique to them—the aim is not to give the customer more for less in accordance with traditional capitalistic economic theory; it is to make him pay more for substantially the same item by increasing the costs of packaging and distribution with utter disregard to volume. That has certainly been profitable for the manufacturers who have sponsored the system. The average cost of a casket rose from $83.53 in 1944 to $127.18 in 1954. According to Department of Commerce figures, the value of coffins shipped in the United States in 1958 amounted to $155,176,000. About 700 manufacturing concerns are engaged in that, another 100 are producing embalming fluid, and 75 make burial garments. Scores of other companies are enjoying the rewards of "the American way" by turning out vaults, grave tents, casket-sealing material, vehicles, floral racks, musical records, chairs and furniture, cards and mementos, books, air conditioners, embalming equipment, and even massaging vibrators.

Since competition through packaging is the general policy, smaller morticians have been forced to keep up with the larger operators. They, too, must have one of the fanciest places in town, complete with a chapel and reposing rooms, fountains, selection rooms, slumber rooms, reception rooms, embalmers, cosmetologists, and assorted employees and facilities; some establishments even maintain completely furnished apartments for out-of-town mourners or for members of a family who, as one mortician advertises, "wish to remain near their loved one prior to a service." They have continued to indulge in this folly thanks to careful avoidance of such consistent business practices as cost accounting and by emphasizing instead public relations programs and legislative activity. The cost of accomplishing their aims has been considerable for both individual undertakers, many of whom belong to a number of trade associations, and suppliers. Recently, for example, the National Foundation of Funeral Service in Evanston, Illinois launched a new program for "perpetuating the ideal of more intelligent, more efficient, and more ethical professional standards": the Foundation Associate plan. The primary purpose of that was held in announcements to be the dual one of insuring the foundation program and guaranteeing its future with an endowment fund. In order to raise funds, the trustees have authorized the recognition as "Foundation Associates" all funeral service firms pledging $100 annually and all funeral supply firms pledging from $250 to $1000 annually.

As early as 1927, the late Elmer Davis was protesting the reluctance of the trade to adopt cost accounting. A survey of a considerable number of representative morticians by a firm of cost accountants at that time revealed that they handled half their cases at an actual loss. "Naturally they did not know they were handling cases at a loss," Davis added sharply. "They did not understand their own business." Because they have been generally unaware of what they had to earn to break even, they have continued to be highly receptive to the advice given to them in the 1920's by John M. Byrne, commissioner of the Casket Manufacturers Association. He suggested that a way to simplify coping with tiresome business worries would be to adopt "the average funeral director's method"—that is, merely to multiply the cost of the casket by five or six and set that down as the cost of the funeral. Although the industry denies it, the method has continued to be popular. Of course, many have felt that there was no law against increasing the multiplier to ten or fifteen or twenty—

if the traffic would bear that, and even if the traffic would not.

The public relations campaign has been designed chiefly to give the community the feeling that an undertaker ranks with doctors and lawyers and even clergymen in status, and to head off any protest about rising costs with cries of "traitor" and "atheist." It has thus succeeded in completely diverting attention from business practices and in impressing many—if not most—persons with the belief that conspicuous consumption is not only the *American* way, but the *spiritual* way to behave when a death occurs. The eagerness with which people have indulged in extravagant display and the contumely they have shown detractors—even clerics—have indicated how successful public relations can be.

By way of insuring the continuation of the paradoxical situation in the unlikely event that the public relations program might break down, the trade associations have become expert in the art of obtaining legislation favorable to their profit-making. In many states preposterous statutes have been written into law. In some states courts of law are continuing to uphold an eighty-year-old precedent, since held invalid in both England and the United States, that has prevented persons from willing their bodies to medical schools. Wisconsin recently passed a state law to prevent further erroneous decisions by granting every sane person twenty-one years or older the right to give his body to any medical school or to any bank handling parts of the body to be used for scientific, medical, or educational purposes. In some states, laws require that the body be embalmed and placed in a casket even when being cremated. (In California, where no such law has been enacted, many funeral directors insist that that be done—either through ignorance or greed.) In some states the law requires that the ashes be placed in a cemetery or mausoleum after cremation— a practice that benefits nobody but the owners of such establishments. Although a law in California prohibits scattering human ashes, even at sea or over the desert, it is quite possible to scatter those of Rover or any other cremated pet anywhere in the state—including dropping them into the slipstream of traffic on Hollywood Boulevard. One cemetery owner reported that when a sales crew had canvassed a Los Angeles suburb recently it had flushed out a number of persons who, unaware of the law which had been enacted relatively recently, had been keeping the ashes of various relatives in the house. "It was quite a good thing for us," he stated cheerfully.

In another state, although undertakers have less difficulty than almost any other businessmen in collecting bills, the law gives them first priority on money belonging to the deceased. And in many states an important source of state revenue is channeled into the pockets of morticians by local policies requiring an unusually high sum of money to be set aside for "a good funeral" if a person dies intestate. In Los Angeles, those with estates of up to $1500 are allowed $500; those with estates valued at from $1500 to $7500 may have a $750 funeral and burial, consisting of $475 for undertaking, $250 for a cemetery plot, and $25 for the coroner's fee. (The coroner's office imposes an average charge of $25 for embalming, calculating that on the basis of $12 an hour.) Those who have left estates valued at from $7000 to $10,500 are allowed a total of $900 for undertaking and burial; $1000 is allowed for those services for anyone who has left $10,000 or more. These sums are paid to the morticians, selected from an alphabetical list, who are assigned the 800 to 900 cases a year handled by the Public Administrator. The remainder of the money—often a small sum—goes to the state.

That such a high percentage of the gross estate should be siphoned into undertaking establishments instead of the public treasury to provide services for the living is due, in large measure, to the pressures brought to bear by the trade. Public officials have even adopted trade terminology and speak frequently when criticism is made of "the importance of guaranteeing a good burial."

By contrast, indigents who die leaving no relatives and no money are sent to the county crematory to be disposed of at a cost of $19, including $15 for cremation (figured at the cost of $7.50 an hour) and $4 for transportation. In the relatively small number of cases in which death has not occurred in a county hospital, another $13.08 is added to the total for picking up the body and bringing it to the morgue. Catholic and Jewish indigents are provided for under different arrangements. In the case of the former, the county provides a casket built in the carpentry shop of the general hospital at a cost of $17. It also provides transportation to an outlying Catholic cemetery at a cost of $4 in a hearse that has been remodeled from an old ambulance. The county pays $30 for each grave to the Director of Catholic Cemeteries. According to Senior Hospital Registrar Joseph C. Messina, much of that money has been obtained from the federal treasury. "We have been able to put in many claims since 1954 to social security to recover county money spent," he said in March, 1962. Moreover, his office has been able to include the Catholic welfare group in obtaining social security funds since the grave actually costs something more than thirty dollars. The Jewish welfare groups provide service for Jewish indigents at no cost to the county. No problem has yet arisen in Los Angeles with members of other religious denominations that frown upon cremation.

Thanks to the careful foresight of the funeral industry, a very small number of persons receives either county burial or burial by private welfare groups. Of the 7950 deaths in 1961 handled by the Mortuary Office of the Los Angeles Superintendent of Charities, only 1211 bodies were cremated and 567 sent to religious groups for low-cost burial. All others were released to private persons, relatives of the deceased, who were called upon to provide more extensive arrangements although their ability to do so might be minimal.

In 1961, a report of an investigation of activities in the Los Angeles County Coroner's office, which handles between ten thousand and eleven thousand cases a year, revealed how assiduously undertakers have been working outside the law to obtain bodies. According to County Coroner Theodore J. Curphey, the investigation—which later attracted the Federal Bureau of Investigation's interest—began in the summer of 1959, when he noticed that several Los Angeles funeral directors seemed to be picking up from the central morgue "more Coroner's cases than would normally be their share, when considering their total business handled in previous years." Since most of the cases checked revealed that there were no local relatives, it became apparent that some of the employees were turning over confidential information to undertakers. The undertakers then got in touch with distant relatives to solicit business.

That, in itself, was a violation of state law. It was made more reprehensible by the informed undertaker's announcement to the distant relatives that he had the body, when it was actually still in possession of the coroner's office and could not be released without consent of the relative. Needless to say, the mortician readily received authorization to conduct the funeral, and armed with that consent he went to the morgue and obtained the body. Coroner Curphey revealed how profitable that activity could be when he suggested that the employees in his office acting as "tipsters" were perhaps ten-percenters. If a tipster receives a 10 per cent share of the bill, he pointed out, his net on a two-thousand-dollar funeral is two hundred dollars. "It's equivalent to ambulance chasing in the legal profession," Mr. Curphey said. "It's a reprehensible practice, but a practice that has been established for many years and is fairly common throughout major centers in the United States." It is not illegal for undertakers to try to stimulate their sales by working out arrangements with officials and employees of private hospitals and rest homes. In southern California, where such establishments abound because of the very large population of "senior citizens," competition to effect such a working agreement is very keen and the reward for what some crudely term "bird-dogging" is very considerable.

The Federal Bureau of Investigation entered the case in April, 1961, to determine the extent to which undertakers were violating federal laws by making improper requests for payment of death benefits provided by social security and Veterans Administration programs. The government payment of a $250 death benefit for veterans, which may be collected by the undertaker, has stimulated new enthusiasm among even more snobbish undertakers for "soldiers' funerals." That is particularly true when the veterans' death benefits are supplemented by social security payments of from $125 to $225. In the first announcement of the investigation, it was reported that one mortician allegedly collected twice for a funeral: once from the government, a second time from relatives of the deceased. Another was charged with having collected payment of the undertaking bill from relatives and then filing claim with the government for duplicate payment, forging the name of a relative on the application. Other morticians were accused of having submitted bills for certain types of services and materials while furnishing items of lesser quality and of having charged for a certain type of casket although another was substituted.

These practices are by no means unique to California. The findings of the New York State Attorney General in 1954 revealed a number of abuses involving duplicate payment. One enterprising undertaker there issued three bills for a single funeral: one to the family of the deceased for $362.02, a second to the Department of Welfare for $202, and a third to the Social Security Agency for $363.06. That man had the remarkable audacity to submit affidavits to the Department of Welfare indicating that the agreed price of the funeral was $202 and that he had not been paid, although evidence showed that he had received duplicate payment for identical charges from the family and the Department of Welfare. In addition, he then helped to defraud both the city and state (which shared funeral costs) of the lump sum benefit due them from social security.

In January, 1962, the president of a Los Angeles mortuary was sentenced to prison for two years for overcharging the Social Security Agency for burial expenses; the vice-president of the mortuary was placed on probation for five years. The mortuary was fined five thousand dollars. The case against them specifically involved the funeral of a retired cook, who assertedly received a burial costing less than five hundred dollars, although a bill was submitted to Social Security for a seven hundred dollar funeral. One of the oldest firms in the part of the city where it operated, the mortuary had been saluted by a western trade journal in August, 1961—honored with a cover photo and a feature story to celebrate the new building in English-Gothic style, complete with chapel and late-model equipment it had just constructed with an investment of some $300,000.

The relatively severe penalty imposed by a United States District Court judge may be considered a sign of the changing times. Although a number of convictions have been obtained in federal courts during the last two decades for similar offenses, mortuary proprietors have been fined modestly and set free to continue their profitable operations. However, in recent years the Federal government, which has enacted many laws and established many policies designed to favor mortuary and cemetery owners, has taken a more lively interest in the activities of those persons. That is understandable, since billions of dollars are ultimately involved.

The states have exhibited much less concern about practices. The investigation conducted by the New York Attorney General in 1954 was an exception to the look-the-other-way policy that has generally prevailed in state capitals. The Attorney General made a series of recommendations designed to close loopholes in social welfare policies and to put limitations on supplemental payments by families to prevent their being gouged. The recommendations were promptly protested by the funeral industry, whose spokesmen asserted that "the whole situation has been handled in an entirely unfair manner."

The industry's dedicated lobbying, powerful influence, has withered enthusiasm for reform in many other states. In 1961, an Illinois State representative heading a legislative investigating committee reported to me that his group had been having great difficulty generating public interest and making headway against trade opposition. Concerning one meeting in April, 1962, in the southern part of that state, he said, "Only representatives of the trade associations and lobbyists showed up." In a letter to me in February, 1962, he had earlier expressed his concern about pressures that would be exerted to hinder the work of his committee: "I'm afraid that the funeral directors may have an upper hand in deciding what direction our investigation is going to take. I already perceive, even before we've begun, that every obstacle will be put in our way."

In most states, governmental structure and policies have served to defend and further the fortunes of the undertakers and cemetery proprietors. State laws, which have been generally written with the "help" of those groups and which reflect their interest rather than public interest, are also administered almost exclusively by them.

California, for example, has a Cemetery Board and a Funeral Directors and Embalmers Board. Forest Lawn's Hubert Eaton has headed the Cemetery Board for years, and a leading mortician the latter. Both boards had been made up entirely of members of the trade until 1961 when Governor Edmund G. Brown appointed a lay member to each (and to all other boards). That action, stoutly resisted in many other states, has been minimized in trade publications on the grounds that the public member would not be an important force. An editorial in *Mortuary Management,* October, 1961, had this to say about the new make-up of the boards set up to issue licenses and to police the industries and professions:

Presumably this innovation in the composition of a board is designed for the benefit of the public—a presumably unbiased individual who will use his vote and influence to prevent actions that might be contrary to public interest. Whether the aim will really be achieved is a matter of question.
For one thing, being ignorant of funeral practice, he will be working at a disadvantage. Then, too, being one against four or five, he will probably find it easier to join 'em than to lick 'em. So we have probably gained nothing and lost nothing.

Thus does the industry view public interest. What makes that view of great concern is that they operate almost entirely free of other governmental curbs. The California Attorney General's office, which is supposed to supervise the activities of the various boards, is actually in the position of acting as private counsel for them. "We cannot initiate any action on our own," an aide to the California Attorney General told me on July 2, 1962. "They tell us that they are going to take action, and we provide legal assistance."

In the case of the Funeral Directors and Embalmers Board, the services of the Attorney General's office are dispensed with entirely in favor of those of a private lawyer. As a consequence, if a person wishes to lodge a protest about a violation of state law against a mortician, he makes protest to a board made up until recently solely of members of an industry instructed at all costs to present a united façade. "Always remember," W. M. Krieger, managing director of the National Selected Morticians and director of the National Foundation of Funeral Service, told the California undertakers at the state convention in 1961, "if we can keep a solid front in our dealings with the public we can create the finest public relations that anybody ever dreamed about."

That remarkable way for a state to defend the public has resulted in relatively few actions taken against morticians. The license of the mortician who was sent to jail in 1962 was revoked by the California State board, but only after the FBI investigation had resulted in a court conviction. Many other government investigations and court decisions have had little effect on the board. "The one thing we can do is to try to get these people going," the California Attorney General's press assistant said, acknowledging the problem. But without an active legal staff there is little likelihood that the state boards governing the activities of cemeteries and mortuaries will take any decisive steps to bring about funeral reform.

Indeed, a few days before, the chief deputy in the attorney general's office working with the boards expressed surprise that a system that allows an industry or profession to police itself and to sit in judgment upon itself should be questioned at all. When I said that it seemed to me that the public would have no recourse against abusive practices and such things as overcharging, he answered: "There is no point making a big fuss about a three-dollar or five-dollar overcharge." And reminded that the overcharge might more reasonably be expected to amount to three hundred dollars or five hundred dollars or more, he said that the funeral business is "like any other business. The law is not concerned if a Chevrolet dealer sells a fifteen-hundred-dollar car for seven thousand dollars."

For a lawyer to draw such an analogy is rather unusual. Car dealers have not obtained for themselves the legal statutes that funeral dealers have managed to obtain in order to bring in business. No one insists that anyone buy a car, but the law does insist upon certain requirements being met when a death occurs. Nor does the Federal government provide an allowance of almost five hundred dollars when someone decides to buy a car—as it does when a qualified person dies. Actually, to a large extent, funeral and burial activities have been legally acknowledged to be semipublic enterprises as well as private business activities; laws at all levels specify how and where disposal is to be effected; government provision has been made at all levels to provide adequate services and to allocate public funds to carry them out. (It may not be much assurance to some persons, but if death occurs during a nuclear attack the Civil Defense Mortuary Service will take very good care of the corpses.)

At the moment, there seems to be little likelihood in California that any considerable effort will be made to obtain a better way of death for the public if the hope lies in the hands of one public servant, who identified a group working in the northern part of the state to secure funeral reform as "a bunch of Communists." Admitting his inability to support that charge factually, he later amended the description to "left wingers."

The situation in other states is no more encouraging. At the 1955 convention of the National Funeral Directors Association, it was reported that more than one-half of the states had adopted laws governing the sale of "pre-need" funerals as a result of three years of sponsorship of this legislation by the association. In Michigan, where about sixty thousand union members had been working through a Detroit cooperative to obtain low-cost funerals, it is now against the law for an undertaker to enter into a contractual agreement with an organization. A number of states have enacted laws requiring bodies to be placed in caskets to be cremated.

One rather interesting new trend is the emergence of the mortician as an active political figure—in California, at any rate. Although, as Dr. LeRoy Bowman has pointed out in his fine study of *The American Funeral,* "political activities are regarded as fraught with danger for the business," a growing number have been finding it advisable and advantageous to enter the arena. In the June, 1962, California primary elections a number of undertakers were listed on the ballots for offices at various levels. And the mayor's office in Pasadena is becoming a traditional post for trade representatives; in 1961, the seven-man Board of Directors of the city elected funeral director C. Lewis Edwards mayor to replace Ray C. Wood, Forest Lawn Memorial-Park public relations director.

The emergence of the mortician as political activist does have at least one positive aspect; it shows that we have put aside old shibboleths and regard persons in the funeral trade as necessary and acceptable members of society. That is to the good. However, the undertakers' political activities may be as "fraught with danger" for the public as for the business—if previous behind-the-scenes politicking provides any clue to the nature of the on-the-scene variety.

Chapter 10

An American Solution

IF THE STATES HAVE BEEN SLOW to move against abusive practices, a number of federal agencies have stepped up their revolt against what they have considered un-American, lavish funeral and burial practices. One rather morbidly amusing instance involved the Alien Property Custodian, who was understandably staggered in 1945 to receive a bill from a California undertaker for $3,101 for the burial of a Basque sheepherder who had died leaving no relatives in this country, but a fairly sizable estate thanks to years of utterly frugal living.

On the itemized (a great concession!) bill were included: $2,500 for a metal casket, $50 for the use of a slumber room, $25 for an organist, $12 for gloves and boutonnieres for pallbearers, $10 for a flower arranger, and other assorted sums for various goods and services. The government official, disputing the charges, filed suit against the undertaker. When the case reached the California Court of Appeals, the government position was upheld on the grounds that such extravagance was "not justified" by the manner in which the man had lived. The bill was reduced from $3,101 to $750.

In that case there was not evidence of the flagrant dishonesty that has prompted many government actions. Suits have repeatedly been brought to court against morticians charged with attempting to defraud the government in the handling of veterans' funerals, but the conviction of the undertakers frequently has had little effect. In 1938, for example, five officials of a large California firm were fined a total of nine thousand dollars by a United States District Court Judge before whom they pleaded *nolo contendere* to charges that they had been filing claims with the Veterans Administration for payment for caskets used to bury veterans. Actually, the caskets they were using had been furnished by the government without cost. When the mortuary and allied companies owned by the firm were sold to another corporation twenty years later, the multimillion-dollar sale price indicated that little serious damage had been done to its business by the previous revelation.

Some segments of the industry have been expressing alarm recently about the government's growing interest in protecting federal expenditures. Not long ago, Thomas Glidden, the president of the National Funeral Directors Association, supplemented his warning to undertakers to "steer clear" of serving memorial societies with an admonition against becoming part of atomic banks. The activities of the first undertaker to handle victims of radioactivity in this country had been directed by the Atomic Energy Commission and coordinated by the Army Quartermaster after the first fatal accident in the AEC's reactor testing program at Idaho Falls in 1961. The industry's concern about who gets the "theoretically salvageable" bodies after a possible nuclear attack is understandable; although the Civil Defense Mortuary Service that has been established allows for the preservation of the "traditional relationship" between cadaver and undertaker, it does not envision that the victims will exercise free choice of private morticians. In a speech in 1961, W. M. Krieger warned his colleagues against their efforts to obtain an increase in the five hundred dollar combined allowance from the Veterans Administration and social security. "If you raise these allowances too high," he said, "you are going to create a ceiling and you're also going to create the atmosphere for socialization or government operation of funerals."

The government has also been concerned with some of the larger aspects of many phases of the funeral industry, including the effects of burial insurance on the economic well-being of the country. An antitrust action brought by the Federal government in 1954 against the Liberty National Life Insurance Company of Birmingham, Alabama, offers interesting insight into the scope of operations and the widespread lack of enthusiasm among many traders for traditional capitalistic competition.

At one time, according to widely-published reports, Liberty National, through its wholly owned Brown-Service Funeral Homes, Inc. and Service Insurance Company, "had the whole funeral supply industry and funeral service crafts in Alabama sewed up in a competition-proof bag." In that state, which has a population of about three million persons, Liberty National had 1,400,000 burial insurance policies in force. Of the 275 funeral establishments in the state, 135 were Brown-Service Funeral Homes. The significance of those startling figures is further emphasized by the fact that the company issued policies payable *only* in funeral merchandise and service at retail values stipulated in the policies, with no provision for an alternative cash settlement.

In its civil antitrust action, the Federal government charged that the effect of the operations of the parent company had been to deny other burial insurance firms free access to the market, to exclude from a substantial portion of the market funeral directors not under contract to Brown-Service as well as firms within and without the state who supply funeral merchandise. Moreover, the government cases contended, 55 per cent of the firms in Alabama that conducted funerals for Caucasians and 30 per cent of those conducting funerals for Negroes had been prevented from buying from firms of their own choice.

Under a consent judgment filed in June, 1954—at the same time as the complaint—the defendants were enjoined from "(1) owning or operating any funeral business in Alabama except where there is no acceptable funeral director available; (2) acquiring any interest in any burial insurance company or funeral merchandiser in Alabama; or (3) having any joint officers, directors or employees with any funeral director, burial insurance company or funeral merchandiser in Alabama." Other restrictions imposed by the judgment prohibited the company from entering into any new funeral service contract or claiming any rights under any existing funeral service contract with any Alabama funeral director which prevented the director from selling merchandise or performing funeral services for any other person. It also applied to efforts to restrict the number of funeral homes the director may own or operate and to the old practice of preventing the director from buying funeral merchandise from any person.

An interesting postscript to the court decision was written in 1961, when the Alabama company—with over two billion dollars of life insurance in force—acquired the stock of California's Forest Lawn Life. That was organized in 1943 under the expert guidance of Builder Eaton and is reputed to have become an astonishingly valuable property. In his announcement of the sale, Dr. Eaton refrained from disclosing just how valuable. It is not easy to estimate, although one undertaker said frankly that "insurance is where the real money in this business is."

By minimizing some of the more flagrantly monopolistic practices and by exposing and acting against some of the more sordid abuses, the Federal government has helped to stimulate an interest in reform. The same is true of state government agencies that have expressed a concern for public welfare in the conduct of funerals.

For example, one of the most important consequences of the New York State Attorney General's investigation in 1954 was to strengthen the attitude of some labor leaders in the state that something should be done to protect workers from exploitation. An investigation was made by a CIO union in the same year that corroborated the findings of the government official. In some cases, union investigators learned, when death benefits had been made known to undertakers, funeral bills had been increased between 300 and 600 per cent above normal costs. Some of the charges were extraordinary: $30 for a newspaper advertisement that cost only $8, $35 for the "personal service" of exhibiting sympathy to the bereaved, $740 for the "use" of artificial palms and ferns, the visitor's register, opening the grave, and the use of a flower car to the cemetery.

Overcharging and the sale of overly elaborate funerals to families who are not able to understand how they are being exploited are not always, not even usually, illegal. However, in some cases, judges who have a concern for the spirit as well as the letter of the law have ordered price reductions.

Because there is so little protection, union officials have been inspired to act on their own. At first, many simply acted in an individual way, like Michael Frisch of Santa Monica. He refused to give any information about insurance policies and benefits to morticians who called him as business agent of his union; his explanation is that he learned that some were charging families up to the last cent of the workers' accumulated funds.

During recent years, however, action has become more vigorous and more comprehensive as labor leaders have come to realize that their labor union pension and welfare plans have unwittingly served to subsidize the funeral and burial industry. To what extent that has been done was indicated by the New York State Insurance Department recently. It revealed that 75 per cent of the $11,914,349 paid out in 1958 to the beneficiaries of deceased workers went to New York undertakers.

In the Fall, 1961, issue of the AFL-CIO *I.U.D. Digest,* Abe Magrisso, assistant administrative director of the National Maritime Union Pension Fund, and Donald Rubin, administrator of the Joint Retirement Fund of the Pocketbook and Novelty Workers Union, made a plea for concerted action to reduce funeral costs, particularly for the lower-income families. "A first need, therefore," they said, "is that the labor movement and community organizations acknowledge the urgency of the question and arrange for local conferences to discuss it and to take remedial steps." Among the benefits that could be realized from a concerted drive, they pointed out, would be lower rates for funeral and burial services, savings on flowers and gravestones that could be purchased in quantity and at wholesale rates, and experienced staff members to give advice to the survivors and serve as their intermediaries with morticians.

Some of those benefits are already being received in many places. One union in the Middle West working with a cooperative group was able to obtain rates for funerals for members more than 50 per cent below those commonly paid in the city. In New York City, a trade union has taken advantage of the

low price for cemetery land that is bought by the acre; it is
now offering individual grave plots to unionists for as low as
thirty dollars—about one-fifth of the average price in the area.
Meantime, the union officials have urged members to heed the
following suggestions: (1) Have a friend of the family make
arrangements, since distraught relatives are "no match for an
experienced, cool-headed businessman." (2) Have the funeral
take place as soon as possible after death in order to eliminate
the need for embalming and to minimize the period of most
acute distress for the family. (3) Select an inexpensive casket
since the display is obviously not for the sake of the deceased.
(4) Make arrangements in advance.

The educational campaign being conducted now on a national level by union leaders is as necessary as it is desirable.
The families of workingmen have been the principal victims of
the extravagant funerals and burials that have been in vogue
for the past century. In the Summer, 1960, issue of the *I.U.D.
Digest*, Dr. LeRoy Bowman cited a number of cases which
dramatize that need and that exploitation. A widow of a non-
English-speaking worker was charged two thousand dollars for
her husband's funeral; payment left her absolutely penniless.
Another family of foreign background found itself after the
funeral with a $3500 bill for the casket, burial plot, and under-
taking services—a sum that consumed both the man's industrial insurance and the family's savings and required the
survivors to make stiff monthly payments for more than a
year. A mill worker whose mother died after an illness of
some months was charged seven hundred dollars for her funeral by an undertaker who advertised himself as "the poor
man's friend." Such instances make it obvious, as several union
leaders have insisted recently, that "organized labor can ill
afford to sit on its hands—and for reasons quite apart from
the purely ethical."

Labor has not been doing that, of course, to the dismay of
the morticians. By the mid-1950's, labor unions were offering
direct competition through the ownership and operation of
funeral homes, chiefly in the Middle West, and through arrangements worked out with professional morticians in many
of the major industrial centers east of the Mississippi.

Some employers have shown an interest in the problem, but few have taken action. Few have had the imagination and the shrewdness of the newspaper owner Elmer Davis spoke of in "The Mortician." When one of his employees died, it was that man's custom to tell the widow that he could get her an excellent coffin below cost because of his influence with a casket maker. That was, Davis reported, a "pious fraud." The coffins he obtained were made of pine, covered with black broadcloth for proper concealment. The newspaper owner had no trouble persuading the widows of his dead employees that they had caskets that would have sold for several hundred dollars. The widow was satisfied, the coffin manufacturer had a profit, and everything was in order all around. "But," Davis concluded his story wickedly, "if she had known that her husband was actually being laid away in a forty-dollar coffin she would have dropped dead on the spot in grief and shame."

Since ignorance and susceptibility to the propaganda disseminated so tirelessly by the industry have enhanced the irrational attitude normally experienced when someone important to us dies, education is of tremendous importance. It will not be an easy process, since some of our most ethical beliefs and most generous impulses have been grossly corrupted.

Encouraging progress has already been made in some directions. In some states where it has been held illegal for persons to will their bodies to medical schools, action is being taken to eliminate such extraordinary legislation that benefits no one but the trade. A notable example of such action occurred in Wisconsin in 1961, where funeral cooperatives worked with scientific and educational leaders to obtain enactment of a measure permitting citizens to give their bodies to medical schools during life for delivery after death. In that state and others new laws have been needed because of the confusion about a person's right to bequeath his body. This confusion stems from an English common law decision of about eighty years ago which held that a person could not will his body because it was not his property. Although that decision has since been declared invalid by judges and lawyers in this country and in England, many persons have been deterred from willing their bodies to medical schools because of their uncertainty about their rights. Until recently, in Wisconsin and many other states there was no shortage of dissection material for medical students because schools were permitted to obtain unclaimed bodies of indigents; however, social security allotments of up to $225, state welfare department grants of $200, and Veterans Administration benefits of up to $250 for funeral and burial expenses have generally created serious shortages. According to an article in the Milwaukee *Journal* in 1961, Marquette University was then receiving only forty bodies a year; it needed twice that number. Thanks to a public education program in the Los Angeles area, where the local funeral society has taken an active role, increasing numbers of persons there are taking that rational and constructive alternative to lavish disposal practices. In fact, so many persons in the Los Angeles area have availed themselves of the opportunity to do something useful with their remains that recently two of the largest medical schools—at the University of California and the University of Southern California—were forced to call a halt temporarily because they were overstocked. Smaller authorized medical colleges in that area and larger ones elsewhere are still in need.

It is, unfortunately, wishful thinking to accept the notion that animal dissection is sufficient. Many of the most impressive gains in medical science have been made only because investigators were able to use cadavers in their research—gall bladder operations, heart operations, cancer control. Yet many persons continue opposition; some do so on the basis of religious beliefs, others on the basis of superstition, many simply because of attitudes inherited from the nineteenth century when grave-robbing flourished and when some medical schools were not above procuring cadavers from unscrupulous undertakers charged with burying indigent dead.

Persons who wish to make such a gift of themselves should make arrangements in advance to insure that their intentions are respected. Frequently, it is required that both the donor and his next of kin make witnessed affidavits authorizing his body to be sent to a specific medical school or to be used for medical, anatomical, or surgical science and study. Acceptance by a medical school should also be obtained in advance, and the institution must be notified promptly after death occurs so that the body can be picked up immediately. In such cases, it is not necessary to have an undertaker secure the certificate of death or permit in order to move the body.

A cautionary note is in order. Since many medical schools will accept bodies only under limited conditions, other provisions should also be made. The schools will not accept bodies if death has been caused by a communicable disease. In that event, a licensed undertaker must dispose of it. Many schools also reject bodies that have been mutilated in accidents and bodies on which an autopsy has been performed.

The revulsion many persons feel about willing their bodies to medical schools is a carry-over of attitudes that were common when medical education was in a primitive stage and charity wards, prisons, and almshouses were plagued by applicants for cadavers—refuse that could be utilized. Today, conditions are very different. And gains in medical science have now made it possible for the dead to be of service to the living in such dramatic ways as enabling the blind to see. Operations transferring corneal tissue from the eyes of a dead person to those of a sightless living being were first attempted in 1944; such operations have been successful 90 per cent of the time. Since the cause of death has no effect on the quality of the tissue needed to restore the sight of someone blinded by corneal defect, neither age nor type of illness is a barrier to participation in that program. Blood banks, ear banks, bone banks, and other services offer stirring possibilities. Unfortunately, in twenty-one states there is not yet legal authorization permitting persons to bequeath their bodies to education and science.

For those who prefer immediate disposal, cremation is also an answer. That has been growing in popularity in the western states, although it is still strongly resisted in other parts of the country. Only about 5 per cent of all persons who died in 1955 chose that alternative. During the next decade, acceptance will undoubtedly become much greater, since the leaders of many Protestant denominations have been publicly announcing their enthusiasm for it with great vigor. Rev. Everett W. MacNair, dean of the chapel and professor of religion at Talladega College, Alabama, and formerly a Congregational minister in Wisconsin, wrote an enthusiastic appeal for it in *Social Action* in April, 1959. He pointed out that the 100 per cent increase in the number of crematoriums that had occurred during the thirty years of his ministry offered concrete evidence that "the feeling is growing that this is a beautiful, dignified, self-respecting way to dispose of our 'earthly vessels.' " A number of other churchmen and church-sponsored societies—like the Cleveland Memorial Society—have actively supported cremation on economic as well as on spiritual grounds. Catholic, Jewish, and other denominational leaders have continued to oppose it, chiefly on the grounds that they consider it a desecration of the body that will interfere with the final resurrection.

One rabbi said to me frankly that he thinks his religious group will have to re-evaluate its position on cremation "in light of modern conditions." It certainly can be little comfort to the families of the six million Jewish victims of the Nazi extermination camps to believe that their relatives will suffer in the hereafter for the crimes commited against them in this life.

Other objections have had more worldly bases. For example, many persons have opposed cremation on the grounds that it would increase criminal activity by concealing evidence of foul play. There is much to be said for that point of view. Although the carefully trained persons employed in coroners' offices in major cities in the United States make it reasonably unlikely that murder will go undetected, in smaller towns and rural communities the persons entrusted to establish the cause of death are often so ignorant of criminology, pharmacology, and even the rudiments of medicine that thousands of murders are believed to be committed in the United States yearly—with no one but the murderer the wiser. As long as the body can be exhumed, evidence of the crime may be obtained.

In other countries, however, cremation has become accepted practice. In contrast with the 5 per cent record in the United States in 1955 (the figure has changed remarkably little since),

28.36 per cent of the deaths in England in 1957 were followed by cremation. The percentage has also been growing in Norway, Sweden, Denmark, and West Germany.

If the undertakers continue to have their way, its acceptance will continue to be slowed in most of the United States. Cremation represents a major threat, particularly immediate cremation, which eliminates public display of the body, elaborate burial costumes, embalming, and dozens of other opportunities to turn a profit. In some states, the undertakers have succeeded in obtaining legislation to offset those gains. For example, in Wisconsin a 48-hour waiting period after death has been made mandatory. An extended waiting period usually means that the body must be embalmed. In some other states, laws require that bodies be cremated in caskets. That eliminates another important financial saving. In states where such laws do not exist, many morticians mislead their clients about such matters.

Another alternative would be for the government to assume control of funerals and the funeral industry. In many European countries, the government either operates the industry or works with private morticians through contractual arrangements to provide decent rites for all people. In some cases, the government pays for everything; in others, it provides the basic funeral and permits those who so wish to indulge themselves in extras. However, the government also scrutinizes those costs. The cemeteries are usually run by the government in the interest of public health and welfare.

In the United States, government intervention has taken three forms: the return of dead troops from temporary mortuary centers in other countries or from government-sponsored cemeteries; the establishment of national cemeteries and municipal, county, and state cemeteries; and the operation of crematoriums, usually by county, city, or state, although the crematory in Washington, D. C., is under the jurisdiction of the Federal government.

Efforts to increase such services and facilities have been bitterly fought—with the exception of the return of dead servicemen for private burial. For example, a bill introduced into the New York State Legislature for a number of years proposed the erection and equipping of a municipal funeral plant at a cost of $920,000 on a self-liquidating basis. The carefully calculated plan showed that a funeral that normally cost three hundred dollars could be provided by a municipal authority for sixty or seventy dollars. Lobbies representing the funeral interests defeated the plan on the specious grounds that the service would be of low grade and that people would not want it. The experience of Los Angeles County indicates that cremation can actually be accomplished for a much lower fee when stripped of extras. As late as 1962, the cost for the use of the county facility was fifteen dollars, plus a small transportation charge for picking up the body. The city-operated cemetery in nearby Santa Monica offers proof that such a service can be of great benefit to both the residents and the revenues, even when it is not utilized exclusively as a public service.

Burial insurance programs and trusts have provided some relief by guaranteeing that there will be money at the time of death to meet the expenses incurred. Unfortunately, they are not economically feasible for many persons. And they are so profitable to operators that many large undertaking establishments and cemeteries have set up insurance and trust plans as principal sources of profit.

Life insurance rather than death insurance seems a more sensible buy, particularly since many of the funeral and burial insurance policies can be redeemed at face value *only* by buying the goods and services the company offers. Trusts set up to cover funeral and burial costs usually pay very low interest rates—about 3 per cent—and it would therefore be much more practical for persons to invest the money in some reliable security—banks, credit unions, or United States Savings Bonds—against ultimate need. Many would find that if they saved on a regular basis, the interest alone would be more than enough to cover the cost of funeral and burial; the principal could be devoted to purposes more constructive than enriching persons engaged in all aspects of the funeral industry.

Another alternative had a beginning more than a century ago when the Basque cigar workers in Florida organized themselves into a buying club as a defense against the "coffin trust." Instead of each member buying a casket for himself and others in his immediate family when death occurred—at which time the price would be anything an undertaker felt he could collect—the club obtained them in quantity at wholesale rates, and each member shared in the saving.

The idea of obtaining lower prices through group buying of funeral goods was later adopted by a number of consumer groups in the northwest central area of the country, where the farmers had a long history of cooperative activity. Of the thirty-six cooperative funeral associations reported active in 1939 by the United States Department of Labor, nineteen were in Minnesota, nine in Iowa, one in Nebraska, five in South Dakota, and two in Wisconsin. By that time, only five of the associations limited themselves to buying caskets. Thirty-one handled complete funerals.

The extension took place after a number of unfortunate incidents had occurred. In some cases, manufacturers refused to sell the groups caskets on the grounds that they would be boycotted. As a consequence, the cooperatives set up their own small manufacturing operations. But other suppliers followed the lead of the coffin makers, and within relatively few years the cooperatives found that they had to do a complete job if members were to be protected. They set up funeral homes, hired morticians to staff them, and obtained supplies of all types. During the 1930's and 1940's they were able to provide funerals to the members for between $142 and $200, in contrast to the $300 to $400 minimum that prevailed in the area when the private establishments had the field to themselves. Some were able to operate in a businesslike way at even lower cost, and many of them set up burial funds to take care of hardship cases in a neighborly fashion. Since they were Rochdale cooperatives, whatever margin existed between costs and charges was returned to the members in the form of patronage refunds.

The co-ops naturally created a furor among the morticians in the country. What one group could do, they reasoned correctly, others could too. As a consequence, the morticians harried the co-ops in a variety of ways, attempting to make it difficult for them to get supplies and using the political structure they had helped fashion to work against them. The cooperative groups were involved in many legal battles with private undertakers. Some of the suits, as James Myers, Jr., pointed out in a pamphlet on cooperative funeral associations in 1946, proved extremely beneficial. One funeral co-op greatly increased its membership as a result of newspaper reports of a court case. And other cases and unjust decisions by state officials, he said, "served as excellent publicity and educational material for the co-ops."

Unfortunately, the continual harassment had another side. In 1939, the Department of Labor reported thirty-six active cooperative associations in the country; by 1950, the agency reported, that number had dropped to twenty-eight. Some, of course, have flourished: one cooperative funeral establishment recently added a $30,000 chapel. Another, not long ago, was able to return $20,000 to members in patronage refunds.

The principal gains in bringing about funeral reform, however, have been made through another type of funeral cooperative. Originally in the minority—in 1950 there were only eight —these co-ops have grown with such extraordinary swiftness during the last decade that by 1962 ninety of them were working actively in the United States and Canada to provide thousands of persons with simple, dignified funerals at modest cost. Although they vary widely in size and scope, all of them are concerned with two basic purposes: to educate persons to value simplicity, and to provide them with the opportunity to obtain the kind of funeral and burial they wish at the economic level they consider appropriate. Intelligent consumption rather than conspicuous consumption is the goal.

Some of the cooperative groups originated in churches, where concern had been expressed about pagan practices as well as about the economic hardship wrought by funerals. One of the first of the church memorial societies was founded in 1937 by the Community Church in New York. Others have since sprung up in Unitarian, Congregationalist, Episcopalian, Methodist, Presbyterian, and other denominational groups in Niagara Falls, Toronto, Ithaca, Rochester, Cleveland, Columbus, Dayton, Ottawa, and other cities. Most of them, like the Cleveland Memorial Society, which was established in 1948, have worked out plans in their communities enabling members of the society and their families to obtain simple services at modest cost from funeral directors in the area.

The Cleveland plan, based on that of the Minnesota Cooperative Plan, has also been widely followed. One member of the family joins the society and pays a family membership fee of ten dollars. There are no annual dues. The members and each person in the family fill out cards indicating which funeral director they prefer, whether a memorial service is desired, and the type of funeral service they wish. The Type I service provides that a funeral establishment will transport the body without embalming to a crematory for cremation. Total cost is not to exceed two hundred dollars. The Type II service includes transportation to a funeral home, embalming the body if necessary, placing it in a modest coffin selected by a funeral director, and private burial before the memorial service. The cost of that is not to exceed three hundred dollars. The cards are then filed with the funeral director, ready for use when needed. No negotiation is required about price, and payment is made when the services are rendered.

The educational program to achieve dignity and simplicity has been highly successful. And members of the Cleveland group have, it has been pointed out proudly, made constructive application of their philosophy. A number have bequeathed their bodies to the Medical School of Western Reserve University for medical research and have given permission to the Central Eye Bank of Cleveland to use their eyes for sight restoration.

The church societies satisfied the needs of their members and attracted favorable attention among outsiders. However, since by their nature they were exclusive to great extent, many persons have preferred the nondenominational, nonsectarian cooperative memorial societies. In many instances, church groups have joined with the lay consumer groups; as a result, the movement has gained strength and cohesiveness.

In 1955, the cooperatives were dismissed by the trade as ineffectual opposition. Today, they are being viewed as a major threat. At present there are nearly a hundred groups working to obtain funeral reform in this country and Canada, most of which are reporting rapid gains in membership. In the spring of 1962, sixty-five delegates from twenty-two of the associations and a number of religious, labor, and consumer leaders met with Jerry Voorhis, executive director of the Cooperative League of the U.S.A., and Stanley Dreyer, assistant director, to plan the formation of the Continental Association of Funeral and Memorial Societies.

Some of the groups represented were small: those in Ithaca and Philadelphia had fewer than two hundred families in each, and the Maryland Memorial Society had only thirty at the time of the meeting. Others are very sizable: Seattle has about twelve thousand members and the Bay Area group about half that many family-members. The rate of growth reported by most, however, was astonishing. Guy S. Lerch, delegate from the Cleveland Memorial Society, reported that an average of thirty new member families a month had brought the total of that group up to 2,900; S. Karp of the Greater Detroit Memorial Society said that his group had been organized in February, 1961, and within a year had attracted five hundred families; Carl Wennerstrom reported that the Chicago Memorial Association had tripled its membership in a year; and John Crane of the Channel Cities Memorial Society in California reported that membership in that group had risen from three hundred in January, 1962, to six hundred by the beginning of April.

The progress has been made against formidable opposition. For example, Mr. Karp pointed out that in Michigan the state mortuary board consists of five morticians and it is "impossible to get anything started"; John Crane said that resistance among morticians in the community of Santa Barbara, where the society was first organized, had been so great that his group had to go ninety miles south in order to find a funeral director to handle the business. Some of the opposition has been on an extremely low level: Florence Parker of the San Diego Memorial Society revealed that "we have been the victim of a poison pen letter sent out to cemetery associations and morticians attacking our leadership in a vicious manner."

Victor Duhnke, delegate from the Planned Funeral Society of Wisconsin, reported on the determined efforts in that state to prevent growth. The Milwaukee society, organized in 1957 with twenty-four members, was joined recently by a chapter in Wausau, sponsored by Employers Mutual Insurance Company. When it was announced that the latter group would hold a membership meeting in the insurance company offices, a number of companies told Employers Mutual executives that they would withdraw their policies if the meeting took place. However, executives held firm and the group met. Unfortunately, pressure applied elsewhere had made it impossible for the Wausau chapter to secure an agreement with any funeral director in the community as late as April, 1962.

The associations, which have had a large number of professional persons as members, have so enthusiastically indicated their intention to pursue the goal of obtaining freedom of choice that they have given many the impression of being made up of missionaries. They have received the blessings of many clergymen, and consumer cooperative groups have announced their intention of joining forces. Walter Childers, of Co-op Enterprises, Inc., was vehement about his organization's wish "to add this kind of service to the other services we now have for our eight thousand members." Those services include five supermarkets, and also three optical offices that do 25 per cent of the business in Akron. "The rubber workers that make up most of our membership," Mr. Childers said, "can't afford these high prices for funerals. We want to get the best funeral for the most reasonable price available in Akron. And," he concluded, "we will."

Labor's increasing interest in the matter was emphasized by John Pierce, AFL-CIO delegate from New York. "Labor's sixteen million union members need protection," he said. "That's why I'm here." He stressed again the extraordinarily high proportion of health and welfare insurance benefits that are diverted from the family to the undertaker—about 75 per cent in New York. "The money was collected to help the union member, not the undertaker. We're worried. I think management is concerned. We want our people protected."

It seems apparent, in view of the lack of interest expressed in many legislative groups, that consumers must look to themselves and to each other for protection. The cooperative memorial and funeral groups are the most logical means of achieving that. Believing in freedom of choice and the right to protection against exploitation, they function to eliminate abuses and irrational behavior through an assortment of plans. Although all acknowledge the right of individual members to make the type of final plans each prefers, all place principal emphasis on making group arrangements in advance. One type of memorial association contracts with individual morticians to provide a range of services at stated prices that may be selected in advance—some for less than $100, others in the $150 to $300 range. Other groups focus attention on education and simply recommend mortuaries where members have had satisfactory dealings—although no contracts are signed and the members must work out individual agreements. A third type offers members the opportunity to prepay the costs of final arrangements, principally cremation. The member puts a specified sum into a credit union in a joint account with the association, and at the time of death the association pays the bill.

Obviously, there is a need to obtain a more unified approach among the groups if maximum benefits are to be realized. A number of the societies have worked out reciprocal agreements enabling a member in one community to avail himself of the society's services in another if such a need should arise. However, that would be of only modest value if, for example, a member of a California group which had worked out very desirable minimal prices died in a community where the society had not been able to obtain a contract specifying prices of funerals.

The establishment of the Continental Association of Funeral and Memorial Societies should be of great importance in making it possible for consumers in the various countries and in all parts of them to obtain maximum protection. Publication of a news bulletin began in June, 1962, edited by Ernest Morgan of 130 Glen Street, Yellow Springs, Ohio. An eight-man steering committee, including Mr. Morgan, Jerry Voorhis, Rev. Carl Wennerstrom, Talbot Pierson, Dr. LeRoy Bowman, Milton Klein, Ozzie Kesler, and Edwin Wilson of the American Humanist Association, is studying the possibilities of services that could be rendered, scrutinizing state laws pertaining to funerals, and making plans for a continental conference in the spring of 1963.

Meantime, the Cooperative League of the U.S.A. is continuing to serve as clearing house for information and to distribute educational materials to interested persons. To indicate how three representative groups got under way and to sketch briefly the kind of obstacles and difficulties that have been encountered, the next chapter will offer a brief history of the People's Memorial Association in Seattle, which grew out of a church organization; the Los Angeles Funeral Society, which evolved from the Southern California Cooperative League; and the Tri-County Memorial Funeral Society in California, which developed from one man's determination to "do something about an outrageous situation."

Chapter 11

Organizing the Revolt

ONE OF THE OLDEST AND LARGEST funeral societies in the country is the People's Memorial Association (P.M.A.) in Seattle. Originally a church project, it was founded in 1939 by members of the Congregationalist Church of the People who decided that expensive and elaborate funerals were "inconsistent with spiritual truth and good taste."

Indignant about the stress on the physical and the high costs demanded by conventional funerals which they did not wish, they joined forces with members of a nearby Unitarian Church and set about obtaining what they considered proper. More radical than most programs, the plan they worked out was for cremation without embalming, followed by a memorial service after an interval that would enable the survivors to regain a measure of composure. A committee, headed by Rev. Fred Shorter started the rounds of Seattle mortuaries to work out an agreement. After a number of rebuffs, the committee found one mortician willing to go along with the novel plan, and the P.M.A. was a going concern.

Growth was relatively slow for more than a decade, averaging fewer than thirty new members a year, although the association moved away from its church orientation and invited all persons of similar views to join regardless of creed and other

197

customary excluding factors. Increasing acceptance of cremation and the association's vigorous educational program helped
to increase membership to eleven hundred by 1955. Within
another seven years, more than ten thousand others joined.
By 1963, there were 13,000 members.

The basic plan is simplicity itself. Adult applicants pay a
small enrollment fee (at present, five dollars), with no charge
for children and no annual membership dues. Officers serve
without pay, and are elected at the annual membership meeting where each member is entitled to one vote. When a member dies, his family calls the funeral home where the membership cards are on file; the mortician picks up the body, at-
tends to the death certificate, and after cremation disposes of
the ashes in accordance with the wishes of the members or
their relatives.

Because to a large degree the success of the organization is
dependent upon the board of directors, the P.M.A. has been
extremely fortunate in attracting intelligent and dedicated men
to serve as volunteers. Among them have been doctors, lawyers, clergymen, accountants, union leaders, businessmen,
housewives, journalists, laborers—representatives of the whole
spectrum of community activity. It is, Membership Secretary
Leslie Tostevin said in 1962, "a businessman's board—in full
recognition of our growth from a branch of a church oganiza-
tion to that of a going business."

During recent years the boards have worked out a number
of improvements. Simplified office procedures have been designed to facilitate the work of the volunteers who staff it.
Through affiliation with the Group Health Credit Union, a
prepaid "cremation reserve fund" plan has been developed.
Members may pay the present cremation fee of one hundred
dollars in advance and thus insure themselves against any possible increase. Unlike the prepayment plans most morticians
and cemetery owners have worked out, the Seattle plan benefits
the living. Each dollar paid into the reserve fund is matched
by another dollar in life insurance that will be given to the
survivors. (Lesser amounts in insurance coverage are available
to older persons; after a person reaches the age of fifty-five
each dollar in the fund is matched by seventy-five cents in in-

surance; after the age of sixty-five, a dollar is matched by twenty-five cents.) Instead of eating up insurance, the Seattle plan makes the term "death benefits" meaningful. Prepayment, of course, is a matter of choice.

Leslie Tostevin, a retired expert machine-shop mechanic, and his wife have devoted all their spare time to the organization since they received membership cards No. 299 and No. 300 in 1950. During recent years, they have devoted almost all their time to this work. Both have been utterly dedicated to the cause and in no small measure are responsible for much of the group's recent success.

However, Mr. Tostevin has other ideas about reasons for the phenomenal growth of the association. Among them are three factors that distinguish the Seattle group from most of the other funeral societies now functioning. First of all, the P.M.A. focuses its reform program on cremation. Friends and relatives of members who are not interested in that, but who approve of simplifying the conventional funeral, will be assisted in making arrangements. "We leave the door open for those who wish the conventional funeral at lower cost; none of our members is obliged to have immediate cremation," Mr. Tostevin emphasizes. However, the educational program is largely concerned with emphasizing the value of immediate cremation. "We advocate cremation rather than burial because it brings about the inevitable dissolution of the body quickly, cleanly and inexpensively," the P.M.A. asserts decidedly. Moreover, they feel that more traditional practices serve to emphasize the physical and material "rather than the immortal qualities of the deceased."

A second principal difference is that the P.M.A. has an exclusive contract with one mortician, James C. Bleitz of the Bleitz Funeral Home. Some societies have no contract; they merely recommend an undertaker or more than one whose past performance has been satisfactory. Still others have contractual arrangements with several morticians providing for a considerable variety of final services. And, of course, others have their own establishment—not all on the scale of the Range Funeral Home of Virginia, Minnesota, built by a funeral co-op recently at a cost of two hundred thousand dollars. The Seattle group has had its relationship with the single mortician since 1939. "He went along with us when the going was rough"; thus Mr. Tostevin explains the refusal of the group to entertain offers from morticians who have lately decided to open their doors. "He was ignored in any social gathering where he met other morticians, who maliciously maligned him time and again. Today, he is reaping a well-earned leadership among morticians; he is handling more cases than any other in Seattle —or in the state." Mr. Bleitz is equally pleased. Pointing out that the P.M.A. proposal originally meant working out a new type of service, he said that the arrangement had been worth much to him for several reasons. A principal one was that it brought in additional business. Although the profit margin is narrow (the cost of the service: one hundred dollars in 1962), "nevertheless, this is a plus business and does return us a profit." Also, "and more important," Mr. Bleitz feels, "is the word of mouth advertising we are getting from P.M.A. members." He added that he found to his surprise that he had thousands of "missionaries" out working for him, many of whom are highly educated professional persons. The favorable image his company has developed as a result of his services for P.M.A. has attracted many other clients, including a sizable number who wish to have conventional funerals. The relationship, he wrote, "has been of extraordinary value to us."

A third factor influencing growth, according to Mr. Tostevin, has been the "strong, progressive program" of the association, particularly during the last years of its highly businesslike direction. Although some members protested advertising as improper, the P.M.A. has embarked upon an advertising campaign in the local press. The opponents of advertising were applying the medical code relative to advertising, ignoring the fact that both morticians and cemeteries did consistent daily advertising, Mr. Tostevin said. Support for advertising grew after a study showed that in 1959, when the association advertised with some degree of regularity for five months in a leading newspaper, the gain in members amounted to 2,042—a 65 per cent increase over gains the previous year. More than one hundred communities in Washington are now involved.

Mr. Tostevin, whose group now has reciprocal arrangements

with societies in a number of other areas, is pressing the idea of a national movement with great zeal. A man of glowing good humor and vital drive, he is utterly convinced that funeral reform in the United States can be effected. "Ideas," he insists enthusiastically, "ideas, ideas, and rejecting the it-can't-be-done. I know we can. And we will."

Rather unusual encouragement was given to P.M.A. several years ago by a Californian who had gone to Seattle to attend the funeral of his brother. Affronted by the extravagant display he had witnessed, he called a P.M.A. leader to get further information about the organization someone had mentioned casually. He was so impressed by the motivations and methods of the association that he gave, in his brother's name, one thousand dollars "for promoting education in the Memorial Way, which is not to be thought of merely as a cheap way."

That distinction has also been emphasized by the Los Angeles Funeral Society, whose leaders and members have very strong feelings about simple funerals and burials being a matter of principle, good taste, and common sense as well as economical. Cooperative-oriented from the first, the society was organized in 1957 with fifteen members drawn from the Los Angeles County consumer co-op markets. By mid-1962, it had a membership of nine hundred, growing at the rate of two families a day, including Saturdays, Sundays, and holidays, according to Mrs. Helen Farmer, the executive secretary.

For a while, growth was very slow. Indeed, 1958 was such a low point in organizational history that officers concede frankly that "in that year, we were on the brink of giving up." Oddly enough, in that community, where Forest Lawn is a major attraction and where it is impossible to escape for a mile the importunings of the area's nearly four hundred morticians, the funeral society met with a cool reception from the public. Expectedly, it met with an even cooler one among the funeral directors with whom a committee attempted to work out a contract. "We have been instructed to have nothing to do with you people," some said. A few were even blunter. Several, however, were quite willing to do business with the organization, but would not make any kind of written arrangement.

Sustained only by the knowledge of the success of similar cooperative societies in Palo Alto and Berkeley, the committee continued to ring mortuary doorbells. After almost a year, one mortician said yes, "it won't hurt to try." He agreed to provide members with basic funerals—$95 for immediate delivery to a cemetery in a minimum casket, $130 for immediate cremation and disposal. Other funerals were offered at special prices, depending on the wishes of survivors or the deceased.

Once the agreement had been worked out, membership became less limited. Several ministers called to say that their church members had expressed a wish for simple services and to ask for information; a few congregations that had been planning to organize their own societies decided to join forces. Since 1958, there has been a 100 per cent increase in membership each year.

Teachers, artists, musicians, lawyers, accountants, and others called excitedly when they heard about the group, and many joined, some of them volunteering their services as directors. "We have always been fortunate in our board members," President George Burleigh said in 1962. At that time serving on the board with Mr. Burleigh, who is a retired bookseller, was Frank Neill, a retired teacher and social worker; an insurance broker; a certified public accountant; a minister; and a retired government official. Most were motivated to join by past experiences, which they relate with a great deal of feeling. For example, one recent board member and her husband reported that they still own a crypt at Forest Lawn, which they bought in 1943 after a member of the family died. A few years ago when they went over to make arrangements for themselves, they received a rude shock. "We said that all we wanted was cremation—immediate cremation—and for our ashes to be put into the crypt." They were told that they had to have the complete service; six hundred dollars was given as the minimum price for each "whether you use all the services or not." Outraged, they returned home, called Mrs. Farmer to obtain membership applications, and have been among the most dedicated members since.

Satisfied consumers have also worked to encourage others to join. One of the first was a Los Angeles librarian whose husband died a few months after they had joined. The minimum funeral—"the kind he wanted"—had cost her $130. More important to her had been the simplicity of the arrangements. "I went to the funeral of a friend's husband a few weeks before, and I wondered how she managed to survive that ordeal."

One of the more touching stories involved two elderly persons in a rest home in Los Angeles, who had paid in advance four hundred dollars each for immediate cremation at a large mortuary. At the Unitarian Church they heard of the funeral society. In serious need of glasses and other essentials, they appealed to the minister to help them recover the money they had paid so that they could join the society. He did—an unusual tribute to the integrity of the mortuary, although the blow of parting with the money was softened by the fact that it had had the use of it, interest free, for a number of years. The couple paid for their minimum-cost funerals in advance, and with more than five hundred dollars left were able to buy the things they needed.

Although the group is relatively small—nine hundred families in a county with a population of seven million—many of the area's morticians have construed its existence as a threat to their own. Not all have, of course. Satisfactory contracts have been worked out with two other mortuaries. But most have gone, and continue to go, to great lengths to discredit it, hiring private investigators to "infiltrate" the public meetings and to scrutinize the backgrounds of directors and members, and issuing what one television commentator frankly described as "libelous" statements about the society.

The influence of the group has already reached out beyond the county, however. Mrs. Farmer, Mr. Burleigh, Mr. Neill, and other leaders helped the groups working to organize the Tri-County Memorial Funeral Society, the Channel Cities Funeral Society, the Valley Memorial Society in Fresno, and the Kern County Memorial Society. There are now ten such societies in California, including the very large groups in Berkeley and in Palo Alto. Many of them, as consumer cooperatives, are deeply concerned with pocketbook economics. But they have gone far beyond that; it is not simply that the cost of dying has increased by 46 per cent in recent years in contrast to the cost of living's 26 per cent increase. It is, Mr. Burleigh says, "a matter of human dignity and decency that is involved." Without the freedom to make a choice between that which is vulgar and that which appeals to good taste, that which offends our beliefs and that which expresses them, we are being cheated of one of our most basic rights, members say.

If the growth trend continues, there is a possibility that the rebellion against what most consider funeral barbarism may make life easier for visitors to Los Angeles as well as the residents. "How can you stand this place?" a touring New Yorker asked. "Everywhere you ride, there are undertaking billboards. Whenever you turn on the radio you are invited to be buried. Even when you sit on a bench at the bus stop you're urged to die and do it in style. How can you people enjoy life?"

Ray Rayburn, a brisk, blue-eyed "senior citizen," is determined that the living shall enjoy life. And if he has anything to say, they may well. He has accomplished single-handed one of the most extraordinary feats of organization; within a year, the funeral society he started at the elegant trailer court where the Rayburns live in Anaheim, California, has reached out to cover three counties.

An extraordinarily lively person, Mr. Rayburn came to California in the late 1940's to enjoy his retirement after forty years as a YMCA executive, a period of occupation interrupted only by a four-year stint during World War II to build and furnish fourteen hundred clubs for the U.S.O. He was realizing his goal of having plenty of time to relax and indulge in his hobby of hooking rugs until June, 1961, when he voluntarily set to work again on a schedule of fourteen hours a day.

That was precipitated when a neighbor died of a heart attack, and his widow asked Mr. Rayburn to help her make arrangements for his funeral and burial. He had had some experiences —some so unfortunate that he had been prompted to make his own arrangements with a mortuary in the area. "Unfortunately," he told me, "this time two things were against me: the undertaker had the body, and the widow was with me so that I couldn't be as blunt as I should have been."

Although the woman told the undertaker that her husband

had wished to be cremated, he led them to a display of expensive metal and hardwood caskets, ranging from $675 to $1000 in price. She was understandably bewildered. When Mr. Rayburn said that the caskets were unreasonably expensive since cremation was involved, the undertaker conceded that he had something cheaper. "He led us out to a cluttered garage, where anything she saw would make a bad impression." When the woman made the expected response, the undertaker then led them to a rear corridor and showed them an acceptable casket that he was selling for $550. He then continued to plan the arrangements, including embalming and other services. Reluctant to seem officious and unfamiliar with California statutes, Mr. Rayburn could simply offer mild protest that it seemed unusual to go to such lengths for cremation. "The law requires it," the undertaker insisted.

When Mr. Rayburn returned to his home, he put in a call to the county health department. He learned that the law did not require a casket, nor did it require embalming unless the body was to be shipped by common carrier.

It was too late to alter the arrangements, and the woman was in no mood to pursue the distressing subject. But after the funeral, Mr. Rayburn returned to a mortuary where he had made his arrangements several years earlier to check up on them. The original owner had died; when the owner's son checked on the contract that had been made five years before, he said affably, "Unfortunately, the $360 funeral has gone up. The same thing now will cost you $550." Mr. Rayburn was incensed. He went to five other mortuaries, some of whom had advertised very low prices; response was invariably: "Yes, we do provide charity funerals, but a person in your circumstances wouldn't want one of those cheap deals."

Discouraged by his experience and determined that whatever money he left should not go to benefit a mortician, he went to a nearby medical school and arranged to will it his body, an arrangement, incidentally, that he has not changed. To insure against the eventuality that his survivors might be subjected to the ordeal of negotiating, he also went to a nearby mortuary and worked out an agreement for his cremation. (Such double insurance is necessary since medical schools may not accept bodies under particular conditions.) A few weeks later he picked up a magazine, read an article about the cooperative funeral reform program, and decided on the spot "to do my share."

He obtained permission from the "mayor" of the trailer park to hold a meeting on a Sunday afternoon in August in the clubhouse, and invited Mrs. Farmer to speak about the work of the Los Angeles society. Seventy persons attended the session, and enthusiasm was so high that they decided to incorporate. Within short order, it had a board of directors made up of concerned persons in the neighborhood: Thomas Murray, a retired buyer for Marshall Field in Chicago, agreed to serve as president; Ted Turner, a certified public accountant, was named treasurer; Mrs. C. S. Hollingsworth, an Anaheim teacher, agreed to be secretary. Other members of the board included Frank Hall, a retired newspaper editor; John Kelly, a real estate and mortgage business operator; Allen Sonin, the owner of a wholesale grocery business, and Mr. Rayburn.

Within six months, 168 families had taken out membership, and a man in San Bernardino County who had been trying to organize a group and another who had made similar efforts in Riverside County allied themselves into what has since become the Tri-County Memorial Funeral Society.

After the organization meeting, Mr. Rayburn interviewed twenty morticians in the area before he found one who agreed to work with the new society. This man was new to the business and had conducted only eighty-seven funerals in the three years in which he had been operating. Despite that low volume, incidentally, he told Mr. Rayburn that overhead amounted to $325 a funeral. He agreed to cooperate after being assured that he could have an exclusive right to business: "It will have to be an unwritten agreement, though," he added. "Do you know what would happen to me if I went along with your group? I couldn't buy any more caskets."

Interested in this evidence of restraint of trade and conspiracy, Mr. Rayburn got into his car and went into Los Angeles to call on casket manufacturers. They said that they would sell caskets to anyone, he reported. "But none of the other undertakers I called on would accept our business." After some weeks they found one, the operator of a handsome mortuary in West Los Angeles which had earlier agreed to cooperate with the "Channel Cities" group, originating in Santa Barbara but extending into Kern County. Imposing only a twenty-five-cents-per-mile charge for transportation for handling bodies outside a fifty-mile radius, the mortuary worked out a plan to provide four basic services for the group, ranging from immediate cremation or immediate interment for $150 to complete funeral services, with what Mr. Rayburn described as "beautiful" caskets, for $395.

In his interviews with more than a score of morticians, Mr. Rayburn put several critical questions to them: Does the body have to be embalmed? Does it have to be in a casket to be cremated? Can the family procure the ashes? The correct answer to each question is no. But only at the mortuary in West Los Angeles, did officials tell him the truth. (The family may obtain the ashes if they produce a Certificate of Removal obtained from the local Health Department.) An executive there was very frank about his willingness to go along with the cooperative societies: "I realize that these groups are the coming thing. I also realize that not everyone will join. The profit I make may be small, but those profits will help to carry my overhead." He was also sensible enough to realize that not everyone in the cooperative societies wishes to have a minimum burial. Many enjoy the traditional display—flowers, open casket, services in the chapel, embalming, viewing, and assorted services. But all wish to feel that they have been protected from exploitation.

In the course of his investigation Mr. Rayburn received a number of valuable insights into the mortuary business. One mortician, a man who said he could not work with the society because of his fear of reprisals but who was—in Mr. Rayburn's rather quaint terminology—a "real Christian gentleman," quoted him the factory prices of caskets which have a great influence on funeral prices. At that time, a minimum-cost redwood casket was priced at $37.50; a cloth-covered "flat top" was $38.50, although in twenty different mortuaries checked it was said to cost from $250 to $300. Another popular casket that was being sold all over the county for from $412 to $500 cost only $48.50. A fair price for a funeral, the mortician told Mr. Rayburn, was between four and five times the amount of the casket cost, the base cost. By charging that amount he had been able to put several children through college, to make a good living, and to save something for his retirement.

One member of the society, a woman whose husband was dying when she joined, revealed how far many morticians departed from that "fair price." Her husband had been a minister, working with boys on New York's lower East Side, and had expressed a wish for a simple burial. The cheapest price quoted to her for picking up his body, putting it in a $37.50 casket, and carrying it to the cemetery had been $539. Through the society she had been able to obtain the same service for $145 plus the sales tax of 4 per cent on the coffin.

Another member, an attorney, reported that he had been involved in carrying an estate for probate in the nearby community of Santa Ana. When the judge had seen the $4500 funeral bill, he declared that he would not allow it. The attorney reminded him that he might as well, because "the mortician was shrewd enough to get the signatures of all the beneficiaries."

Since shortly after the society was organized, scarcely a day has passed—until the Rayburns took off for Europe in April on a much needed vacation—that someone has not stopped at their home on West Katella Boulevard with an application for membership and some "horrid example" to relate.

One friend in the park told Mr. Rayburn that when a close friend died and his wife asked for help, "I stood there and watched the undertaker exploiting the woman's grief until I couldn't stand it, and I asked, 'What are you trying to do? Ruin this woman financially?' " Another woman in the park, whose husband had been killed in the crosswalk at the entrance, showed bills to prove that the modest funeral had cost her more than two thousand dollars. A woman two doors away went to her sister's funeral in Modesto in the central part of the state; she reported that although her sister and the husband had both been working people, the funeral had cost nearly $2100. Those things are bad enough, Mr. Rayburn acknowledged, "but how about the young widow with two children who was taken by a mortician for $3300?"

Mr. Rayburn's next project is to continue his survey of cemeteries. Although not one mortician he interviewed recommended anything but a memorial park, he found that a number of cemeteries in the area operated by various government agencies offer thousands of low-cost vacant grave spaces. One cemetery that he discovered near his dwelling charged $40 for the grave, $35 for opening and closing it, and $18 for a concrete vault for the casket. In all the memorial parks recommended by the undertaker the costs—the minimum costs—were at least five times that amount.

Mr. Rayburn's voluntary labors have already affected the lives of a great many persons and have demonstrated that one informed and concerned individual can wield great influence. At an age at which many regard themselves as superannuated, he has embarked anew on the exciting task of making the world a safer place for people to live in.

Undeniably, his work has brought him a great deal of pleasure. It is nonsense to imagine that persons in the funeral reform movement are lugubrious types, morbidly preoccupied with well-wrought urns. The many I have met are characterized by a zest for living and an acute awareness of life. They have, for the most part, learned that all-essential lesson of facing death cheerfully and with good sense.

Moreover, they have made it possible for others to do that. One of the rather curious results of the reform movement is that it opened the floodgates and enabled others to talk about something that is of tremendous importance to them but which they have suppressed because of the widespread notion that "nice people don't talk about things like that." Dr. Herman Feifel, of the University of Southern California School of Medicine and the Veterans Administration Outpatient Clinic, reported in *The American Behavioral Scientist* in March, 1962, an interesting experiment he conducted in discussing death with eight seriously ill patients. Over the protests and objections of many hospital authorities, he continued to interview others. Not only were there no untoward incidents, he reported, "but an unanticipated felicitous by-product was the seeming psychotherapeutic effect in some of the patients" as a result of being able to discuss their attitudes toward that, for them heretofore, rigidly taboo subject. Mrs. Farmer reported that after she and several members of the Los Angeles Funeral Society had been interviewed over the air on the Joe Dolan Show in May, 1962, more than one hundred persons called and wrote to her. "Most of them," she said, "seemed terribly relieved to be able to express their feelings to someone."

In his fine series of studies of the adjustive behavior of bereaved families, Dr. Thomas D. Eliot of Northwestern University stressed the importance of breaking down the barriers that have been built up by our social attitudes about death. Although it is a universal experience, when death comes to the individual or family, he pointed out, "it seems a new experience if not a unique shock." As a consequence, most of us are powerless to deal with it in even a relatively objective way; we are hopelessly unprepared to face the facts. Our emancipation from the sex taboo has made it possible to react realistically in that area; "Sex," he pointed out, "is no longer exclusively associated with its morbid aspects." Dr. Eliot and others have, consequently, appealed for removal of the taboo and an education that will enable us to accept death with a minimum of "abnormal *dis*tresses."

The cooperative movement is a way of achieving that education. By encouraging persons to respond rationally to the economic aspects of death, it is also encouraging them to respond in an emotionally appropriate way to that overwhelming experience.

Chapter 12

Requiem for Everyman

THE QUESTION TO WHICH WE ARE inevitably led is whether or not anything can be done to make American funerals more meaningful and less costly. Can we bring ourselves to acknowledge our own mortality and thus free ourselves from the Egyptian bondage of the effort to keep up with the Pharaohs?

To come to terms with the fact of death is the only solid foundation on which to construct a satisfactory life. How straight and clear would be the impersonal history of man, and the personal histories of billions of men, if each day had been lived with an awareness that it might be the last. All civilized religions and philosophies have, of course, attempted to bring about such awareness; but resistance has been strong, and the belief in a perpetual tomorrow when the dark web may be unraveled and all debts paid has continued to provide a convenient escape from present reality. So the quarrels and the strivings and the wars continue. Few things symbolize that mode of thinking and being more clearly than the barbaric and ostentatious funeral practices in which we indulge: an extension of our unavowed belief that the expense of spirit in a waste of shame is less taxing than facing up to essentials.

There is no small amount of truth in the dogged assertions of the industry that people are getting the kind of funerals they want. Falsely, however, industry spokesmen fail to mention that people are getting the kind of funerals they have also been persuaded to want. However attractive as a compensatory gesture many persons find elaborate funerals for relatives to be, few emotionally stable and mature people wish—or would even tolerate—an extravagant finale for themselves. Viewed in relation to our religious and philosophical tradition, such a wish is as symptomatic of psychological and spiritual sickness as the condemned man's pitiful desire to stuff himself with pie *à la mode* before he is led off for execution. One of the more revealing clues to the disordered mentality of the Florida skipper who murdered his sixth wife and four members of a Wisconsin family in 1962 was the suicide note he left. Omitting all mention of the crime, the retired Air Force lieutenant-colonel instead spent his last moments writing down elaborate instructions for his final disposal—twelve miles off the coast of Miami, with his corpse shrouded in red velvet and "fitting" honors accorded. Although the industry rejects the notion, it cannot be denied that the warped tastes of gangsters, megalomaniacs, and other psychopaths have helped to incorporate lavish funerals into the American dream of success.

Less dramatic, but of increasing importance as taste makers in matters funereal, are the millions of elderly persons in America, many of whom are frankly suffering emotional and psychological dislocation. These senior citizens are being enthusiastically exploited by morticians and cemetery operators because of their responsiveness to the idea that post-mortem luxury will enable them to realize the dream that life has denied; they have greatly influenced rising funeral costs. In Southern California, where elderly persons are heavily concentrated, funeral costs have soared during the last quarter of a century. Between 1936 and 1960, the average price of a funeral in Los Angeles rose from about $325 to $1,100. By mid-summer of 1962, the average was estimated to be almost $1,400. In the next decade, funeral costs may be expected to rise at an even faster rate, with the aged population continuing to grow rapidly: during the ten years from 1950 to 1960, persons in the sixty-five and older age group increased by 34.7 per cent, while the general population increased by only 18.5

per cent. Unable to cope properly with the present, dissatis-
fied with the past—with "nothing to look backward to with
pride, and nothing to look forward to with hope"—many of
the millions of aged persons are finding ultimate solace in the
promises of mortuary and cemetery salesmen that the rich, full
life-in-death will be theirs for only twenty-five or fifty dollars
a month, cash on the here-and-now barrelhead. For those who
can afford three or ten or even a hundred thousand dollars at
a single check writing, it will be even richer and fuller; the
American dream of wealth and fame will be theirs in all its
glory.

As a consequence of this naïve view, death insurance policies and "before need" arrangements of a costly nature on and
off the installment plan have become exceedingly popular
among the elderly and exceedingly profitable for the merchan-
disers. A colleague, who supported himself through two advanced degrees by working for a Los Angeles undertaking
establishment, reported recently that there is a "mad scramble"
among morticians for exclusive rights to business in the scores
of rest homes, sanitariums, and nursing homes in southern California in which hundred of thousands of elderly persons are
waiting out death. Competition is, he said, "really cut-throat."
In addition to making substantial gifts to the proprietors or
directors of the establishments, along with any employees who
might be of service—gifts, incidentally, that may be written off
as necessary business deductions—funeral industry representatives ingratiate themselves in other ways. Cutbacks, although
considered unethical, are fairly standard, my colleague reported, with five or ten per cent of the total cost of a funeral being
held a reasonable sum to pay for referrals. Even if the inmate
had no insurance or pre-need plan at the time of death, undertakers may benefit by a friendly arrangement with the rest
home owners and employees. Relatives and friends can be
encouraged—counted upon—to do the handsome thing, partly
as a compensatory gesture and partly because it enables them
to assume the momentarily important role of master of ceremonies. Not long ago, when an elderly neighbor died after
several months in a rest home, she made a final appearance
wildly at odds with the modest manner in which she had lived.

With the aid of an undertaker recommended to them, two close friends had done the occasion up in a style to which forty years as an insurance company employee had not permitted the deceased to become accustomed. Elaborately made up, with her hair in a new coiffure, wearing a chiffon "burial gown" and holding a sheaf of orchids, the dead woman lay on public display for several days. More than a thousand dollars had been spent to impress the fifteen or twenty persons who signed the "Visitors' Book" in the mortuary before her body was taken off to a grave with a good address. "Wasn't it lovely?" one of her friends demanded later. "I know it was just what she would have wanted."

Undoubtedly her friend was right—not, perhaps, the way the dead woman had wanted the trip she had felt she could not afford, but the way she had been educated to want a funeral that would seem proper and right to the neighbors. For whatever their demerits and deficiencies may be in other areas, the undertakers—individually and collectively—have demonstrated themselves remarkably effective teachers. Aligning themselves indiscriminately with the men of science and the men of faith, propping themselves against the flag and the pillars of commercial establishments while keeping careful check on the latest developments of advertisers and promoters, they have so thoroughly instructed both the nine and the ten o'clock scholars that many of their pupils regard any protest as heresy.

Grimly humorous evidence of the extent of indoctrination was given in September, 1962 by Ann Landers, whose columns of advice to readers are syndicated in scores of newspapers throughout the country. A few weeks earlier, a reader had asked about the propriety of taking pictures in a funeral home; Miss Landers had answered that movie cameras and flash bulbs were, in her opinion, out of place in such circumstances. "Dozens of readers," Miss Landers wrote, "called me hard-hearted and cruel." A Missouri woman had chided her, saying: "We run the movies of grandfather's funeral every time relatives come from out of the city. They are so grateful, especially the ones who couldn't make it." A reader in Kentucky, Miss Landers reported, had written: "I wouldn't take a million dollars for the pictures I made of my husband laid out in his blue suit.

He looked better in that box than he had anytime in the last ten years."

Nihil nisi bonum with a vengeance!

As glad to learn as to teach, the undertakers have whole-heartedly (the abstract intelligence could not possibly be involved) absorbed the information given to them by trade association leaders. With due respect to the more professional pedagogues in the mortuary science colleges, it has been the industry associations' publicists and accountants who have written the philosophy and established the methods of operating and the modes of thinking that prevail among the members; it is they who have formulated the guidelines, given the individual entrepreneurs their sense of mission and the techniques with which to implement it. For information on how this has been effected, few works are more revealing than Wilber M. Krieger's basic text for the trade, *Successful Funeral Service Management*. After an introduction to the "profession"—an introduction that stresses the importance of tact, honesty, hard work, perseverance, self-discipline, a carefully developed personality, and the "ability to sell yourself," Mr. Krieger's manual moves rapidly to such essentials as financing a funeral home and attracting and holding business. Expectedly, he emphasizes the importance of advertising through a continuous program, particularly in newspapers—although telephone directories, billboards, radio, and television can be employed profitably. The latter is somewhat expensive, it is conceded, but effective; as illustration of its effectiveness, a detailed account is given of an enterprising undertaker who sponsored Dickens' *Christmas Carol* on TV during the holiday season. "He got a much greater response than hoped for," Mr. Krieger tells readers, when he contracted to subsidize the cost of retailing the simple prayer of Tiny Tim. Calendars are also recommended, particularly when a tie-in can be made with churches for their distribution; and the scattering of neckties, thermometers, pens, pencils, church directories, and assorted largesse can all be considered bread upon the waters by those eager to have bodies brought in.

Undertakers are urged vigorously to associate themselves with churches, clubs, and other community institutions and groups—from the Red Cross to Parent-Teacher Associations—

as a means of drumming up trade. So conscious are many funeral home proprietors of the value of those ties that they will not employ persons who do not participate in church programs or do not belong to service organizations. Since doctors and ministers are principal sources of business referrals, members of the trade often scrutinize membership lists carefully before joining an organization to make sure that it offers the "right" contacts. Mr. Krieger stresses the importance of community and religious activity more than some industry leaders do; even Boy Scout work should not be overlooked: "It may be a long time before you can think of this work in terms of bringing business, but you will meet many people in connection with your work in the Scouts." And memberships in the Masons, Knights of Columbus, Odd Fellows, Rotary, Chamber of Commerce, and other groups are all guaranted to produce the kind of friends who call when funeral service is needed.

Personal acquaintance and church affiliation rank high among the reasons for patronizing a particular undertaker, which grossly minimizes the claim of leaders that the funeral business is a profession. In the recent study conducted by the National Selected Morticians among 400,000 families who had had experiences with undertakers, those two reasons were cited with frequency. Although professional reputation, ability, and technical skill were revealed as minor factors in the determination of which undertaker to call, the N.S.M. has repeatedly insisted that undertaking is a profession. So has the National Funeral Directors Association—although a study made for the N.F.D.A. in 1948 showed that of the twenty "professional" duties listed, only six were known to 50 per cent of the persons questioned. Technical competence and professional skill are, despite efforts of the trade to achieve status, of relatively little significance. To be sure, the nine-month or twelve-month courses offered by colleges of mortuary science do provide some basic instruction in bacteriology, inorganic chemistry, anatomy, and pathology for those who wish to obtain licenses as embalmers; however, not even that rudimentary knowledge is required for those who wish to set themselves up in business as morticians. It is, therefore, not surprising that "professional" gatherings rarely evince a concern for professional activities. Consider, as a representative example, the twenty-eighth annual convention of Preferred Funeral Directors International, which took place in Los Angeles in September, 1961, with Maytor H. McKinley, president of Utter-McKinley Mortuaries and Inglewood Park Cemetery, acting as host. After a Sunday meeting of the board of directors and a tour of the host's establishments, the convention got down to business on Monday with a speech by Los Angeles Mayor Sam Yorty, reports of the board and of the legislative, membership, convention, awards, publicity, audit, and by-laws committees. After lunch, the principal feature was a debate on price advertising, followed by election of officers and a cocktail party and banquet. Tuesday morning was devoted to speeches on "Selling the Public on Our Rising Costs," "Successful Mortuary Operation," and "Insurance as a Pre-Need Vehicle." Tuesday afternoon was highlighted by two talks—"Merchandising" and (mirabile dictu) "Importance of Our Professional Work in Securing Patronage." Wednesday morning was given over to a discussion of "Public Relations" by Mr. McKinley and an address by the president of a large advertising agency. Wednesday afternoon, the group participated in round table discussions on "How to Secure Patronage," "Merchandising," "Our Professional Services," and "Collections." During the entire event, only twice was mention made of the professional aspects of funeral directing, in both cases suitably tempered with financial considerations. But of what consequence is systematized knowledge to men whose principal profits are derived from "knowing their way around"?

It is not the smattering of scientific and technical information picked up at a short-order school that has paid off, but the clichés about God, country, and the_____Funeral Home delivered at endless service club luncheons and fraternal conventions to sympathetic "brothers." The willingness of a medical man to recommend to the family of a dead patient a friend—or at any rate a fellow lodge member—is what really counts. Church congregations can also be counted upon to exhibit a loyalty to the "in's." When the mother of a friend died recently, she sought out an officer in the women's guild for aid in arranging the funeral. "Mr._____belongs to the church. He'll take good care of your mother," my friend was told. He did—at what she later found was twice the price in the area.

It is not surprising that such old-fashioned avenues to enhancing "professional" status are still considered safest and surest; and "don't ride, walk," Mr. Krieger advises his readers: it is the way to save money, meet more people, and attract more business. However, technology has its uses even if technical skill and scientific ability are regarded as of minor importance. Technology has recently invaded not only the preparation rooms, where bodies are treated and made ready for public display, but also the "selection rooms," where shoppers are turned loose among the caskets and urged to pick out "something nice." Not long ago, a friend and her brother, a police captain, went to a recommended mortuary to make arrangements for the funeral and burial of their mother's body, which was still in the hospital where she had died. They were left in the selection room with a cheery invitation to make themselves at home. Realizing after a few moments that her brother had stopped talking, my friend asked about his silence. He took out a small pad and wrote on it: "Let's get out of here. This place is bugged." After they had managed to make their way out of the mortuary over the protests of the insistent salesman, who had reappeared with remarkable swiftness, her brother told her that shortly after they had been left alone he noticed that the room had been wired. It was not a particularly obvious job of planting the devices, he agreed, but then police captains have a greater familiarity with wire tapping equipment than most persons.

Another rather unusual mechanism, and one that is making great progress with the trade, is the one-way window in the selection room wall; that enables the salesman, who is invisible to those inside the room, to watch the expressions and gestures of prospective buyers. He is thus able to determine the strategic moment to return in order to keep their taste in caskets on a suitably high plane and to close the sale while his commission prospects are brightest.

Further to insure themselves and their followers against any failure in their program of persuasive education, industry leaders have constructed a supporting program of legislation guar-

anteed to keep profits and prices high and to maintain the fiction
that such current practices as embalming are necessary in fact.
The laws and ordinances and regulations which they have
coaxed and coerced governing bodies on all levels to enact,
many of them utterly in defiance of reason, are a source of
pride to the trade groups. They are also a source of profit:
leaders find them impressive selling points in obtaining new
members at $300 or $500 or $1,000 a year. Understandably,
the associations have hailed as triumphs such "milestones" as
state laws making it mandatory that bodies be cremated in
caskets (although many undertakers have doubly benefited from
that law by removing the body from the casket just before cremation), and making it a legal requirement that cremated
remains be kept permanently in urns at registered cemeteries
or mausoleums. One southern California cemetery proprietor
told a committee from the Los Angeles Funeral Society that
the measure had been "a real bonanza." Other activities have
also been profitable; in 1955, the National Funeral Directors
Association was able to report to members that after only three
years of assiduous sponsorship it had been instrumental in having more than one half of the states adopt legislation control-
ing sales of "pre-need" plans.

One of the rather amusing consequences of the industry's
influence is the regulation in many places that prohibits pets
from being buried on their owners' property. In Los Angeles,
as in many other cities, animal burial grounds have become
fairly numerous, some of them of considerable size. In Pet
Haven, for instance, more than nine thousand dead animals
lie in individual plots at prices (in 1962) ranging from $69.10
for cats and small dogs to $79.60 for large dogs. Horses and
larger animals are more costly to bury, although the cemetery
offers "special" prices for Great Danes and other out-size
breeds. In addition, cement vaults are offered "from $127.50
up." Although those prices include a casket, grave, and flow-
ers(!), many pet owners have insisted on something better than
the basic casket—not infrequently favoring made-to-order hardwood models lined with silk and bolstered with satin pillows—
and have insisted on having the creatures embalmed. Final
rites are often very elaborate, and many owners have carried

the farcical display even beyond that point. Not long ago, two grieving owners of a pet arrived with all of the paraphernalia employed at a child's birthday party and settled down at the grave of their dead dog to celebrate his birthday. During the Christmas season, the pet cemeteries are brightened by hundreds of tiny decorated trees set on the graves "in loving remembrance."

More serious evidence of how influential mortuary and cemetery forces have been in shaping public policy and obtaining extraordinary concessions was given in Los Angeles in 1948. Forest Lawn's brazen display of political power enabled it to obtain for graveyard use nearly five hundred acres of some of the most valuable residential land in the city. The episode, which rated front-page headlines in several of the local papers for months, began with Forest Lawn's application for a zone change that would enable it to exploit the land it had acquired adjoining Griffith Park, the largest municipal park in the United States.

The five members of the city Planning Commission rejected the application. Under normal procedures, their decision could have been superceded only by the enactment of a city ordinance by the fifteen-member city council. That path was risky in the extreme since all fifteen would have to consent to the ordinance, which would then have been subject to veto by the mayor—who was pressured to oppose the zone change by thousands of individuals and many influential organizations on the grounds that the large central area could be and should be made available for public use. Reluctant to offend either side, the mayor proposed that another alternative—rarely used and costly—be taken: that the Forest Lawn proposal be submitted to the people of the city through a referendum. But with public sentiment strong against the zone change, the cemetery was loath to hazard that avenue. Instead, working cautiously, but effectively, it accomplished its goal by reviving a generally forgotten measure providing that the decisions of a city commission could be over-ridden by a resolution of eleven members of the city council and that such a resolution would not be subject to veto by the mayor. On a spring morning, eleven members of the city council met and passed a resolution granting Forest Lawn its petition.

Outraged opponents, including the son of the donor of Griffith Park, promptly filed an injunction suit against the city council and Forest Lawn on the grounds that the action of the eleven "graveyard councilmen" was illegal. They were vigorously supported through their court battles by the Hollywood *Citizen-News*. Charging that Forest Lawn had been guilty of improper lobbying, exertion of undue pressure, and "the liberal expenditure of money" to effect its goal, the paper editorialized with frank contempt:

Griffith Park, the gift of one man, is worth millions of dollars. In appreciation, 11 Councilmen voted to hand Forest Lawn five or more million dollars of profits, at the expense of the park and the public.

Pointing out that Forest Lawn has made "many millions" by selling graves, flowers, and undertaking services to the people of the city, the editorial said, the cemetery "owes" something to Los Angeles; instead of acknowledging its indebtedness, the cemetery "demanded and got from the City Council a gift worth at least five million dollars through the changing of the zoning of the property to permit its sale for graves." The attitude of Colonel Griffith G. Griffith, who had left the park to make life happier for millions of persons, was contrasted sharply with that of the city councilmen who had acted to grant Forest Lawn its request. "In voting to hand Forest Lawn a profit of millions of dollars," the editorial concluded, the public officials had "voted a monument to their own shame."

The fray, in court and out, was easily won by Forest Lawn, which cinched the victory by secretively burying a number of persons in the disputed tract—an action calculated to paralyze the opposition since the inhumation of six bodies in a piece of ground gives the plot cemetery status. Moreover, because California requires consent of the nearest of kin before a body may be exhumed, Forest Lawn's action was, for all practical purposes, irreversible. (It was to guard against a repetition of such tactics that West Covina residents organized their night and day vigil when Forest Lawn sought a similar zoning change twelve years later in order to establish another branch in that suburban community.)

Such overt engagements between public interests and mortuary-cemetery programs for making profits have been—if generally successful for the latter—detrimental to the image that the industry has sought to fabricate. So, too, have been the encounters with clergymen and critics of the economic aspects. As a consequence, the morticians and cemetery operators have adopted a new defensive strategy, claiming that funerals "serve the living." Without such an outlet, N.F.D.A. Executive Secretary Howard Raether told delegates to a convention in 1961, bereaved persons "would repress their emotions, probably causing either mental or physical harm or both."

There is no question at all that funerals do serve the living, both publicly and privately—and often in highly questionable ways. Since long before Mark Antony made his crowd-swaying oration over the body of dead Caesar, demagogues and casuists have used funeral rites to advance their ambitions. In his remarkable study of a communist organizer in *In Dubious Battle*, John Steinbeck shows how effectively a corpse may be put to use as a rallying force. When little Joy, the gnome-like agitator who is "slug-nutty" from police clubs, is killed by vigilantes as he leads a group of scabs to join the strikers, Mac speaks frankly of the usefulness of his dead friend's body. "We'll get a hell of a lot of people on our side if we put on a public funeral. We got to get public opinion."

In like manner, the heads of the dying empires in May, 1910 shrewdly seized upon the funeral of Edward VII, "whose two passions in life were correct clothes and unorthodox company," to present a show of strength in the hope that it might recover their lost prestige. So, too, a young Negro was given importance in death that had been denied him in life in May, 1962 after he was killed in a fracas with the Los Angeles police near a Black Muslim temple. Welcoming the opportunity to stir anti-white feeling, leaders of the radically rightist Negro sect organized a mammoth funeral procession of more than two hundred cars and delivered passionate eulogies celebrating the "martyrdom" of Ronald Stokes.

Privately as well as publicly, millions of persons have used funerals for suspect purposes. It would be no easy matter to calculate how many have ordered elaborate funerals for the late and often unlamented solely to impress neighbors and relatives, or to "pay off" debts of neglect and abuse in what has come to be considered a highly acceptable way of squaring accounts with the dead. For the size and scope of a man's obsequy have come to symbolize, more than any other thing about his life, the extent to which he realized the American dream. In one of the most bitterly ironic parallels of fiction and fact in our literary history, F. Scott Fitzgerald made his final appearance as his hero-victim Gatsby had—with the perennial guests departed, the audience faded away. Laid out in lonely splendor in the William Wordsworth room of a Los Angeles mortuary, looking—as Frank Scully reported—like a cross between a tailor's dummy and a floor walker, Fitzgerald's suffering humanity was denied by the "A production in peace and security." Even beyond death the illusion continued—the spurious dream that had ultimately destroyed both Gatsby and his creator. At the conclusion of Arthur Miller's *Death of a Salesman* is a requiem for Willy Loman, the pathetic victim of our machine civilization whose defeated and self-defeating life is summed up with final irony in the dialogue between his wife and his best friend. "Why didn't anybody come?" demands Linda. And Charley answers stolidly: "It was a very nice funeral." The scene, which has been condemned by critics as sentimental and indicative of Miller's confused values is significant chiefly because of the sentimentality and confusion of the attitudes it realistically presents. It is inherent in the modern tragedy that "everyman's" right to have attention paid him is deferred beyond death.

Even what many consider a "really nice" funeral—with all the people there—can be just as meaningless, just as much a mockery of a life. I witnessed such an event recently when a good, a genuinely great teacher was sent to her grave in a manner considered suitable by several distant relatives. Birds twittered in the chapel of the undertaking establishment and the organ played some lively tunes; her small, still body, calling attention to the terrible progress of the disease that had finally and fatally afflicted her, lay on public display in a velvet and satin-lined casket for inspection by friends and strangers. A minister summoned from a nearby church delivered a fulsome eulogy, during the course of which he mispronounced her name each time he uttered it. In what sharp contrast had been her retirement celebration four years earlier, when hundreds of her former students sponsored a banquet for her, subscribed enough money for a trip to Europe, and personally delivered their thank-you notes: the man for whom the world of music had opened when she gave him a ticket to hear Marian Anderson sing; the woman who could forget the horrors of the past because the teacher had helped her to obtain plastic surgery to remove the number tattooed on her arm in a German concentration camp; the scores who delivered thanks for the food and clothing she had given them when they were in school during the wretched days of the depression, for the jobs she had found for them, the learning she had shared, and for the knowledge of truth and honor and beauty she had given them. What need had she for a lesser epitaph?

Unfortunately, too few people are ever made aware while they are able to comprehend that their lives have not been meaningless. If, instead of indulging in extravagant post-mortem gestures, we concentrated on the fulfillment of pre-mortem needs, many of the social ills that make this world a vivid approximation of hell for millions might be minimized drastically. Indeed, the question of whether or not any funeral can be meaningful is one that must be given serious consideration if our belief in human values is to be preserved. To imagine that a ceremony after death is adequate compensation for a life of emotional and intellectual and economic deprivation is to share the view of the Brazilian landowner who protested furiously in 1962 the growing spirit of revolt among the sharecroppers of northeast Brazil with their current way of life. In that region, where the average wage is thirty cents a day, the human span is also measured out with coffee spoons: 463 of every 1000 children born die during their first year from malnutrition and endemic diseases. Yet, speaking to a *Time* reporter for his fellow *patrãos*, landowner Joacil Pereira insisted: "We are generous men. If a peasant dies, or his wife dies, or his child dies, who pays for the funeral? The landlord." With values so perverted among the few, it is not surprising that in northeast Brazil, like much of Latin America, the many tremble on the brink of revolution.

In our Western culture, most persons are agreed that some kind of final acknowledgement is fitting and proper. For who, indeed, is so unworthy that his passing should go unnoticed, unmourned, unmarked? A funeral is not, of course, the only alternative. There are other ways in which death may offer the means of achieving dignity. If prisoners, who are generally characterized by feelings of insecurity about themselves, are able to realize a moral and emotional elevation by risking their lives to participate in medical and scientific experiments without thought of personal gain, would it not be more practical and meritorious for others to make such a contribution rather than to attempt to acquire status through a costly funeral and burial? To help the advancement of medical science in a general way would certainly be to end life on a commendable note. More personally, to make contributions of sight, of health, of life itself—through such agencies as eye, bone, artery, and blood banks—would be to express in the highest sense of the word that *magnanimity*, that large-souled generosity, that is the mark of a noble man and the goal of a civilized one.

Not all, of course, are willing to do that. Many feel that some kind of funeral ceremony is necessary. And it must be conceded that a funeral can be of value; it does provide during a period of crisis a set of customs and rituals that minimize the traumatic effect of the experience and offer other members of the group an opportunity for spiritual and secular communion. Bereavement for all who genuinely feel grief is a shock that disrupts and disturbs and devastates; for some, it is such an intolerable experience that their incoherent response may be suicide or moral and emotional disintegration. Funerals can help to alleviate the pain of individuals affected by offering a series of actions that must be performed and by offering the solace that grief is shared by others. The social unit—the family, the tribe, the nation, and even, as in the case of Mrs. Roosevelt's funeral, the community of nations—gains a feeling of cohesiveness and fraternity from participating in an affecting ritual.

Unfortunately, current funeral practices do not serve those ends, but negate them. They encourage irrational responses by enhancing the feeling of unreality survivors often experience when death occurs. By forcing bereaved persons to play publicly their parts as chief mourners during the first terrible wave of grief, funerals intensify their emotional shock and dislocation. The social value has also been minimized because the undertakers, the entrepreneurs, have appropriated the members' traditional roles and usurped their functions. Even though a number of mourners may show up somberly clad for the ceremony, they have surrendered to the florist the expression of their thoughts and feelings and to the mortician the expression of their ritualistic gestures. The occasion, therefore, merely isolates and alienates them from other members of the group. Spiritually, death is the one human event that makes us most acutely conscious of the dignity and divinity of man and most completely aware of the folly of our preoccupation with getting and spending. But a theatrical production starring a theatrically made-up corpse enhances the illusion of the importance of the world and the flesh and makes the spiritual realities of the occasion as remote as any Grade B motion picture does—all at tremendous cost to the living.

A first step has already been taken by many religious leaders to simplify the funeral service and strip it of its pagan emphasis on the material: the extravagant casket, the heaps of floral offerings, the embalmed corpse decked out brighter than life with fancy garb and layers of cosmetics. Most religious groups in the country have endorsed the idea that the funeral should be conducted in a church rather than in a commercial establishment and that the spiritual implications once again be emphasized so that the occasion may, as the Psalmist wrote, "teach us to number our days, that we may apply our hearts unto wisdom." Many churches are now precluding elaborate ceremonies conducted by fraternal organizations. A considerable number have also, like the Los Angeles Episcopal diocese, made it mandatory that the casket be closed before the beginning of the service on the grounds that it is pagan, just as parading past the open casket "is an ugly survival of paganism, when the mourners danced around the funeral pyre, beating their tom-toms."

Although some religions do not adapt themselves to the practice, many churches are encouraging the substitution of

memorial services for elaborate funerals. At a specified time—
a week, two weeks, or a month after death has occurred—
members of the family and friends meet at the church or home
to commemorate the person who has died. The delay is held
important since it gives the persons most deeply affected an
opportunity to appreciate the gathering of friends to honor
the dead at a time when they are less likely to indulge in un-
controllable emotional outbursts. At the service, whatever is
appropriate in the way of homage is paid to the person as an
individual. "What is important," one Unitarian minister said,
"is to express something true about the person, to acknowledge death as a deep break in the experience of the living. . . .
In the frank acknowledgment of the meaning of death and in
identifying the person who has died, what may be achieved is
a celebration of life in its full dimension."

Squandering money on flowers that cannot be enjoyed by
the recipient has become so repugnant to many that it has now
become common practice to urge that instead of sending floral
offerings to the funeral home or cemetery a check be sent to
some worthwhile organization. Opportunities to make one's
death a contribution to the living are numerous, although not
all are of equal value since many of the charity promoters can
put the funeral entrepreneurs to shame in the matter of exploiting decent human emotions. The most satisfactory solution is for the donor to select a charity he knows and
approves. Although the family of the deceased may have specified the .... Fund, there is nothing to prevent
the mourner from sending the five or ten or fifteen or more
dollars he might have spent on flowers to the principal of a
nearby school, for example, to be used to help some youngster
achieve his goal. Such a gift could only add to the stature of
the person thus commemorated.

If funeral services were simplified and limited to relatives
and closest friends, the living might be better served. Grief
and anguish are not buried with the corpse, and during the
long period of adjustment that inevitably follows the day of
the funeral, life might be made more bearable for the survivors
by having those who would normally have attended the funeral spend that amount of time with them. By restricting

attendance at the funeral, the persons closest to the dead would be freed from the obligation of putting on a show designed to impress casual on-lookers. Economically as well as emotionally the saving would undoubtedly be great; many an otherwise sensible person has indulged in extravagance against his or her better judgment and at great cost to the members of the family merely to protect the memory of the dead against the accusations of neighbors whose only standard of measurement about death as life is "How much did it cost?"

Post-funeral activities may also be simplified in the interests of the living and the dead. The bomb-proof vaults and elaborate air-tight caskets with and without hospital beds are an essential blasphemy—a denial of all of our philosophical and religious beliefs. To accept that dust shall be returned to dust is to commit ourselves to what we call our deepest beliefs—an acceptance that enables us to feel, like Socrates, that "neither in life, nor after death, can any harm come to a good man."

One of the great values of the memorial societies and the funeral cooperatives is that they encourage us to think in a realistic way about the practical aspects of death. By concerning ourselves with the economics, we are led to question the worth. From there, it is not a long step to making pertinent and ultimate inquiries about the meaning of death. When we have answered them in a reasonable way, we shall have gone far toward establishing the meaning of life and toward the establishment of a satisfactory conduct of life for ourselves and the world we live in. To do that is really to have lived.

Directory of Known Memorial Associations and Funeral Societies in the United States and Canada
(As of April, 1962)

Continental Association of Funeral and Memorial Societies
Suite 400
59 East Van Buren Street
Chicago 5, Illinois
Carl Wennerstrom, Chairman

Arizona

Valley Funeral Society
4205 North 11th Street
Phoenix, Arizona

California

Bay Area Funeral Society
1414 University Avenue
Berkeley 2, California

Central Coast Memorial Society
Box 679
San Luis Obispo, California

Channel Cities Funeral Society
482 Vaquero Lane
Santa Barbara, California

Christian Service Society
1508 Locust Street
Chico, California

Kern Memorial Society (formerly the Desert Memorial Society)
Box 674
China Lake, California

Los Angeles Funeral Society, Inc.
c/o Dr. Fremont Higgins
1714 So. Ardmore Avenue
Los Angeles 6, California

Peninsula Funeral Society
Box 366
Palo Alto, California

Sacramento Valley Memorial Society, Inc.
2112 Edison Avenue
Sacramento 21, California

San Diego Memorial Society
c/o Miss Florence Parker
3656 Eugene Place
San Diego 16, California

Tri-County Memorial Funeral Society
3675 Lemon Street
Riverside, California

Valley Memorial Society
c/o Mrs. Grace Longenecker
1510 E. Loftus Lane
Fresno, California

Connecticut

The Memorial Society of Connecticut
10 Lyon Plains Road
Westport, Connecticut

District of Columbia

All Souls Unitarian Church Funeral Society
c/o E. D. Opie, Secretary
16th and Harvard Street, N.W.
Washington 9, D. C.

Illinois

Chicago Memorial Association
5707 S. Woodlawn Avenue
Chicago 37, Illinois

Indiana

Bloomington Memorial Society
419 North Indiana Avenue
Bloomington, Indiana

Indianapolis Memorial Society
5805 E. 56th Street
Indianapolis 3, Indiana

Iowa

Benton and Adjoining Counties Cooperative Burial Association
c/o Robert J. Fellmet, Manager
Keystone, Iowa

Cooperative Funeral Service
c/o Will Winterfeld, President
Sioux Center, Iowa

Cooperative Funeral Service of Sioux Center
c/o Walker Bleeker, Secretary
Ireton, Iowa

Eddyville Cooperative Burial Association
c/o Frank Jager, President
Eddyville, Iowa

Fremont Cooperative Burial Association
c/o H. A. Triplett, President
Fremont, Iowa

Iowa State Federation of Cooperative Burial Associations
c/o Reuben Schakel, President
Pella, Iowa

Lyon County Cooperative Burial Association
c/o L. W. Baumann, President
Little Rock, Iowa

O'Brien Co-op Funeral Association
c/o O. D. Koontz, Director
Drawer 190
Sanborn, Iowa

Pella Cooperative Funeral Home
c/o John W. Boot, President
R.R.
Sully, Iowa

Whiting Cooperative Burial Association
c/o Glen Deyloff, President
Whiting, Iowa

Winneshiek Cooperative Burial Association
c/o Albert Womeldorf
Decorah, Iowa

Maryland

Maryland Suburban Memorial Society
c/o Bruce Bowman, President
707 Ludlow Street
Takoma Park, Maryland

(This group is organizing chapters in Greater Baltimore,
Cumberland, and Annapolis.)

Massachusetts

The Berkshire Memorial Society
c/o Rev. H. V. Kafka
175 Wendell Avenue
Pittsfield, Massachusetts

Memorial Society of Massachusetts
874 Beacon Street
Boston 15, Massachusetts

Springfield Memorial Society, Inc.
292 Worthington Street
Springfield 3, Massachusetts

Michigan

Grand Rapids Funeral Association
24 Fountain Street, N.E.
Grand Rapids, Michigan

Greater Detroit Memorial Society
c/o S. Karp
6129 Highland Road
Pontiac, Michigan

Minnesota

Cooperative Burial Association of Cokato
Cokato, Minnesota

Freeborn County Funeral Association
Albert Lea, Minnesota

Greenwood Prairie Burial Association
Elgin, Minnesota

Kandiyohi-Meeker Co-op Funeral Association
Lake Lillian, Minnesota

Minnesota Co-op Burial Association
Farmington, Minnesota

Minnesota Memorial Society
900 Mount Curve Avenue
Minneapolis 5, Minnesota

Minnesota Valley Funeral Home
c/o M. F. Witt, Manager
New Ulm, Minnesota

Northland Co-op Mortuary
Cloquet, Minnesota

Range Funeral Home
c/o Eli Ranta
Range Cooperative Federation
Virginia, Minnesota

Sunset Burial Association
Echo, Minnesota

Sunset Funeral Association, Inc.
Glyndon, Minnesota

Tri-County Burial Association
Prinsburg, Minnesota

Missouri

Kansas City Memorial Society
c/o Ray Watson
Hallmark Cards, Inc.
Kansas City 41, Missouri

Memorial and Funeral Society of Greater St. Louis
c/o Rev. Webster Kitchell
Eliot Unitarian Chapel
Kirkwood, Missouri

St. Louis Memorial Society, Inc.
5007 Waterman Boulevard
St. Louis, Missouri

New Hampshire

Memorial Society of Greater Nashua
58 Lowell Street
Nashua, New Hampshire

New Jersey

Central Memorial Society
156 Forest Avenue
Paramus, New Jersey

Memorial Society of Plainfield
c/o Harold M. Honig
428 Vine Street
Elizabeth, New Jersey

Princeton Memorial Association
c/o Mrs. G. W. Loos
8 Erdman Avenue
Princeton, New Jersey

New York

Community Funeral Society
c/o Miss Lillian D. Stollow, Chairman
40 East 35th Street
New York 16, New York

The Greater Buffalo Memorial Society
695 Elmwood Avenue
Buffalo 22, New York

The Ithaca Memorial Society
P.O. Box 134
Ithaca, New York

Memorial Society of Chemung Valley
P.O. Box 643
Elmira, New York

Niagara Falls Memorial Society
639 Main Street
Niagara Falls, New York

Rochester Memorial Society, Inc.
220 Winton Road South
Rochester 10, New York

North Carolina

Burial Committee; Robert Barrus, Chairman
Celo Friends Meeting
Route 5
Burnsville, North Carolina

Ohio

Cleveland Memorial Society
21600 Shaker Boulevard
Cleveland 22, Ohio

Columbus Memorial Society
93 W. Weisheimer Road
Columbus 14, Ohio

Dayton Memorial Society
665 Salem
Dayton 6, Ohio

The Greater Cincinnati Memorial Society
6 Linton Street
Cincinnati 19, Ohio

Yellow Springs Branch, Columbus Memorial Society
c/o Mrs. Kenneth Tregillus
Kurt Street
Yellow Springs, Ohio

Yellow Springs Friends Meeting
Burial Committee; Ernest Morgan, Chairman
130 Glen Street
Yellow Springs, Ohio

Oklahoma

Memorial Society of Northern Oklahoma
c/o Francis F. Campbell
123 East 26th Place
Tulsa 14, Oklahoma

Oregon

Oregon Memorial Association, Inc.
4312 S.E. Stark Street
Portland 15, Oregon

Pennsylvania

Lehigh Valley Memorial Society
701 Lechauweki Avenue
Bethlehem, Pennsylvania

Philadelphia Consumer Service Coop., Inc.
c/o Charles R. Nelson, President
604 Bailey Building
1218 Chestnut Street
Philadelphia 7, Pennsylvania

Philadelphia Memorial Society
2125 Chestnut Street
Philadelphia 3, Pennsylvania

Pittsburgh Memorial Society
c/o David Weintraub
605 Morewood Avenue
Pittsburgh 13, Pennsylvania

South Dakota

Community Burial Association
Castlewood, South Dakota

Community Burial Association
Vienna, South Dakota

Fraternal Burial Association
Viborg, South Dakota

Minnehaha County Burial Association
Baltic, South Dakota

Virginia

Fairfax Memorial Society
380 Maple Avenue, East
Vienna, Virginia

The Memorial Society
4444 Arlington Boulevard
Arlington 4, Virginia

Washington

People's Memorial Association, Inc.
309 Areis Building
2366 Eastlake Avenue, E.
Seattle 2, Washington

West Virginia

The Charleston Burial Society
c/o Charles W. Wilson, III
835 Carroll Road
Charleston 4, West Virginia

Wisconsin

Planned Funeral Society
c/o Victor Duhnke
P.O. Box 4444
Milwaukee 7, Wisconsin

Reedsville Co-op Association Funeral Home
c/o Steve Dvorachek, Manager
Reedsville, Wisconsin

Valley Cooperative Services
Appleton, Wisconsin

Wausau Chapter, Planned Funeral Society
c/o Rev. Carleton Fisher
504 Grant Street
Wausau, Wisconsin

Wisconsin Burial Association
c/o M. Marshall Taylor
2624 Van Hise Avenue
Madison 5, Wisconsin

Canada

Edmonton Memorial Society
12210 88th Street
Edmonton, Alberta

Manitoba Mortuary Association
c/o W. F. Oldham
205 Maplewood Avenue
Winnipeg 13, Manitoba

Memorial Association of Montreal
P.O. Box 106, Sta. N.D.G.
Montreal 28, Quebec

The Memorial Society of British Columbia
P.O. Box 917, Sta. A
Vancouver 1, B. C.

Ottawa Memorial Society
Box 239, Sta. D
Ottawa, Ontario

Regina Memorial Society
3042 Angus Street
Regina, Saskatchewan

Toronto Memorial Society
c/o Mrs. A. J. Elder
60 Dalbeattie Avenue
Weston, Ontario

Information about funeral societies and memorial associations may be obtained from any of those groups or from The Cooperative League of the U.S.A., 343 South Dearborn Street, Chicago 4, Illinois.

APPENDIX II

Notes on Sources

I AM INDEBTED to many persons and publications for the material in this book. Friends, acquaintances, even strangers who had learned of my interest in the subject provided anecdotes of interest, offered bills for undertaking services to substantiate their statements, and guided me to books, newspapers, and magazines that were very helpful. I have, wherever possible, attempted to identify sources in the text itself. Because it has not always been possible to do that and because I did not wish to burden readers with footnotes, I have added this brief appendix indicating some of the principal sources used in writing each chapter.

Special mention should also be made of some books and pamphlets on the subject that are of particular value. Indispensable aids have been Bertram S. Puckle's delightful and detailed *Funeral Customs: Their Origin and Development* (New York, Frederick A. Stokes Company, 1926); LeRoy Bowman's authoritative and objective *The American Funeral* (Washington, D. C., Public Affairs Press, 1959), and *The History of American Funeral Directing* by Robert W. Habenstein and William M. Lamers (Milwaukee, Bulfin Printers, 1955). The latter, a remarkably scholarly and comprehensive work, is unfortunately marred by its assumption of the role of apologist for undertakers in general and in particular the National Funeral Directors Association of the United States, Inc., which copyrighted the book. Of great value have been the pamphlets published by the Cooperative League of the U.S.A. and some of the publications of the Associations of Better Business Bureaus, Inc. Any student of the subject will find, as I did, the files of the trade journals—in particular, *Casket and Sunnyside, Mortuary Man-*

238

agement, the *American Funeral Director,* and the *Southern Funeral Director*—of tremendous assistance.

Chapter 1

Some of the material in this chapter was derived from an article on funeral extravagance that I wrote for *The Progressive,* March, 1961. Details about costs of undertaking imposed for the funerals of the California State Polytechnic College football players were obtained from Donald Nelson, Memorial Fund Treasurer, on July 2, 1962. Additional information about the event came from newspaper clippings and from Melvin Durslag's "Aftermath of an Air Crash," the *Saturday Evening Post* (February 10, 1962). Information about the Crawford family was provided by Margaret Parton's "No Father to Turn To" in the *Ladies' Home Journal* (December, 1961). Comments about the funeral cost were made in the same issue by Sidney Margolius, consultant on family finances for the Family Service Association of America. Some of the background material was contained in the *Psychology of Funeral Service* by Edward A. Martin (Grand Junction, Colorado, *c.* 1947), which is widely advertised in trade journals as "the only book on psychology written for the funeral profession." The clergyman's quote was from an article by Ernest Havemann in *McCall's* magazine (March, 1956). Robert L. Fulton's survey of attitudes of clergymen was published in 1959 by the National Funeral Directors Association of the United States, Inc. A later analysis by Dr. Fulton of his findings, "The Clergyman and the Funeral Director: A Study in Role Conflict," appeared in *Social Forces* (May, 1961). Information about the number of morticians needed to cope with the volume of business was obtained from Elmer Davis' "The Mortician," reprinted in *The American Mercury Reader* (Philadelphia, 1944) and LeRoy Bowman's *The American Funeral.* An amusing account of W. W. Chambers' appearance before the congressional investigating committee was contained in an article by Decca Treuhaft (Jessica Mitford), "St. Peter Don't You Call Me," in *Frontier* (November, 1958). The study of costs made for the N.F.D.A. by Eugene F. Foran of Funeral Service Facts and Figures appeared in *Mortuary Management* (June, 1961). Material about profits from Negro funerals was derived from an article on "America's 100 Richest Negroes" that appeared in *Ebony* (May, 1962). A detailed account of the New York Attorney General's investigation appeared in *Consumers Look at Burial Practices,* an excellent pamphlet on the subject by Allan Earnshaw Backman, published by the Council on Consumer Information of State Teachers College, St. Cloud, Minnesota, in 1956.

For several months in 1958, I worked with a committee of the Los Angeles Funeral Society to negotiate a contract with local undertakers; their quotations were obtained during those visits. The exploitation of workingmen's families is graphically described in "Tricks of the Undertaker's Trade" by LeRoy Bowman, AFL-CIO *I.U.D. Digest* (Summer, 1960) and "Death's High Toll" by Abe Magrisso and Donald Rubin, *I.U.D. Digest* (Fall, 1961). The account of the row between the Secretary of the Army and House Armed Services Committee Chairman Carl Vinson was given in *Newsweek* (February 25, 1957).

Mrs. Londa S. Fletcher of Palo Alto and Robert Treuhaft of Oakland provided much information about the activities of the funeral societies in those areas. Tom Franklin of KTLA-TV made his files available to me, including the letter from the president of a Los Angeles mortuary and scripts of three programs he presented on funeral costs on the *Big 3 Final* on December 26 and 27, 1961, and January 15, 1962. Information about court actions against the mortuary came from the files of the Los Angeles *Times*.

Chapter 2

The material in this chapter was derived from a paper I prepared in 1962 for a seminar in epic poetry conducted by Professor Walter M. Crittenden of the University of Southern California. In this, I have limited myself to those epics that seemed to have the most profound effect in shaping Western funeral practices. Books that were of particular value and which are quoted in this chapter include C. M. Bowra's *The Greek Experience* (New York, 1959); Alexander Heidel's *The Gilgamesh Epic and Old Testament Parallels* (Chicago, 1949); W. F. Jackson Knight's translation of Virgil's *The Aeneid* (London, 1960); E. V. Rieu's translation of *The Voyage of Argo* by Apollonius of Rhodes (London, 1959); W. H. D. Rouse's translation of *The Iliad of Homer* and *The Odyssey of Homer* (both New York, 1960); N. K. Sandar's translation of *The Epic of Gilgamesh* (London, 1960); Dorothy L. Sayers' translation of *The Song of Roland* (London, 1960); Robert Southey's translation of *The Chronicle of the Cid* (Garden City, New York, n.d.); and Mary E. Waterhouse's *Beowulf in Modern English* (Cambridge, England, 1949).

Chapter 3

Excellent material about the eschatological beliefs of the early Jews and Christians and important pagan groups is contained in *The Gilgamesh Epic and Old Testament Parallels* by Alexander Heidel, *The History of American Funeral Directing* by Robert W. Habenstein and William Lamers, Bertram S. Puckle's *Funeral Customs*, Thomas Mann's *Joseph in Egypt* (New York, 1940); James H. Breasted's *A History of the Ancient Egyptians* (New York, 1903), and Alfred C. Rush's *Death and Burial in Christian Antiquity* (Washington, D.C., 1941). All of those works have been used in preparing this chapter. Also important for Jewish and Christian beliefs are the *Jewish Encyclopedia*; the *Catholic Encyclopedia*; and the *Jewish Code of Laws*, Books I and IV. The information about the funeral of Charles "Lucky" Luciano appeared in newspaper accounts in January, 1962. The letter from the mortuary college student was published in *Mortuary Management* (September, 1961). Description of the French funerals and the quotations from the *Bishop of Angiers* and *Le Monde* appeared in an article in *Time* (September 8, 1958). Dorothy Sayers' translation of *The Song of Roland* and Robert Southey's translation of *The Chronicle of the Cid* were also helpful in preparing this chapter. The material about Norse funeral beliefs and customs was derived largely from Hilda Roderick Ellis' *The Road to Hel* (Cambridge, 1943).

Varying attitudes toward funerals during the Middle Ages were exemplified in Eileen Power's *Medieval People* (New York, 1924). John Evelyn's *Diary* (Oxford, 1955) was, on funerals as on all other seventeenth-century matters, a rich source of information. Material about the effects of the bubonic plague on European funeral practices was taken from C. H. Clarke's translation of Johannes Nohl's famous chronicle of *The Black Death* (New York, 1960) and Daniel Defoe's *Journal of the Plague Year* (Boston, 1919).

Chapter 4

In writing this chapter, again I found that Bertram Puckle's *Funeral Customs*, Habenstein's *The History of American Funeral Directing*, and the various religious encyclopedias were very useful. George Willison's *Saints and Strangers* (New York, 1945) was extremely helpful in obtaining material about early American funeral customs, as was Alice M. Earle's *Customs and Fashions in Old New England* (New York, 1894) although to a somewhat lesser degree. Samuel Sewall's *Diary* (Boston, Massachusetts Historical Society, 1878–1882) is of value in any historical study. Minor details were provided by Sir Richard Steele's *The Funeral* or *Grief à la Mode*, the *Oxford University Dictionary*, the *Encyclopedia Britannica*, the *Encyclopedia Americana*, Robert Blair's *The Grave* (London, Routledge, n.d.), Charles Dickens' *Martin Chuzzlewit* (New York, Heritage Press, n.d.), and "Tract" by William Carlos Williams from *A Little Treasury of Modern Poetry*, edited by Oscar Williams (New York, 1952).

Chapter 5

Material on the Civil War and the growth of corporations in this country is amply detailed in *The Rise of American Civilization* (Book 2) by Charles A. and Mary Beard (New York, 1930). *The History of American Funeral Directing* provided much information on embalming during the nineteenth century and before. Although some of the details given about Dr. Thomas Holmes by Trentwell M. White and Ivan Sandrof in "The First Embalmer" in the *New Yorker* (November 7, 1942) have been disputed, it is a lively and informative study of that unusual man. Early files of the trade journals and recent catalogues of the mortuary colleges were helpful in obtaining information. Rail, air, and ship fares were obtained from Los Angeles employees of the various companies mentioned and from tariff conference reports.

Both *Funeral Customs* and *The History of American Funeral Directing* provided information about the development of the hearse, and recent issues of trade journals were also helpful. All those were also useful in describing the evolution of coffins in Jewish and Christian cultures, as was Thomas Mann's *Joseph in Egypt*. A detailed description of the modern manufacture of Jewish coffins was contained in an article in the May, 1962, issue of the *National Hardwood Magazine*. William Faulkner's *As I Lay Dying* (New York, 1946) carefully describes the manufacture of an old-fashioned coffin. Material on the various subjects in this chapter is also printed in W. H. F. Bavesi's *The Burial of the Dead* (New York, 1920). The description of middle-class Mexican practices today was given to me in April, 1962, by Brita Bowen de Canto of Mexico City College.

Chapter 6

The disposal plan operated by the Friends Meeting in Yellow Springs, Ohio, has been described in *The American Funeral* and a number of other publications. Ernest Morgan, chairman of the burial committee, is currently preparing a book about the activities of his group and other practices. Interesting information about Mexican funerals is presented in Frances Toor's *A Treasury of Mexican Folkways* (Mexico, D. F., 1947), Frederick Peterson's *Ancient Mexico* (London, 1959), and Neill James' *Dust on My Heart* (New York, 1946). *Funeral Customs* and *The History of American Funeral Directing* are both cited in this chapter. Further material about the Egyptian practices is contained in Herodotus' *The Persian Wars* (New York, 1942). Brief references are made to John Donne's *Devotions*, Shakespeare's *Macbeth*, and Poe's "Bells." Johannes Nohl's *The Black Death* is again cited. Purification rites among primitive peoples are described in careful detail in E. Bendann's *Death Customs* (New York, 1930).

The quotation by the early president of the trade association was taken from the *Proceedings of the American Funeral Directors Association, 1886*, cited in Habenstein's *History*. W. M. Krieger's speech to the California convention in 1961 was reprinted in *Mortuary Management* (especially the issue of October, 1961). Informative accounts of the California convention and Nicholas Daphne's protest appeared in *Time* (June 2, 1961) and *Mortuary Manage-*

ment (June, 1961). W. W. Chambers, Jr., made that comment to Roul Tunley, according to the latter's article "Can You Afford to Die?" in the *Saturday Evening Post* (June 17, 1961). The higher figure was set by William C. Cowan, president of the Los Angeles County Funeral Directors Association, on Tom Franklin's *Big 3 Final* (January 15, 1962). Much of the information about Hubert Eaton and Forest Lawn was taken from Adela Rogers St. Johns' *First Step up toward Heaven* (New Jersey, 1959). Less flattering pictures of Dr. Eaton appeared in articles in *Playboy* by Al Morgan ("The Bier Barons," June, 1960) and in *Fortnight* by Eustace Cockrell ("O Death, Where Is Thy Sting?" June, 1955). Evelyn Waugh's brilliantly satirical *The Loved One* (Boston, 1950) and Aldous Huxley's equally biting *After Many a Summer* (The New Phoenix Library, 1950) were, in spite of protests, obviously influenced if not directly inspired by Dr. Eaton's creation.

Chapter 7

Many of the sources used in preparing Chapter Three were helpful in obtaining information for the first part of this chapter: Puckle's *Funeral Customs*; Rush's *Death and Burial in Christian Antiquity*, Habenstein's *History of American Funeral Directing*, Ellis' *The Road to Hel*, and Bavesi's *The Burial of the Dead*. Also of assistance in preparing the history of cemeteries was a booklet, "Remembering through the Ages . . . The History of the Cemetery," by James Worley, Executive Vice-President of the American Cemetery Association (1959), and a news release with a Columbus, Ohio dateline, issued by that organization, scheduled for publication May 1960. *Stories on Stone* by Charles L. Wallis (New York, 1954) contains interesting material about epitaphs. The exposé about Forest Lawn's ownership of Mount Sinai Memorial-Park was published in the Los Angeles *B'nai B'rith Messenger* (January 13, 1961).

Information about the Los Angeles practices was obtained during personal interviews in March with Allen Parken, cemetery caretaker; Joseph Messina, senior registrar of the county hospital, and representatives of the coroner's office and the public administrator's office. During March and April, I also interviewed a number of cemetery operators with George Burleigh, president of the Los Angeles Funeral Society, and other officers of the society. An account of the Forest Lawn controversy with the residents of the West Covina area appeared in *Time* (February 10, 1961) and other accounts were published in many issues of the Los Angeles *Times* and *Examiner* during October and December, 1960, and January and February, 1961. Information also appeared in *Mortuary Management* (July, 1961). Some of the material was obtained during interviews with Mrs. Frank Rupert and other members of the West Covina committee. In this chapter, too, Mrs. St. Johns' *First Step up toward Heaven*, Waugh's *The Loved One*, and Huxley's *After*

Many a Summer were extremely helpful. The student's reaction was written by Pat Riley, editor of *The Associate*, and appeared in the Claremont Men's College paper on April 5, 1962. Perhaps the most significant information was given to me during May and June, 1962, by a Forest Lawn salesman who called at our house to persuade us to buy some "property" there. The pamphlet put out by the Associations of Better Business Bureaus, Inc., "Questions You Should Ask about Cemetery Lot Promotions," is available from that organization at 723 Chrysler Building, New York 17, New York. The cautions printed in that publication were later repeated in articles in the *Reader's Digest* and *Changing Times* and *Good Housekeeping*.

Chapter 8

The widely protested article by Roul Tunley appeared in the *Saturday Evening Post* (June 17, 1961). The trade journals, particularly *Casket and Sunnyside* and *Mortuary Management*, carried vigorous attacks on the magazine, the article, and the writer during June, July, and August. Judge Westover's comments were printed in the Los Angeles *Times* (March 13, 1962). A humorous account of Rudolph Valentino's funeral, "Farewell Great Lover," by Beverly Smith, Jr., appeared in the *Saturday Evening Post* (January 20, 1962). H. L. Mencken's sharp comments about morticians are contained in *The American Language*, Fourth Edition (New York, 1936) in the section on "Euphemisms." Elmer Davis' "The Mortician," appeared in *The American Mercury Reader* (Philadelphia, 1944). The Thomas Wolfe quotations are from *Look Homeward, Angel* (Modern Library edition). *The Catcher in the Rye* by J. D. Salinger (New York, 1953) is also quoted. James Agee's *A Death in the Family* offers a marvelously detailed account of a funeral and a memorable picture of an undertaker. William Faulkner's comments about undertakers are from "That Evening Sun" *The Faulkner Reader* (New York, 1946) and *As I Lay Dying*.

The account of the controversy begun by the Middletown ministers is from "A Foray into Funeral Customs" by Hugh Stevenson Tigner in *The Christian Century* (October 13, 1937). *The American Funeral* offers a detailed discussion of the controversy stirred up by the bulletin published by the (then) Federal Council of Churches in America. Perhaps the most comprehensive discussion of the position of many Protestant churchmen is that contained in the "Christian Burial" issue of *Social Action* (April, 1959), which contains the widely printed and distributed articles by Paul E. Irion and Everett W. MacNair. The quotations protesting clerical interference are from an editorial in *Casket and Sunnyside* (March, 1962). Robert L. Fulton's analysis of his survey of clerical attitudes toward undertaking and undertakers was published in *Social Forces* (May, 1961). The discussion of efforts to achieve harmony was based on an account contained in *Mortuary Management* (September, 1961), in which issue also appeared W. M. Krieger's attack on "the European theological approach."

Chapter 9

The opening anecdote appeared in Mark Twain's *Life on the Mississippi* (New York and London, 1901). Quincy L. Dowd's *Funeral Management and Costs: A World Survey of Burial and Cremation* (Chicago, 1921) unfavorably contrasts United States customs with those of many European countries. W. M. Krieger's comment is taken from LeRoy Bowman's *The American Funeral* (Washington, D. C., 1959). Graham Taylor's *Pioneering on Social Frontiers* (Chicago, 1930) presents some touching anecdotes about settlement clients in Chicago, anecdotes that have been matched by those of social workers in New York, Los Angeles, and other urban centers. Puckle's observations about the British poor come from *Funeral Customs.* The classic study of funeral extravagance is still John C. Gebhart's *Funeral Costs* (New York, 1928).

Information about Dane County was reported by Elliott Maraniss in *The Capital Times*, Madison, Wisconsin (August 2, 1961). Helpful background material on funeral costs is also given in *Cooperative Funeral Associations* by James Myers, Jr., published by the Cooperative League of the U.S.A. in 1946, and Allan Earnshaw Backman's *Consumers Look at Burial Practices.* Material about costs of public burials was obtained from personal interviews in March, 1962. Accounts of the investigation of the Los Angeles County Coroner's Office appeared in local papers on October 11, 12, and 13, 1961. The sentencing of the Los Angeles county funeral directors occurred on January 15, 1962. The information about the Illinois legislative investigating committee was sent to me by Anthony Scariano, First District Representative, in February and May, 1962. The conversation with the California Attorney General's chief deputy took place on June 27, 1962.

Chapter 10

W. M. Krieger's speech was reprinted in *Mortuary Management* (September and October, 1961). A detailed discussion of the Liberty National case also appeared in that magazine in September. The program for unions was presented in the *I.U.D. Digest* (Fall, 1961) by Abe Magrisso and Donald Rubin. Material about the Wisconsin efforts to make it legally possible to will bodies to medical schools was sent to me by H. Marshall Taylor of Madison. Much of the information about cremation was provided by the "Christian Burial" issue of *Social Action.* LeRoy Bowman's *The American Funeral* contains a more detailed account of the effort to obtain an appropriation to erect a municipal funeral plant in New York. James

246 / Appendix II

Myers Jr.'s *Cooperative Funeral Associations* and Jerry Voorhis' *The Cooperatives Look Ahead*, published by the Public Affairs Committee, 1952, provide much information about cooperative activities in this area. Much of the information about the progress of the cooperative funeral and memorial societies was obtained from the conference held in Chicago on April 16, 1962 under the sponsorship of the Cooperative League of the U.S.A. *Proceedings of the April 16, 1962 Meeting of Funeral and Memorial Associations, University of Chicago*, were published in June, 1962 by the League.

Chapter 11

For the case histories of the three funeral societies presented in this chapter, I owe much thanks to Mrs. Helen Farmer, Ray Rayburn, and Leslie Tostevin. Herman Feifel's "Scientific Research in Taboo Areas—Death" appeared in *The American Behavioral Scientist* (March, 1962). Thomas D. Eliot's outstanding studies of grief have appeared in many publications; those cited in this chapter are "The Adjustive Behavior of Bereaved Families: A New Field for Research," *Social Forces* (June, 1930) and "War Bereavements and Their Recovery," *Marriage and Family Living* (February, 1946).

Chapter 12

It would be difficult and excessively lengthy to acknowledge the assistance I received in writing this chapter from many religious groups and individual clergymen concerned with funeral reform. In addition to the pamphlets and statements referred to in other chapters, readers may find of interest the material on funerals prepared by the American Unitarian Association, 25 Beacon Street, Boston 8, Mass. *A Humanist Funeral Service* by Corliss Lamont (Boston, 1947), and the detailed exposition of funerals and the Episcopal Church by Rev. Enrico C. S. Molner, Th.D, in *The Episcopal Review* (July, 1962). Thomas D. Eliot's detailed studies of bereavement are still among the best and most useful on that subject: among his publications referred to in this chapter are articles that appeared in *The Family* (June, 1930); *The Annals* of the American Academy of Political and Social Science (March, 1932); *Social Forces* (June, 1930); and *Marriage and Family Living* (February, 1946). Other interesting comments are contained in John Dewey's *A Common Faith* (New Haven, 1934), and Erich Fromm's *The Sane Society* (New York, 1955). The quotations by Ann Landers appeared in her column published in the Lincoln Heights *Bulletin-News* (September 15, 1962). Wilber M. Krieger's text for the trade, *Successful Funeral Service Management* (New York, 1951), offers valuable insights into the funeral industry. The program of the Preferred Funeral Directors International convention was carried in full in *Mortuary Management* (September, 1961). The editorial in the Hollywood *Citizen-News* quoted appeared in the issue of April 10, 1948. Brief references have been made to John Steinbeck's *In Dubious Battle* (New York, 1936); *The Guns of August* by Barbara W. Tuchman (New York, 1962); an account of the funeral of Ronald Stokes, Los Angeles *Times* (May 12, 1962); Arthur Mizener's *The Far Side of Paradise* (Boston, 1951); and Arthur Miller's *Death of a Salesman* (New York, 1951). The quotation of the Brazilian landowner was taken from an article about Brazil that appeared in *Time* (May 18, 1962). The quotation about the Los Angeles Episcopal diocese position was taken from Canon Molnar's article in *The Episcopal Review*, and that about the memorial service from a sermon by John W. Cyrus preached at the Unitarian Church, Milwaukee, Wisconsin, on October 19, 1958, which has been printed and distributed by the Planned Funeral Society of Wisconsin. A detailed article about how blood from the dead may help the living, a new scientific breakthrough made by Russian scientists, appeared in the New York *Times Western Edition* (November 13, 1962).

Index